The Burden of Modernity

The Burden of Modernity

≡ THE RHETORIC
≡ OF CULTURAL DISCOURSE
≡ IN SPANISH AMERICA

Carlos J. Alonso

New York   Oxford
Oxford University Press
1998

Oxford University Press

Oxford   New York
Athens   Auckland   Bangkok   Bogotá   Buenos Aires   Calcutta
Cape Town   Chennai   Dar es Salaam   Delhi   Florence   Hong Kong   Istanbul
Karachi   Kuala Lumpur   Madrid   Melbourne   Mexico City   Mumbai
Nairobi   Paris   São Paulo   Singapore   Taipei   Tokyo   Toronto   Warsaw

and associated companies in
Berlin   Ibadan

Copyright © 1998 by Oxford University Press, Inc.

Published by Oxford University Press, Inc.
198 Madison Avenue, New York, New York 10016

Library of Congress Cataloging-in-Publication Data
Alonso, Carlos J.
The burden of modernity : the rhetoric of cultural discourse in
Spanish America / by Carlos J. Alonso.
    p.   cm.
Includes bibliographical references and index.
ISBN 0-19-511863-4
1. Spanish American prose literature—19th century—History and
criticism.   2. Spanish American prose literature—20th century—
History and criticism.   3. Narration (Rhetoric)   4. Latin America—
Intellectual life—19th century.   5. Latin America—Intellectual
life—20th century.   I. Title.
PQ7082.P76A69   1997
868'.08—dc21   97-37363

PQ
7082
.P76
A69
1998

9 8 7 6 5 4 3 2 1

Printed in the United States of America
on acid-free paper

Preface

IN THE BROADEST TERMS, this book is an examination of the repertory of strategies used by Spanish American writers and intellectuals to take their distance from their otherwise explicit adoption of and commitment to the discourses of modernity. As such, it is an attempt to give a historical and contextual dimension to reflections that were first presented *in nuce* in the introductory chapter of my previous book, *The Spanish American Regional Novel: Modernity and Autochthony*.[1] My contention there was that the lexicon, the presuppositions, and the projects of modernity that serve as foundation to cultural discourse in Spanish America are invariably weakened—when not expressly undone—by some dimension of the very text that invokes them. I further argued that this movement away from modernity had become institutionalized both discursively and politically as a continual search for identity that had paradoxically provided the foundation for an intrinsically Spanish American cultural enterprise that could never be challenged or foreclosed. I then went on to study a specific manifestation of this phenomenon, the so-called *novela de la tierra* or regional novel of the 1920s and 1930s. The necessarily circumscribed scope of the earlier project called for a complementary effort that would put in evidence the existence of this contradictory movement in the larger realm of Spanish American cultural discourse. That, in short, is the purpose of the present book: to document in a number of specific works, ranging from the beginning of the nineteenth century to the present, that moment in which the gesture of allegiance and obeisance toward the modern is eschewed—however ambiguously or paradoxically—by recourse to a given textual practice that renders that gesture problematic. Hence, I will argue that Spanish American intellectuals ultimately became masters of the intricate code of the discourse of modernity for two related—if opposite—reasons: because its acquisition expressed their intense desire to be modern, and also because that knowledge turned out to be indispensable as a way of expanding the repertoire of possibilities and opportunities to *deviate* from it. The obsessive readings of the latest books; the scrupulously documented travels to the metropolitan countries; the incisive, painstaking, and pained studies of local reality—they all served first to measure the distance still to be traveled to become modern, but they also helped to identify and master the most effective strategies for never leaving home. The Spanish American house of discourse is indeed divided against itself, but the building not only stands on its own but displays the arresting architectural force that issues from its tortuous yet balanced rhetorical framework. Simón Bolívar once argued that the Spanish American *letrados* would serve only "para amontonar escombros de fábricas monstruosas y para edificar sobre una base gótica un edificio griego al borde de un cráter" [to pile up the remains of monstrous factories and to build a Greek edifice on a Gothic foundation at the border of an abyss][2] In this study I wish to reclaim for that radically heterogeneous structure that is Spanish American cultural discourse the rhetorical verve and audacity that characterizes Bolívar's own formulation on the subject.

Given the topic and the objectives of this work, I was confronted from the outset with an essential choice regarding the structure of my argumentation: I could (a) construct a catalogue of those contradictory rhetorical moves that occur repeatedly throughout the history of cultural discourse in Spanish America, thereby arriving at a repertoire of fundamental tropes around which Spanish American discourse articulates itself, or (b) choose specific texts, authors, and discursive formations that in my mind saliently exemplified those particular strategies. I have chosen to follow for my exposition the second option because it is the one that best wards against the danger of reifying modernity as a transhistorical category (and therefore of reifying also whatever is posited as modernity's negation or opposite), a shortcoming that has been a consistent characteristic of Spanish American cultural discourse. "Modernity" is a concept with a historical dimension that is privative to every context in which it is invoked and that must be accounted for—not only because the *idearium* of modernity and what is regarded as "modern" evolve both in metropolitan and peripheral circles but also because the historical circumstances in which every claim for modernity is made in Spanish America lend concrete specificity to each claim, however repetitive or derivative the gesture may seem. For instance, what Sarmiento understood modernity to be was quite different from the modernity that the Cuban polymath Domingo del Monte was striving for, a discrepancy that is directly attributable to their particular and unique historical contexts, even if the two wrote within twenty years of one another and are therefore roughly coeval. Sarmiento's idea of modernity was a composite created out of his personal experiences—readings, travels, and so on—but was primarily articulated from within the port city/province dichotomy that arose in various guises throughout the nineteenth century as a leitmotif of Argentine political life. By contrast, Del Monte's modernity was forged as a direct challenge to the by then anachronistic institution of slavery that confronted him and his intellectual cohort as they attempted to envision a future configuration of Cuban identity that could be invoked in order to legitimate their ideological program for autonomy from Spain. Hence, a thorough comprehension of each proposal for modernity and its simultaneous rejoinder to the latter can be achieved only within the scene delimited by the particular historical circumstances from which it arose. Historical events have an ineradicable facticity that must be given its due. At the same time, my argument is that the discursive appropriation of historical events has a textual nature that in the Spanish American context inevitably sets in motion the rhetorical dynamics that I have described.

Nonetheless, it is impossible not to notice at the same time the repeated occurrence of certain motifs and strategies in the history of cultural discourse in Spanish America. The charting of the ambivalent displacement away from modernity that is the principal objective of this study reveals the existence of a number of rhetorical strategies that seem to recur in the consistent historical manifestation of that discursive maneuver. This circumstance can be accounted for in two ways: to begin with, there is indeed a transhistorical dimension to the definition of modernity, which has its roots in the various strands of eighteenth-century thought that are laid claim to time and again in disparate historical and geographic contexts. In his perceptive study of Greek modernization, Gregory Jusdanis has summarized these strands as follows: industrial expansion, constitutional restrictions on the exercise of political power, the rise of civil bureaucracies, the growth of urban centers, the spread of literacy and mass educations, secularism, and the appearance of the interior psychological self.[3] Second, it is possible to argue, without minimizing the ideological and historically bounded dimension of all discourse, that cultural discourse inevitably acquires an internal life of its own—that is, that the fiction that sees all the participants in a cultural enterprise as collectively engaged in a permanently ongoing process of cultural foundation and interpretation inevitably creates internal echoes, citations, and polemics in the historical deployment of that tradition. In other words, the inter-play of continuities and disjunctions with previous texts as well as each work's capacity to become itself the site of future contestation are effective immanent generators of the textual tradition to which they belong. The danger would lie, however, in succumbing to the temptation of claiming for these recurrent thematic and strategic moves some sort of absolute or primordial rhetorical status, a temptation that must be resisted under whatever seductive guise it may present itself. Hence, one of my cares in this monograph has been not to allow the claim of exemplarity made on behalf of the authors and works chosen for this study to be purchased at the expense of their specificity—both rhetorically and historically. It will be, of course, up to the reader to determine the degree to which I have succeeded.

The authors that I have selected to substantiate my thesis—Sarmiento, the Cuban antislavery writers, Mansilla, Quiroga, Vargas Llosa, García Márquez, and Fuentes—encompass among them roughly 150 years of Spanish America's history and literary production. Although that tem-poral expanse almost coincides with the actual chronological age of Span-ish America as a distinct political entity, this book is not aspiring to claim absolute coverage of cultural production in Spanish America during that entire period, even if I am in fact claiming that the rhetorical difficulties they exemplify are intrinsic to Spanish American cultural production in general. The works discussed here have been selected because they offer as a collection a varied sampling of the ways in which modernity has been interpreted throughout time in the Spanish American context. Each text is meant to be representative of a historically grounded concept of how "the modern" has been defined at various times in Spanish American history: Europeanization (Sarmiento), abolitionism (Del Monte), the ur-ban milieu (Mansilla), literary professionalization (Quiroga), postmodern-ism (Vargas Llosa), the end of modernity (García Márquez and Fuentes). I then attempt to show how each work engages in a surreptitious ques-tioning of the authority of that chosen paradigm of modernity; by the same token, how that maneuver is effected in each text is also part of the exemplarity that I claim for the works selected for study. This accounts for why some likely candidates have not been included—the literary movement called *modernismo*, for instance—as well as why other choices may at first seem surprising to the reader. In the case of *modernismo* it seemed to me that the most evident rendition of the rhetorical proble-matics I study in this book is the recurrent insistence on a local Spanish

American referent in the midst of a rarified universe derived from Symbolist and Parnassian poetics, a disjunction that evolved finally into the embracing of nativist topics that characterized the movement's denouement. Yet, I judged this reading to be too conventional a development to be indicative of the interpretive opportunities allowed by the perspective described here.

As may be evident by now, in this study the category of "text" is used in a broad and pliable fashion. Sometimes it refers to an individual work; at other times it alludes to the oeuvre of an author; at yet other times it is utilized to encompass a series of texts that compose a given discursive body or moment in Spanish American cultural history. This flexibility is necessary because the rhetorical phenomenon I am attempting to describe does not necessarily observe the discrete boundaries of individual texts. The embracing and turning away from the modern that I propose to survey in this book sometimes articulates itself in the larger body of an author's several works or in the relationships that are entertained among the texts that conform a particular discursive horizon. I am aware of the pitfalls entailed by this hermeneutical maneuver, yet I would argue for its appropriateness given the peculiarities of the object under scrutiny.

The nature of my argument makes the list of possible works to be examined almost inexhaustible, since I am contending its comprehensive applicability to Spanish American discourse as a whole; yet that same nature also requires close textual readings of works chosen because of their usefulness as exemplars of a specific rhetorical maneuver. The contradiction inherent in these two claims has produced, inevitably, a selection of texts that may be perceived as too idiosyncratic, as too discomfiting on account of its heterogeneity. I trust that in the end the book will make its case above and beyond—and perhaps because of—the heterogeneity of the material treated in it.

The writing of a book is a protracted and somewhat enigmatic process to which many people contribute, sometimes unbeknownst to them. The present one has benefited from the encouragement I have received and the intellectual stimulation I have derived from the works of Antonio Benítez Rojo, Sylvia Molloy, Doris Sommer, Julio Ramos, Josué Harari, Nancy Armstrong, Leonard Tennenhouse, Stephanie Merrim, Patricia Seed, Richard Morse, Claudio Véliz, Nelly Richard, Beatriz Sarlo, Eduardo Subirats, and my colleagues and graduate students at Emory University. My best friend, Servando Echeandía, has proven deserving of that adjective in too many late-night conversations about literature and life in general that I have imposed on him and that he has suffered patiently throughout the many years we have known each other. Aníbal González Pérez and James D. Fernández read the first version of this manuscript and made unsparing critiques; I unsuccessfully parried those critiques, but they have made this book as strong as it could ever hope to be. I would like to express my gratitude to the two anonymous readers of the manuscript, whose critical rigor and exacting critique was accompanied by an uncommon intellectual generosity. Also, portions of this book appeared in abridged form in *Modern Language Notes, Hispanic Review, PMLA*, and *Revista de Estudios Hispánicos*. I am grateful to the editors for permission to reprint them in revised and expanded form.

Finally, Anne Lubell, my unfailing intellectual interlocutor and the love of my life, has patiently taught me to be happy. This book is dedicated lovingly to her and to the wondrous things that we have accomplished together—Miguel and Ari foremost among them.

Atlanta, Georgia   C. J. A.
October 1997

Contents

The Burden of Modernity

CHAPTER ONE

Modernity as Ideal and Curse

América Latina, donde las tradiciones aún no se han ido y la modernidad no acaba de llegar.

Latin America: Where traditions have not yet departed, and modernity has not yet arrived.

—Néstor García Canclini, *Culturas híbridas*

El Arte y la Cultura es [sic] *la única forma de salvación a que pueden aspirar los pueblos pequeños.*

Art and Culture is [*sic*] the only kind of salvation to which lesser peoples can aspire.

—Mariano Picón Salas, "Las formas y las visiones"

THE TWO QUOTATIONS that serve as introduction to this chapter are opening statements in more than one fashion. Beyond their formal liminar function as epigraphs, I wish to invoke them as a point of departure for the discussion of a rhetorical characteristic that I will argue is typical of most Spanish American texts. In this regard, the two fragments are particularly useful since by all accounts they are representative of two diametrically opposed attitudes concerning the problems of cultural identity and cultural politics, as well as of their mutual articulation. The quotation by García Canclini is tinged with the knowledge of a presumably failed timetable, with the awareness of a thwarted historical development, and is shaped by an uneasy mixture of a feigned exasperation regarding the deficiencies of the present and a sense that something has been lost, perhaps irretrievably. There is also a redundant character to it, since the advent of the phenomenon described by the first clause is contingent on the earlier occurrence of the phenomenon depicted by the second: that is, almost by definition traditional ways are presumed to disappear or be otherwise displaced as a result of modernity's advent. Hence, in this context the conjunction expresses a false coupling, since the two clauses describe phenomena that are in reality simultaneous rather than sequential. Writing almost fifty years earlier, Picón Salas confronts the same distressing cultural scenario but offers instead the palliative of an affirmative cultural project. That the project is described in salvific terms substantiates that there is an acknowledged need for deliverance from the sort of fall or lack that is the backdrop to García Canclini's remark. Furthermore, in Picón Salas's statement, Art and Culture are proposed as the only dimension in which the avowed deficiencies of marginal cultures are no longer hindrances to performance, since the context configured by them is presumed to constitute a level playing field: one in which redemption can be achieved despite whatever failures in the other realms of historical existence one may be forced to admit or outsiders may wish to point out. Notice, however, the sentence's problematic grammatical coordination, with its initial attempt to separate Art and Culture as distinct entities, only to fuse them immediately afterward through the use of the singular verbal copula: "El Arte y la Cultura *es* . . ." As against García Canclini's quotation, in this case the conjunction is expressive of a desire to insure the discreteness of the elements involved, only to have this differential specificity disappear in its grammatical reduction to a single subject category through the employment of the copula conjugated in the singular.[1]

The two fragments quoted here are drawn from larger texts that address in turn some of the central questions of cultural life in Spanish America; in fact, they are representative of two very distinct perspectives on those issues: García Canclini's statement concerning the existence of an impasse in historical/cultural development contrasts sharply with Picón Salas's affirmation of a way out through the empowering vehicles of Culture and Art. In a sense, they could even be said to represent prototypical and contrary postmodernist and modernist attitudes, respectively, regarding the transcendent capabilities of cultural agency. Nonetheless, a closer examination has revealed that both remarks are characterized by a similar rhetorical incongruity, one that involves the use of a grammatical connective that is subsequently weakened by the logical structure of the very sentence in which it is employed. The sort of rhetorical disjunction exemplified by these two passages I take to be—not in its specificity but rather in its occurrence—a consistent trait of cultural discourse in Spanish America. This is not a restatement of the hackneyed assertion that Span-

ish American discourse is inherently marked by inconsistency and contradiction: such a diagnosis would only confirm the long-held and unproductive view that regards the peripheral writer as an imperfect wielder of
metropolitan discourses. My proposal is that such intrinsic discordances
and disjunctions, which are characteristic of *all* writing, become more
salient in the Spanish American text given the particular nature of the
rhetorical situation in which it is inscribed—a situation whose specificity
will be the main concern of this chapter. The works of Derrida, De Man,
J. Hillis Miller, and several others have alerted us to the fissures that exist
in all language, to the ways in which texts invariably manage to dismantle
themselves under the gaze of a scrutinizing reader; or, as Barbara Johnson
has put it, this sort of reading "follows the misfires, losses, and infelicities
that prevent any given language from being *one*. Langage, in fact, can
only exist in the space of its own foreignness to itself."[2] Yet my contention
is that in the Spanish American work these fissures and warring forces
within the text are exacerbated and brought to the surface by the tensions
inherent in the rhetorical circumstances from which it springs.

The enterprise of engaging in a study of the rhetoric of Spanish American cultural discourse has to be clarified from the start on two separate
but related grounds. First, it is not my intention to analyze this discourse
with the purpose of studying it against a register of tropes codified by
any rhetoric—classical or modern; hence, I am not seeking to produce
what would be commonly referred to as a rhetorical analysis of this tradition. This does not mean, of course, that rhetorical terms and concepts
will not be used in the course of my examination of these works. Second,
by studying the rhetorical dimension of this tradition I do not propose
to ignore or underestimate in any way the specific historical circumstances
that gave rise to these texts, thereby echoing the colloquial use of the
term "rhetorical" as referring to "mere words," devoid of truth or referential value. In fact, I have in mind quite the opposite, for I believe the
most rigorous account of the Spanish American discursive circumstance
is necessarily indissoluble from a consideration of the precise historical
conditions under which Spanish American writers and intellectuals labored to produce their works. Hence, the adjective "rhetorical" is used
throughout this study not as a marker of a certain modality of analysis
but as indicative of the way in which historical circumstances have created
a predicament that has in turn constituted the context for the Spanish
American performance of cultural discourse. In this regard, the category

"rhetorical" does not point at all to a purely textual milieu and should be interpreted as alluding to a context that is no less determining and compelling than historical circumstances are conventionally assumed to be.

The source of what would eventually manifest itself as this rhetorical predicament can be found in the amply studied phenomenon of the appropriation of the New World by European economic interests and its translation into narratives of knowledge and desire that arose to provide both an ideological justification and a cover for that incorporation. From the Discovery onward, the New World became defined by Europe intrinsically by its novel quality and by European projections onto it of the evolving interpretations of what constituted that novelty.[3] Sixteenth-century Europe's conceptions of America may have been quite different from romantic mystifications of the new continent, for instance, but they had as a common thread an explicit affirmation of the latter's capacity to evoke amazement on account of its infinite undiscoveredness, its ability to elude being known totally and for all time—that aspect of the New World that Stephen Greenblatt has subsumed under the apt term of "marvelousness."[4] Just as, for instance, the discovery of the island of the Amazons was perpetually imminent and forever postponed at once, the total knowledge of the New World—the moment in which the adjective "new" in the locative "New World" would cease to have a reason for being—was always simultaneously announced and deferred.[5] In this regard, the novelty of the New World functioned as the central conceit of an ideological narrative that propelled the spread of empire into ever wider exploration and acquisition of territory and ever more intricate epistemological constructs with which to encompass it.

This narrative of novelty was not without its problems, since at times its emphasis on the quest for the new came into direct conflict with the foundational and inescapably sedentary needs of the empire's colonizing project. But by and large, the narrative was sustained—with modifications, to be sure—into the Colonial period on account of its usefulness for metropolitan interests: first, as a facilitating backdrop for the ensuing colonial enterprise of raw material exploitation and uneven mercantile exchange of commodities, and second, as a coadjuvant to the New-World-as-imperial-frontier myth that was meant to enhance its desirability as an assignment to that class of bureaucrats designated by the Crown to administer it.

Yet it is important to underscore that from the Renaissance to Independence the new continent's relationship with Europe was inescapably defined in terms of complementarity, since newness and novelty are by definition relative and relational concepts: in other words, "the new" presupposes a place and a perspective from which it is perceived as such. It follows necessarily also that during that entire period America and Europe existed in a shared temporal frame: the chronological frame of the beholder who provided the continuity needed for the complementing operation. Mario Góngora has summarized this situation in the following fashion: "There is . . . a certain characteristic peculiar to America which has made it the stimulus and pretext for ambitious eschatological and Utopian schemes. . . . In both cases, they were ideal historical interpretations of great importance, because they incorporated the newly discovered lands into the spiritual history of Europe, even though, paradoxically, the precise manner of this incorporation resulted from the concept of them as countries which were new and different from Europe."[6]

Hence, in spite of the distancing mechanisms that were put in place to sustain the rhetoric of amazement and wonder about America, Europe and America were posited as coexisting in the same temporal/historical framework, even if the former was regarded as a perpetual source of novelty and wonderment for the latter. The European rhetoric of amazement depended heavily on the deployment of what anthropologist Johannes Fabian has termed "the denial of coevalness": the use of strategies to posit the other as a distant object of cognition.[7] In his powerful book Fabian argues that this denial of coevalness is perhaps the foundational strategy of anthropological thought. According to him, as a praxis ethnographic description places the Other *discursively* in a temporal and spatial dimension different from that of the researcher in order to create an epistemological space that will then be filled with the content of anthropological knowledge. Europe's rhetoric of amazement vis-à-vis America used some of the same distancing techniques alluded to by Fabian, since amazement necessitates the ceaseless deferral of total cognitive mastery. But rather than being deployed in order to maintain an irreducible alterity, the European figuration of the New World as new posited a continuity between itself and the new territories that made possible European appropriation of the recently discovered lands while simultaneously affirming their exoticism. In both cases we have obvious ideological strategies of incorporation disguised as their opposite—that is, as the seeming recognition of the Other's autonomy and ultimate unknowableness. But the peremptory and inescapable materiality of the colonial enterprise—as opposed to the predominantly intellectual character of the anthropological encounter—

precluded the total denial of coevalness, even if the new lands were posited as endlessly receding from the advancing European epistemological thrust. This predicament resulted in the sort of logical aporia involving both continuity and cleavage between the two worlds that Antonello Gerbi has studied in detail in his classic book *La disputa del Nuevo Mundo*.[8]

Nevertheless, though the discussion to this point describes in broad strokes the discursive and tropological relationship between Europe and the New World during the Colonial epoch, one can also point to the existence throughout that period of a counternarrative that was slowly acquiring shape. This alternative narrative was predicated on the positing of a shift in the relative temporal spaces occupied by America and Europe with respect to one another. For almost imperceptibly, the coevalness that the narrative of newness required was replaced by a narrative paradigm in which America occupied a position of *futurity* vis-à-vis the Old World. This transformation from novelty to futurity was significant because, among other things, it created the conditions for a permanent exoticization of the New World—the sort that cannot be undermined or dissolved by actual experience or objective analysis: safely ensconced in an always postponed future, America could become the object of a ceaselessly regenerating discourse of mystification and perpetual promise. In time, the resulting narrative would be taken up explicitly from this side of the Atlantic as an instrument to curtail European hegemony in the New World.[9]

Rafael Gutiérrez Girardot has alluded to a phenomenon that may help us locate the origin of this parallel counterplot in which the essence of America came to be identified with the future rather than with the quality of novelty. Speaking about the colonial *barroco de Indias* in Spanish America, an aesthetic modality for which there is no exact European counterpart, he avers the following:

> La especificidad del arte y la literatura barrocos hispanoamericanos . . . [es] la expresión del lujo que surgió del ascenso social. Si se acepta el sintético juicio de Alfonso Reyes sobre el barroco español, esto es, que expresa un "ansia de precipitación hacia lo absoluto," entonces cabe decir que el barroco literario hispanoamericano no es ansia de lo absoluto sino voluptuosa satisfacción del ascenso social, del triunfo sobre la pobreza peninsular que proporcionó a los primeros pobladores y conquistadores del Nuevo Mundo el descubrimiento de que el mundo fantástico de las novelas de caballería no era sólo un sueño sino que parecía real. (46)[10]

> The specificity of Spanish American baroque art and literature . . . is the expression of the luxury that arose from social mobility. If one accepts Al-

fonso Reyes's pithy comment about the Spanish baroque as expressing a "desire to rush headlong toward the absolute," then one could perhaps say that the Spanish American literary baroque is not a desire for the absolute but rather the voluptuous satisfaction of social ascent; the triumph over peninsular poverty that was offered to the first settlers and conquerors of the New World by the discovery that the fantastic world of chivalric romances was not just a dream.

Although Gutiérrez Girardot's observation concerns itself exclusively with the *barroco de Indias*, his insight has implications that transcend the aesthetic realm as well as the temporal specificity of the Spanish American baroque. The proposition that there has been a long-standing effort to link the New World constitutively to the possibilities of the future is, of course, not new with Gutiérrez Girardot. Nonetheless, Gutiérrez's comment differs quite significantly from earlier conceptions in that it offers a *material* basis for the explanation of why such an association between the future and the New World should have arisen in the first place. For, if I understand him correctly, in his view the American continent came to be identified with futurity because it was perceived from the outset as a scenario where individual social mobility was possible—where the static social categories of metropolitan Spain could be made permeable through the instrument of personal agency.[11] In this fashion, the surfacing of a previously unknown possibility of social fluidity would translate itself into a concrete sense of the future as the realm of the possible-but-not-yet-realized. From there it is not difficult to imagine how after a while what may have been understood or felt at first strictly as a social venue for personal advancement would later come to be identified, through a simple metonymical operation, with the geographic, material, and historical specificity of the New World.

As should be evident by now, the two master narratives of novelty and futurity arose from the sharp and ever diverging interests of the metropolis and those of the colonial *criollo* elites, respectively. This clash of interests was founded on the ample privileges originally bestowed on the founding settlers and their descendants by the king—privileges that the Crown would very quickly endeavor to curtail. But as Richard Morse makes clear, it was also abetted by geography and its implications for a centralized authority: "The centrifugal movement of settlers out into farms, ranch, and mining lands, far removed from seaports and administrative centers (with these in turn distant from Spain by a long and arduous sea voyage), created the danger of virtually sovereign satrapies, each enjoying absolute control of Indian workers."[12] The concept of America as novel was in the interest of the metropolis because it brought implicit with it, as we saw earlier, the possibility and the promise of the former's reduction to the coordinates of the Old World. The fact that from this perspective the new continent and Europe shared the same temporal frame—even if America was defined as a constant source of new phenomena—was a guarantee that they also shared the same epistemological plane; hence, the narrative of novelty was by extension an affirmation of the conceptual accessibility and eventual mastery of the New World. Equally important, the coevalness that this view assumed both guaranteed the success and certified the legitimacy of the *traslatio imperii*, that is, the faithful and uncontaminated reproduction in the colonies of the social and political structures of the metropolis. In this regard, the narrative that identified the Americas with novelty can be seen to have functioned as an ideological façade for an operation that aspired in fact to maintain stasis and the permanence of existing structures of authority through time.

In sharp contrast, the master plot of futurity posited a break in the absolute continuity espoused by the metropolitan narrative of novelty, emphasizing instead the political and ideological terrain in the American continent left uncovered or unaccounted for by the metropolis's hegemony. Its ultimate aim was to put in suspension or challenge the unproblematic *traslatio* assumed by the narrative of novelty. This was achieved principally by using as a most effective armament the double-edged quality of the newness invoked in that narrative, for the mobilization of a master story based on the concepts of novelty and amazement carried with it the danger of allowing the "new" reality to slip insensibly into a refractory difference instead—in other words, the discourse of the New could turn into a discourse on the insurmountably Other. The activation of this potential fissure at the core of the concept of the new provided a foundation for the contestatory plot in which America was identified with an ever postponed future, a tactic that inaugurated a discursive space in which alternate possibilities could be legitimately envisioned, if not essayed outright—as Gutiérrez Girardot's comment implies. This strategy— which I would like to call the "subjunctification" of political language— would be of immediate usefulness to the descendants of the original *conquistadores*, attentive as they were to any circumstance that would permit the redefinition of their relationship with the metropolis in such a fashion as to protect and advance their class interests.[13] This explains how, for all their political and economic conservatism—their unwillingness to change substantively the political and economic structures against which they were presumably revolting—the Creoles and mestizos who declared themselves autonomous from Spain during the first decades of the nineteenth century nonetheless could and did deploy for their rebellious purposes a rhetoric that was solidly identified with modernity, change, and futurity.[14]

Political independence was unquestionably the historical culmination of this narrative centered on the avowedly indissoluble relationship between America and the future. One sees this in that, on the whole, arguments for independence were founded as much on complaints about Spanish abuses of power as on the fundamental allegation that Spain was hopelessly tied to a past that was now judged discontinuous with Spanish America's essence and needs.[15] Furthermore, it is significant in this regard that simultaneous with the first stirrings of the emancipation campaign, the appellation "Nuevo Mundo" was reactivated in reference to the American colonies and given wide circulation after centuries of disuse.[16] But the use of a figurative historical scheme that projected the newly liberated continent's core reality into the future had momentous consequences, results that reached far beyond the period of the struggle for independence.[17] These ramifications become evident when the postcolonial experience of the former Spanish possessions of the New World is compared with that of other nations throughout the globe at the moment in which they managed to cast off the yoke of metropolitan domination.

What such a comparison reveals immediately is the essential distinctness of the Spanish American case, a uniqueness that I argue is directly attributable to the Creole reliance on the narrative of futurity that I have been discussing to this point. To begin with, the very concept of postcolonialism arose in order to describe and examine the relatively recent twentieth-century historical experience of decolonization in its various manifestations; as such, the circumstances of its formulation and the realities that it was meant to encompass are removed by more than a century from the comparable moment in Spanish American history. More decisive still, however, is the fact that the Spanish American postcolonial circumstance differs substantially from other such conditions in that there was an attempt to identify the new countries (when not the entire liberated continent) with the future rather than with some autochthonous cultural reality that preceded the colonial imposition of power, as was the case in other postcolonial situations. To conceive of Spanish America's predicament after the defeat and expulsion of the Spanish presence as a postcolonial condition is highly problematic because what is perhaps the most powerful impulse behind colonial revolt (and likewise the most determining principle in the subsequent postcolonial reality) is to understand the period of colonial occupation as a sort of historical parenthesis, as an interruption or hiatus that, once ended, should allow the formerly colonized culture to retake the forcibly abandoned thread of its authentic historical existence. There are, indeed, a number of modern postcolonial projects that evince a commitment to modernization, some of which have been intelligently examined by Neil Lazarus in his book *Resistance in Postcolonial African Fiction*. Almost invariably, though, the argument there is for a participation in modernity that ought to be preceded by the recuperation of traditional cultural ways, which should then make possible the nation's partaking of and contributing to the modern world from a sui generis and locally grounded location. In Spanish America such nuances were hardly ever entertained. This essential difference in the Spanish American postcolonial circumstance has seemingly become "visible," as it were, only in the past few years, and its manifold consequences are only beginning to be explored. The Mexican anthropologist Jorge Klor de Alva has argued along similar lines in a recent article in which he proposes the distinctness of the Spanish American situation in a forceful and rigorous critical performance.[18] His conclusions on the matter deserve to be cited at length:

> Given that the indigenous populations of the Americas began to suffer a devastating demographic collapse on contact with the Europeans; given that with minimal exceptions this population loss had the effect, by the late sixteenth century, of restricting those who identified themselves as natives to the periphery of the nascent national polities; given that the greater part of the mestizos who quickly began to replace them fashioned their selves primarily after European models; given that together with Euro-Americans (criollos) and some Europeans (peninsulares) these Westernized mestizos made up the forces that defeated Spain during the nineteenth-century wars of independence; and, finally, given that the new countries under criollo/mestizo leadership constructed their national identities overwhelmingly out of Euro-American practices, the Spanish language, and Christianity, it is misguided to present the pre-independence non-native sectors as colonized, it is inconsistent to explain the wars of independence as anti-colonial struggles, and it is misleading to characterize the Americas, following the civil wars of separation, as postcolonial. In short, the Americas were neither Asia nor Africa; Mexico is not India, Peru is not Indonesia, and Latinos in the U.S.—although tragically opposed by an exclusionary will—are not Algerians. (3)[19]

Klor de Alva's thesis is indisputable in its description of the specificity of the Spanish American case, to wit: the Creole and mestizo classes who fashioned the new nations of Spanish America (a) did not belong to the indigenous element, which had been banished almost from the start to the periphery of the social body, and (b) used European language, religion, and cultural models in the construction of their emerging national identities. These factors together make it very difficult to subsume the Spanish American postindependence period under the rubric of the postcolonial because, as I stated earlier, the quintessential postcolonial gesture is one of recuperation of the indigenous group's interrupted historical existence. Furthermore, as Klor proposes, if there was no decolonization during the presumed period of postcoloniality, one can also throw into question the existence of a preceding colonial reality. Yet I believe that the conclusions arrived at by Klor de Alva on the basis of his otherwise accurate description can be challenged in at least two of its key aspects.

According to Klor, the principal difference in the Spanish American case is the fact that the mestizo and Creole classes that took over after the defeat of Spanish hegemony had no ethnic identification with the colonized indigenous population and fashioned themselves after European models, thereby presumably weakening the ties to a group that possessed an identity that could have provided the foundation for a legitimate claim of cultural autochthony. All of this is of course true; but in itself it does not explain why that should have been in fact the case. Moreover, Klor's argument is composed against the presumed backdrop of an archetypical postcolonial situation, the one against which the difference entailed by the Spanish American case becomes not just visible but measurable as well. Yet when one examines the elements of what Klor would regard as the model postcolonial condition, one finds that the distinctness and specificity of the Spanish American case are not as transparent as he would have it.

Let us consider for a moment the definition of the traditional postcolonial circumstance invoked by Klor, as depicted now in its African rendition by Kwame Anthony Appiah in his gripping book *In My Father's House: Africa in the Philosophy of Culture*: "Postcoloniality is the condition of what we might ungenerously call a comprador intelligentsia: of a relatively small, Western-Style, Western-trained, group of writers and thinkers who mediate the trade in cultural commodities of world capitalism at the periphery. In the West they are known through the Africa they offer; their compatriots know them both through the West they present to Africa and through the Africa they have invented for the world, for each other, and for Africa."[20] Appiah's description is of interest to us because of the similarities between the situation he describes and the supposedly distinct Spanish American circumstance discussed by Klor de Alva. The cultural producers of so-called "conventional" postcolonial societies share with their Spanish American counterparts their intellectual upbringing and self-fashioning after Western models; the paradigms they have invoked in order to bring to life the postcolonial nation are more likely than not derived from nineteenth-century European conceptions of nationalism; they speak the colonizer's language equally well as—if not anxiously better than—it is spoken by educated speakers in the metropolitan capital. It could be claimed in response that in the typical postcolonial circumstance the members of the national postcolonial ruling groups described by both Klor and Appiah have ethnic ties to the indigenous population and were therefore discriminated against and thus hampered under the colonial regime by diminished opportunities. But if it is true that the Spanish American Creoles and mestizos eschewed identification with the original native populations, their lives under the colonial regime were so routinely exposed to impediments to their advancement and to arbitrariness in their treatment that, as Benedict Anderson has argued, the sense of belonging to a cohort of oppressed second-class subjects became one of the principal realizations impelling them to seek autonomy from Spain.[21] Michael Hechter has stated this idea in more general terms by saying that "the persistence of objective cultural distinctiveness in the periphery must itself be the function of the maintenance of an unequal distribution of resources between the core and peripheral groups."[22] Therefore, the claim for the distinctness of the Spanish American postcolonial case must rest—if it is to hold at all—on categories or circumstances that either are different from those mentioned by Klor de Alva or constitute a distinctly American rendition of them.

My answer is that Klor is correct in asserting the specificity of the Spanish American postcolonial circumstance but that his analysis misdiagnoses mostly symptomatic events as if they were the underlying root condition instead. The difference of the Spanish American case cannot reside in those qualities that Klor identifies since, as we have seen, they are not by any means unique to Spanish America. In fact, the similarities revealed make it not just possible but entirely accurate to refer to the wars of liberation as an anticolonial struggle and thus to speak about the existence of a Spanish American postcolonial condition. The truly important difference in the Spanish American case stems from the fact that the narrative that was used to give an ideological underpinning to the anti-colonial effort was not one in which the idea of recovering or returning to indigenous cultural ways played a significant role. Klor is doubtless cognizant of this narrative "deviation," and he proposes to explain it by underscoring the social marginalization of the indigenous element, on the one hand, and the many cultural qualities that the Creoles and mestizos had in common with the colonizers from whom they nevertheless wanted to secede, on the other. But these are not in themselves explanations but rather circumstances that arise from the narrative departure from the norm; that is, the adoption of Western ways and the marginalization of the autochthonous element by Creole and mestizo groups can be explained as coextensive with a desire to eschew identification with the indigenous past rather than as the markers of an essential ethnic and cultural difference that prevents identification with that element and then reflects itself in the anticolonial narrative used (again, mistaking the symptom for the disease). In other words, the Creole and mestizo groups *willed* themselves narratively white and Western, and the denial of the autochthonous element issued from that, and not from their *being* different from that element.[23] This is why I believe we must look elsewhere if we are to identify the origin of the narrative deviation from which the Spanish American postcolonial situation ensues.

I would like to propose that the root of this distinctness lies in the dominance achieved by the narrative of futurity examined earlier, through which the New World came to be identified comprehensively and unequivocally with the future. Since all formulations of national character are artificial abstractions—imagined communities—in any event, theoretically there were no compelling ethnic, linguistic, or demographic reasons preventing the Spanish American Creoles who defeated the Spaniards from constructing a narrative of national origins based on the indigenous past;[24] witness the atypical and truly singular case of Paraguay, in which the Indian presence was decisively incorporated into the myth of national foundations by the Creole elite;[25] or the fringe Mexican neo-Aztec movement of the late eighteenth century, which concocted the very term "Aztec" in the process of advancing a mythologized version of the pre-Columbian past.[26] What did indeed serve as an impediment to even considering the plausibility of this option was the compelling drive behind the narrative of futurity that had been nurtured and finally taken up explicitly by the Creoles as the ideological justification for the secessionist movement. In the specific context of this narrative, with its tropological framework of futurity, the idea of founding the postcolonial nation on the project of reactivating an indigenous past would have been difficult to envision, let alone articulate. In reality, though, this option had effectively been foreclosed long before the independence moment and the ensuing postcolonial phase of national redefinition. The marginalization of the indigenous population in Spanish America began with the colonizer's sense of superiority—that is, as a facet of an ideological ploy to justify the denial of political participation, as was the case in almost every other colonial situation. But it was also abetted by the natives' growing irrelevance, an irrelevance that arose from the ideological constructions of the Creole and mestizo elites in their efforts to devise formulas to contest Spanish hegemony. The dominant one of these was, I am arguing, the narrative in which Spanish America was identified with a vision of the future, a prospective reality that was always announcing itself in the telltale signs of its imminence and that unavoidably condemned the autochthonous element to historical and narrative invisibility.

Interestingly, the indigenous populations received the same treatment in this ideological narrative of Creole hegemony as their erstwhile Spanish oppressors: they as well as the Spaniards were simply written out of it by being subsumed under the mantle of the preterit, by being assigned to what from the perspective of the narrative of the future could only be described as the *non-place* of the past. Through this maneuver Spain and everything associated with it was placed in a hopelessly archaic and static temporal location by the Creole anticolonial struggle, which is wryly ironic because the liberal and forward-looking policies of the Enlightened metropolitan administrations of the second half of the eighteenth century had been bitterly opposed by the emerging and later triumphant Creoles.[27] In the end, the narrative of futurity admitted of the past only to mark its distance from it, and of the present only as an imperfect harbinger of things to come. It sometimes found expression in paradoxical affirmations of nonidentity, such as the following one by Bolívar: "Nosotros, que no somos nada y que empezamos a ser" [We, who are nothing and are beginning to be . . .] notice the rhetorical similarity between this phrase and the quotation by García Canclini that serves as an epigraph to this chapter).[28] But by the same token, this narrative opened a wide rhetorical space for the formulation of potentially new emplotments of nationalism and nationality, at least when compared to the narrower repertoire of the paradigmatic postcolonial narration, which is principally articulated around the recuperation of indigenous origins.[29] On the other hand, the richness of possibilities seemingly available and the open-ended quality of the discursive realm hence inaugurated would also bring unsuspected anxieties and difficulties—as we shall see later.

The discourse of futurity, which had served so efficiently in the context of the anticolonial struggle against Spanish hegemony and authority, became the essential framework for the construction of novel ideological narratives during the postcolonial phase of nation building. But the integral tenets of this script clashed with the essentially conservative models for the definition of a nation and a people that were contemporaneously available. In fact, the narrative of the future was forced to undergo a transformation in order to allow it to serve the ideological needs of the nation-building phase. As I have argued elsewhere, the then recent paradigms for the definition of a people and a nation could not be applied unproblematically to the Spanish American cultural situation for two basic reasons: first, the specific linguistic and territorial characteristics and circumstances of Spanish America confounded the model; second, the paradigm's strength derived in great part from its rigid, unyielding simplicity, which made impossible any adjustments or modifications that would allow it to fit a recalcitrant reality.[30] The decisive postcolonial contribution of the discourse of futurity was precisely to mask this ill-fitting implementation of the imported paradigm of the nation by shifting the conservative, backward glance of the people/nation model to a forward-looking projection into the future. This ideological resolution was expressed in an uneasy arrangement that allowed for the parallel coexistence of both the narrative of futurity and the imported model for the nation and that could be summarized in the following fashion: each country would engage in the formulation of a national myth of origins that would identify and locate its presumed beginnings somewhere in the colonial period, while it would also be possible for each country to assert simultaneously that the final configuration and image of that national identity would be revealed only at an unspecified yet certain future date. In this way the monadic and static European model for the formulation of a national identity was infused in its Spanish American acceptation with a chronological dimension that made for a contradictory but nonetheless ideologically useful discursive space.

Eventually these contradictions compelled yet another modification in the narrative of futurity that would attempt to conceal them by displacing them to a different terrain—by projecting them now to the *continental* plane. That is, each country would exercise the option of affirming a national distinctness arising from the colonial past, while emphasizing at other times its essential connection to a wider continental identity that was to achieve its consummate expression at a future point in time. The concept of a continent wide identity had first surfaced during the independence struggle and had carried on briefly into the early years after victory. In the beginning it was a manifestation of the intense collective polarization that was inherent in the anticolonial contest, as well as a possible ideological ground for one of the several options of geopolitical organization that were being contemplated for the liberated territories: a republic that would putatively encompass the entire geographical expanse of the former colonies. But this was all before the territorial claims of the various local elites had had an opportunity to manifest themselves as discrete nationalistic aspirations. Yet the idea of a supranational continental identity survived the fragmentation of the vast colonial territories into separate and avowedly distinct republics. Its long history can be gleaned from the several versions of *americanismo* that have been a constant in Spanish American discourse on culture, a longevity that attests directly to its usefulness as an ideological instrument for the defusing of political, social, and narrative contradictions.[31]

To recapitulate: the narrative of futurity and its various transformations can be seen as having served important ideological purposes during both the colonial and postcolonial periods. What must be underscored, though, is that the reliance on that narrative for the fulfilment of those peremptory ideological needs also created an uncompromising commitment to the discourse of the future and its rhetoric that extended well beyond the anticolonial struggle against Spain. Here lies the source of the self-identification of the new countries with modernity, since the concept of time at the core of the latter was exactly coincident with the one displayed by the Spanish American narrative of futurity. That is to say that regardless of its richness and possibilities, in both perspectives the present was significant mostly inasmuch as it constituted the anticipation of a final and always future epiphany. Hence, modernity became from the outset the cri de coeur for the Spanish American republics because the former's narrative repertoire dovetailed perfectly with the rhetorical demands of the cultural myth of futurity that had been forged to oppose the discourse of Spanish hegemony. In a number of salient ways my aim here is to explore the ultimate consequences of this ideological and rhetorical commitment to the discourse of modernity made by Spanish American intellectuals and cultural creators. Yet to begin to appreciate the depth of this compact and the extent of its repercussions, we must remember that political independence did not so much mark the end of colonialism for Spanish America as its entrance into a neocolonial arrangement in the historical context provided by nineteenth-century imperialist expansion. For the concrete world-historical backdrop in which Spanish America experienced its postcolonial circumstance is another important element in the determination of the latter's specificity and distinctness.

The Spanish American Discursive Situation

Very soon after emancipation, European imperialist powers penetrated Spanish America swiftly and effectively in a script that is all too familiar to need rehearsing here. The vast destruction wreaked by the wars of independence and the need to build an economic infrastructure—even one that would simply enable the new countries to carve a peripheral niche in the prevailing mercantile system—imposed almost immediately the reliance on foreign capital for internal development.[32] This form of neocolonial penetration had the insidious advantage of being seemingly invisible, since it took the form of accords, loans, and guarantees between supposedly sovereign nations or between sovereign nations and foreign trusts, a formula that rendered unnecessary the sort of overt colonial take-over that was contemporaneously being exercised by the same metropolitan countries in other areas of the world. The economic results for Spanish America were nevertheless virtually indistinguishable from those in other colonial scenarios: the region was quickly relegated to the periphery of an economic and commercial system that had global scope and territorial ambitions to match.

In this international order the economic, spatial, and cultural arrangement of center/periphery was endowed with legitimacy by a collection of ideological narratives and categories that sought to naturalize the hierarchy that had been created, in effect, by the economic relationship just described. The most significant and all-encompassing of these narratives was, of course, the myth of Modernity: the belief that there were metropolitan foci out of which the modern emanated and which by means of a rippled and delayed expansion through time and space would eventually transform the material and cultural orders of those societies that languished in the outer confines of the system—if only they were fittingly receptive to its beneficent effects. A case could indeed be made that Modernity was the master trope of Western hegemonic authority, the one that provided the foundation for the countless other hierarchical arrangements of categories employed by the relentless *ratio* of the metropolitan discourse of domination.[33] For the imposition of a universal time line made possible the annulment of local chronologies in their heterogeneity, which in turn provided the leveling of the field needed to allow the operation of cross-cultural judgment to obtain. In the words of Nelly Richard,

> All the extensions of the idea of modernity work towards confirming the position of privilege, and to this end negate any particular or localized expression which could possibly interfere with the fiction of universality. Transferred to the geographical and socio-cultural map of economic and communicational exchanges, this fiction operates to control the adaptation to given models and so to standardize all identifying procedures. Any deviation from the norm is classified as an obstacle or brake to the dynamic of international distribution and consumption. Thus modernity conceives of the province or periphery as being out of step or backward. Consequently, this situation has to be overcome by means of absorption into the rationality of expansion proposed by the metropolis.[34]

In this sense "modernity" is always more than just a category: it is an operation of exclusion that always has already taken place.

In all colonial situations the indigenous ruling classes that had been displaced or forced by the metropolitan power into the diminished role of mediators eventually developed a number of strategies to progressively challenge more openly metropolitan authority and its legitimizing institutions and ideological conceits—the narrative of modernity chiefly among the latter. This is the process that historically results in the final expulsion of the imperial power after a protracted and multilevel anticolonial struggle and that has been the proximate cause of the various waves of decolonization that have punctuated the last two-thirds of the present century. In Spanish America, however, the situation was much more complicated and ambiguous, since the essential tenets of the myth of futurity on which the cultural foundation and distinctiveness of the new countries rested harmonized rather than conflicted with the narrative of Modernity that sustained the legitimacy and prestige of metropolitan rule. Hence, at the precise moment when Spanish American intellectuals moved to assert their specificity or made a claim for cultural distinctness, they did so by using a rhetoric that unavoidably reinforced the cultural myths of metropolitan superiority. In this way what could have constituted a space for a contestatory intervention was thoroughly compromised by its reliance on a set of tropes that it shared with its putative rhetorical antagonist. This is the essential contradiction that resides at the root of Spanish American cultural discourse and the one that has dictated until very recently the contorted intensity of its rhetorical force.[35]

Hence, for Spanish American writers authority resides in the prestige of the discursive models of modernity that they invoke and that are appropriated precisely to lend status to their writing. This maneuver would appear to be predicated on the complete absence of the anxiety of influence; on the unproblematic appropriation of the Other's voice; on a practice of citation that is actually eager to acknowledge its sources rather than conceal them. Examples of this sumptuous display and conspicuous consumption of "modern" metropolitan rhetorical models are so numerous in the history of cultural discourse in Spanish America as to be overwhelming. Yet in his philosophical analysis of discourse, *L'Inconscient malgré lui*, Vincent Descombes has examined the difficult logic of the argument that invokes the authority of another in order to vouch for itself.[36] In employing the "authority argument," as he calls it, those who do not know identify those who supposedly know in order to substantiate their formulations. But a difficulty arises immediately, one that can be summarized in the following terms: "How does someone who does not know, know enough despite his ignorance to know that there is a third person who is absent and knows?" (112). But further complications ensue:

> And how does the one who does not know, know where to find the knowledge that he is missing? He has faith, of course, on the reputation, the glory attached to a certain name by universal opinion. . . . *Everybody* knows who the third person is that must be invoked in the discussion between a subject and his audience. That third person is finally *everybody*, personified in this circumstance by the subject who answers to the illustrious name. . . . The authority of general opinion founds the authority of the supposed sage; in other words, the authority of the Other as a third person rests on the authority of the Other as the place of universal discourse (what everybody says). Hence, the argument on authority concludes by quoting in fact universal thought. (113)[37]

The difficulty lies in that "common knowledge"—that is, what everybody knows—is not a dependable warrantor of the authority of an individual to back another's argument, since in fact this person is being singled out from the mass of people as a privileged voice of knowledge. The "authority argument" can thus be shown to be a contradiction in terms, since it bases its authority on its identification of a Master as a source of knowledge, when in reality that identification has been effected from the outset by "the crowd."

Descombes is describing a situation that arises out of the strategic and limited use of the invocation of another's authority in order to substantiate or buttress one's point. Furthermore, his analysis of borrowed authority studies the implications of that practice in the context of a homogeneous universe of discourse, that is, one in which it is assumed that every writer is in a position to speak with authority in the first place—even if that authority may be occasionally borrowed from another person who belongs to that same discursive circuit. But what happens when the citation of authority extends to entire discursive modalities—philosophical, literary, scientific, and so on—which are appropriated by virtue of their avowed prestige? And how does the dynamics that Descombes identifies play itself out when the "knowledgeable" source and the text that cites it belong to different discursive universes, mutually imbricated, furthermore, in an asymmetrical relationship?

The first consideration pertains to the discernment that the designation of an authority figure is in the ultimate analysis a reflection of collective opinion. The Spanish American writer perceives himself as occupying an extrinsic position vis-à-vis the metropolitan rhetorical collectivity that would designate his model as an authority: therein lies the reason for reaching for the model in the first place, since the aim is to bring this model to bear on a reality that will be avowedly illuminated by the model's application to it. This circumstance makes the invocation of the model at once both easier and more difficult. It is easier because authority can be equated simply with provenance from the metropolis so that *any* author coming from that discursive realm could potentially be an authority figure. But this possibility simultaneously makes it harder to make the claim of authority for *any one* figure as against all the others that could nominally be invoked for that purpose. Hence, the Spanish American writer collectivizes and multiplies a category that in order to function effectively as a warrantor of his authority has to be thoroughly identified with a particular individual instead. In this regard the situation of the Spanish American intellectual reveals the mechanism that is intrinsic to all writing that uses "authority arguments," but in this case the dynamics that Descombes underscores becomes readily manifest on account of the relative positionality of the speaker with respect to the metropolis that is inherent in the Spanish American discursive event.

Equally problematic is the fact that the unrestricted use of the "argument of authority" effected by the Spanish American writer produces a crisis in its operation, which is supposed to be ruled by its strategic employment to temporarily support a rhetorical authority that is nonetheless assumed to be always already there. Descombes's dismantling of the "authority argument" is effective only because it overturns the authority that the citing text thought it possessed. But the extended and comprehensive resort to the argument of authority by the Spanish American text underscores that its authority is founded primarily on the citational operation that it encompasses, thereby turning what defines itself as a limited practice of authorization into the text's foundational strategy of legitimation. This surfeited and wholesale use of the argument of authority reveals to us that the authority of *all* discourse is founded in effect on the repeated citation of other texts and authors; but that deconstructive realization cannot compensate for the rhetorical disempowerment that the excess produces in its wake. Hence, the seemingly unproblematic appropriation of the Other's voice that characterizes much of Spanish American discourse reveals at another level a thorough problematization of the writer's discursive authority.

Furthermore, the condition of being economically and culturally peripheral to the metropolis (a dependency that, as I argued earlier, was no less real for being less overt) created yet another difficulty for the Spanish American writer: given the objective economic and social circumstances of the new continent—semifeudal agricultural economies; flourishing slavery in some instances; masses of illiterate Indians, blacks, and so-called mixed-breeds; precarious urban life; political instability—Spanish American reality was always in danger of becoming the negative object of Western knowledge, of Western modernity and its discourses; that is, it was forever on the verge of turning into the consummate example of an untoward deviation from a supposed norm established by those same metropolitan discourses that were themselves confidently wielded by Spanish American writers and intellectuals. This situation constituted a permanent danger to the latter: the threat of passing from being the brandishers of a discourse to becoming their object instead. This predicament, coupled with the problematic dynamics of the argument of authority, reveals that the rhetoric of Modernity constituted both the bedrock of Spanish American cultural discourse and the potential source of its most radical disempowerment.

My discussion of the elaborate implications of these contradictions be-

gins with a brief survey of two recent and influential works on the topic
of modernity in the Hispanic world. This review will enable us to understand the need for a sweeping reconceptualization of the concept as it
is employed in the larger Hispanic context, especially in the Spanish
American milieu.

The two books I am referring to are Beatriz Sarlo's *Una modernidad
periférica: Buenos Aires 1920 y 1930* and Eduardo Subirats's *La ilustración
insuficiente*, both of which constitute perhaps the most significant revisit-
ings of the topic of modernity in Spanish America and Spain, respectively,
in recent years. Subirats, a philosopher by training, proposes to address
in his study the *idée reçue* concerning the innate frailty if not the outright
absence of Enlightenment philosophy in Spain. Indeed, it would be difficult to provide a thorough account of the various dominant cultural and
historical paradigms that take as their point of departure the feebleness
of modern thought in the Spanish context—a deficiency that is then ex-
trapolated to the Spanish American scenario as well. Sarlo's book in turn
examines cultural discourse in the Buenos Aires of the 1920s and 1930s.
Recognizing her debt to British cultural historian Raymond Williams, she
endeavors to identify the "structures of feeling" created by the experienced sensation of participating in "lo nuevo" that was characteristic of
the times—that is, the various ways in which Argentine cultural production of the two decades she addresses in her essay reflected the urban
dynamics of modernization.[38]

Aside from the influence they have exerted in the rethinking of modernity in the Hispanic context, these works are significant for two other
reasons: first, the authors and periods addressed by them—Feijóo, on the
one hand, and the Argentina of the 1920s and 1930s on the other—
roughly stand at the two chronological boundaries of the experience of
modernity in the Hispanic world.[39] Second, the titles of both monographs
explicitly reflect the fact that they intend to be corrective of received ideas
regarding the experience of modernity in the respective cultural contexts
examined by each. Subirats's book is an attempt to dismantle the tired
yet still almost universally accepted notion concerning the feebleness of
Enlightenment thought in Spain. By striking directly at this cardinal conceit, Subirats proposes to create a novel space for the reconsideration of
the status of modernity in the Spanish circumstance. His strategy is to
engage in a subtle analysis of Feijóo's critical discourse in an effort to
expose its close filiation with the more conventionally acknowledged discursive practices of a generalized European Enlightenment. Sarlo, on the

other hand, is interested in taking to task the commonplace idea that modernity in the peripheral milieu of Argentina was nothing but a simpleminded reflection of metropolitan cultural motifs and models regarding the modern. By focusing on the aesthetic movements and forms that emerged from the historically grounded experience of the modern in Buenos Aires, she purports to provide a distinctive face to an Argentine— and, by extension, Spanish American—modernity, a sui generis face to counter the indictment of servility to metropolitan sources.

Both of these works forcefully propose the need to rethink the experience of modernity in the Hispanic world. All their examples argue convincingly for a reconsideration of Enlightenment and liberal thinking in Spain and Spanish America that will not dismiss them as inadequate either because they did not manage to go far enough or because they were merely an echo of metropolitan discourses of modernity. Yet Subirats's and Sarlo's books position themselves respectively *against* each one of these prejudices in turn and are therefore inescapably caught in a dialectics of restoration through the affirmation of the opposite. The way to a thorough understanding of the experience of modernity in the Hispanic context does not lie in the careful overturning or the rigorous denial of received notions—maneuvers exemplified by these two otherwise admirable works—however indispensable that step may be. It requires a radical reconsideration of that experience and its historical determinants. Hence, I now retake the thread of my discussion in order to delineate an alternative possibility for understanding the phenomenon.

As I stated earlier, the adoption of the discourses of modernity placed Spanish American writers in an overwhelming rhetorical situation, since they and their reality were perpetually in danger of shifting from the subject to the object position of that discourse. Consequently, their discursive authority was just as unfailingly threatened by this ambiguity regarding their proper grammatical and epistemological location within their own elocution. In semiotic terms it could be stated that the danger confronting Spanish American writers was their employment of a discourse that threatened to turn them from *sujet d'énonciation* into *sujet d'énoncé*.[40] In order to address such an untenable situation—one that entailed the persistent undermining of their rhetorical command—Spanish American writers and intellectuals had to devise ways in which to subvert the authority of the discourses of modernity even as they wielded them ostentatiously. In the most general terms, this subversion can be described as the opening of a dimension within the text in which the latter's chosen rhetorical mode is contravened, thwarted, or rendered somehow inoperative. The result is that even while arguing for the adoption of the ideology of modernity and its values, Spanish American writers also moved simultaneously to delimit a space impervious to that rhetoric as a strategy to address the threat with which the discourse of modernity unremittingly confronted their discursive authority. This contradictory rhetorical situation manifests itself textually in that the work adopts a rhetorical mode identified as "modern" and simultaneously proceeds to argue in a way that suggests that this rhetorical mode is somehow not commensurate with the Spanish American circumstance. The outcome of this textual maneuver is a rhetorical difference that resides at the center of the Spanish American work, a turning away from itself that is expressive of its incongruous discursive predicament; for the text is engaged at some level or another in this attempt to effect a cultural claim to exception from modernity, a claim that is the expression of a discursive will to power, an attempt to stave off the rhetorical disenfranchisement with which modernity threatened the Spanish American writer at every turn. It is a strategy designed to fashion a rhetorical foundation, to arrive at a position of rhetorical authority out of the difficult discursive situation outlined earlier—a stratagem to rhetorically empower the Spanish American writer in the face of modernity's threat to undermine the legitimacy of his discourse. Hence, the Spanish American text argues strenuously for modernity, while it signals simultaneously in a number of ways its distance from the demands of modernity's rhetoric as a means of maintaining its discursive power. In this way, the discourse of modernity constitutes both the core of the Spanish American work and the center from which it has to flee in a centrifugal flight for the preservation of its own rhetorical authority. The uniqueness and particularity of the Spanish American postcolonial/neocolonial cultural situation is founded on this radically ambivalent movement toward and away from modernity.

Given this circumstance, it follows that the study of Spanish American cultural discourse demands a critical perspective that is attentive to and is able to discern the various strands of this contradictory textual maneuver. More exactly still, what is required is in fact a radical reformulation of the concept of cultural resistance, one that will not be founded on a symmetric, zero-sum relationship of interaction between the metropolis and the colony, between center and periphery, which inevitably operates under a more or less complex logic of restitution.[41] Recent developments and debates in anthropology and cultural studies have shown us that resistance is never simply an aggregate of oppositional strategies but a complex dialogic negotiation that involves all the parties in a multilevel relationship of constant and mutual reaccommodation. Richard Terdiman's study of counterdiscursive practices in nineteenth-century France offers the following enlightening paragraph: "[Counterdiscourses] are more than simple antinomic formations dependent upon their antagonist in the manner of some perverse mirror image. We cannot deduce their tactics or their contents by mechanically negating elements of the dominant discourse. On the other hand, neither is the process that produces them simply an election of chance. Counter discourses are the product of a theoretically unpredictable form of discursive labor and real transformation. No catalogue of them can ever be exhaustive."[42] But further than that, a formulation of resistance that is relevant to the Spanish American context must also be able to account for the quite explicit desire of appropriation and quotation of metropolitan discourses that is intrinsic to it; in other words, it has to be a reformulation capable of incorporating the passionate commitment to a modernity articulated in hegemonic terms that is also very much a part of Spanish American cultural discourse.

This is why the various attempts to describe the relationship between Spanish American cultural production and metropolitan models as founded on some conception of parodic appropriation will necessarily offer an incomplete view of its subject. For the idea of parody implies a process of distancing from an original model that cannot represent accurately the relationship that obtains between the Spanish American work and its hegemonic models. I use the term "parody" here to refer to any critical perspective for which colonial discourse is ultimately a "savage" appropriation and repetition of metropolitan paradigms, however much ideological resistive value one may wish to place on that deviation from the original. This critique extends particularly to the concept of *transculturación* in the several creative renderings of it that have been advanced by a number of recent works on the topic.[43] Ever since the coining of the term by Cuban anthropologist Fernando Ortiz in the 1940s, all of the various acceptations of transculturation have presupposed from the start a detachment from an original that is measured in the distinct peculiarities that result from its appropriation and subsequent rendition of it by the colonial subject.[44] Ortiz may have intended—as Mary Louise Pratt has argued—"to replace the paired concepts of acculturation and deculturation that describe the transference of culture in a reductive fashion imagined within the interest of the metropolis."[45] But as Pratt's quotation clearly implies, advocates of transculturation endeavor to change the perspective on the cultural exchange process between the metropolis and the periphery by proposing to look at it from the optic of the subordinate cultural party instead. Nonetheless, this exercise always leaves intact the avowed original in order to then describe its decomposition, reshaping, reincorporation, or cannibalization into a novel cultural object produced by the colonial "savage" mind.[46] The assumption here is that the work of recomposition done on a metropolitan discursive modality by its "savage" appropriation inevitably undermines the former's claims to being an organic discourse, which in turn is a way of questioning its authority. But the reality is that this maneuver does not entail any concrete exploration of the plurivocal, self-contradictory, and open-ended dimension of metropolitan discourse, which is therefore left to stand as the self-same, monolithic authority it purports to be, regardless of its supposed disfigurement in the periphery.[47] The second objection is that in its desire to identify an active strategy of resistance in the process of appropriation of the "original" it does not account sufficiently—and this is especially limiting in the Spanish American case—for the desire that led to the "original" in the first place. In other words, from this critical perspective the "subaltern's" voice is *forced* to reside in an essential difference and negativity with respect to hegemonic discourses that places an outside limit on the exploration of their interplay. In Spanish America the determined invocation of the prestige of the metropolitan discursive model is a fact that cannot be elided by underscoring any other aspect of its appropriation that may reveal a resistance to the model's authority. I believe that we must aim to formulate a critical discourse that is faithful to that contradictory movement of both embracing and marking a distance from the model, simultaneously, and that in my view is characteristic of cultural enterprise in Spanish America. The specificity of the Spanish American cultural circumstance requires a critical instrument that is still in the process of being devised.[48]

This characterization of cultural discourse in Spanish America has myriad implications for critical approaches that assume a chronological perspective on cultural matters in which models, currents, and movements succeed one another.[49] Temporal relations between works, or the larger historical sweep of cultural movements in Spanish America, become less of a determining factor than the effective play of this primordial tension around which each work articulates itself. If we conceive of the double movement at the core of the Spanish American text metaphorically as a displacement toward modernity that is "followed" by a recoil from it, we can project a temporal dimension onto the work that would recapitulate its rhetorical and tropological structure, even if the latter exists in simultaneity rather than succession. The Spanish American work would then possess an internal "chronology" that may or not be consonant with the developments or currents in any proposed broader frame of cultural history. Indeed, one must envision the way to reformulate the received cultural history of Spanish America from a perspective that will discern this internal textual dynamics and will derive its categories and major conceptualizations from its paradoxical nature.

The foregoing discussion has been grounded on a series of assumptions regarding the concept of modernity that must be unpacked in order to address questions that have undoubtedly arisen. Of special concern is the determination of the relationship between the experience of modernity in hegemonic circles and my depiction of that experience, up to this point, in the Spanish American context. My intention now is to dwell for a moment—and to whatever extent is allowed by the dialectics of blindness and insight—on the problems and opportunities afforded by conceptualizing the experience of modernity in Spanish America in the terms I have already proposed.

One possible critique of my argument could be stated in the following fashion: the latter appears be to be founded on the conflation of two distinct meanings of modernity—modernity as a concept or aesthetic ideal as manifested in several discursive modalities, and modernity as a socioeconomic reality, as a phase of Western historical development. Matei Calinescu has summarized most economically these two acceptations and the relationship they entertain:

> It is impossible to say precisely when one can begin to speak of the existence of two distinct and bitterly conflicting modernities. What is certain is that at some point during the first half of the nineteenth century an irreversible split occurred between modernity as stage in the history of Western civilization—a product of science and technological progress, of the industrial revolution, of the sweeping economic and social changes brought about by capitalism—and modernity as an aesthetic concept. Since then, the relations between the two modernities have been irreducibly hostile, but not without allowing and even stimulating a variety of mutual influences in their rage for each other's destruction.[50]

The intellectual/aesthetic category of modernity would therefore be an abstraction that could be wielded by anyone, irrespective of context, while the former term represents a moment in the economic development of Western societies that presupposes an asymmetric relationship in which some can make an effective claim of participation, while others cannot. Hence, it should be possible for a writer in a nonmetropolitan circumstance to invoke the discursive category of modernity irrespective of the degree of socioeconomic advancement of his or her society—that is, irrespective of its relative compliance with the requirements posited by the second acceptation of the term. According to this view, the aesthetic/intellectual concept of modernity would not be inescapably tied to—or tainted by—its European origin and would therefore be transportable to other contexts without incurring loss or contradiction. Once displaced to its "new" milieu, the discourse of modernity would evince the same internal dynamics of self-questioning that characterize its metropolitan existence as well, a dynamics that could be summarized in the following fashion: modernity's desire to break with the past and to align itself with the impermanence and sweep of the present has as one of its well-known consequences the undermining of the text that invokes that desire as its own. Faced with this danger, the "modern" writer reacts with a defensive gesture that disallows modernity's reach in order to safeguard his or her authority. Benjamin, De Man, Calinescu, and others have shown this aspect of modernity's discourse in their consideration of Baudelaire as a paradigmatic case. For his part, Marshall Berman has shown this dialectics at work in Marx's contradictory consideration of modernity and its relation to the working class in his now classic *All That Is Solid Melts into Air*.[51]

The combined effect of these two arguments strikes at the heart of my conception of modernity in the Spanish American context. For it would appear that the problematics that I have identified as intrinsic to the Spanish American rhetorical situation in fact characterize the experience of modernity in metropolitan circles as well, thereby complicating if not outright disallowing its viability as a marker of discursive specificity. From this perspective, the Spanish American rhetorical predicament would not differ substantially from the one in which every modern writer has been immersed since the advent of modernity as an intellectual and textual modality in hegemonic circles. The principal advantage of this view is that it allows us to speak about a Spanish American modernity as a local instance of a more generalized Western phenomenon—"without asterisk"—without having to make a special claim as to its peculiarity or specificity. Given the abuses to which assertions of cultural specificity in Spanish America have been prone traditionally, this critique would move the discussion away from such equivocal terrain by disallowing from the outset the ground in which such claims could be predicated.

Nonetheless, the outline of a rejoinder to this critique begins to emerge from a close reading of Calinescu's earlier comment concerning the two acceptations of modernity. In his view, aesthetic or textual modernity and socioeconomic modernity have followed essentially divergent trajectories, a fact that would seem to buttress the proposition that the aesthetic manifestation of modernity can indeed thrive in the absence of the material conditions of the modern. But what is also evident from the quotation is that the seeming autonomy of the two concepts is an illusion, a mirage created by their very claims of absolute exclusion that each concept makes with respect to the other. Calinescu is correct in diagnosing the hostility between the two versions of modernity, and it is precisely out of that stated desire to negate each other that their proclamations of autonomy with respect to one another arise. Yet what is important to highlight is that the two modernities entertain a relationship that makes possible, in Calinescu's words, "a variety of mutual influences in their rage for each other's destruction"; hence, what we are confronting, in reality, is a dialectics that requires a fortiori the mutual engagement of the two terms, even if their interaction cannot be understood in the mechanical terms of action and reaction or the vocabulary of zero-sum games. In other words, the discourse of modernity purports to be autonomous, but this autonomy is beholden to its negation of the material conditions from which it springs. Claudio Véliz says as much when he refers to the "awesome process of industrialization without which there would have been no dissolution of traditional community, no tortured transition from *Gemeinschaft* to *Gesellschaft*, no isolation in the midst of the metropolis, no anomie, no alienation, no repression, angst or ennui."[52] Likewise, Marshall Berman has identified quite accurately the essential traits of this phenomenon, which he calls the "modernism of underdevelopment" and to which he devotes a substantial portion of his discussion:

> The contrast of Baudelaire and Dostoevsky, and of Paris and Petersburg in the middle of the nineteenth century, should help us to see a larger polarity in the world history of modernism. At one pole we can see the modernism of advanced nations, building directly on the materials of economic and political modernization and drawing vision and energy from a modernized reality—Marx's factories and railways, Baudelaire's boulevards—even when

it challenges that reality in radical ways. At an opposite pole we find a modernism that arises from backwardness and underdevelopment. . . . The modernism of underdevelopment is forced to build on fantasies and dreams of modernity, to nourish itself on an intimacy and a struggle with mirages and ghosts. In order to be true to the life from which it springs, it is forced to be shrill, uncouth and inchoate. It turns in on itself and tortures itself for its inability to singlehandedly make history—or else throws itself into extravagant attempts to take on itself the whole burden of history. It whips itself into frenzies of self-loathing, and preserves itself only through vast reserves of self-irony. But the bizarre reality from which this modernism grows, and the unbearable pressures under which it moves and lives—social and political pressures as well as spiritual ones—infuse it with a desperate incandescence that Western modernism, so much more at home in its world, can rarely hope to match.[53]

In Spanish America the appropriation of the discursive modalities of metropolitan modernity have had to contend with the absence of its material antagonist in its midst, or more precisely, with its phantasmatic presence as the always distant and assumed reality of the metropolis. For the Spanish American intellectual the modern has always been "somewhere else," regardless of the relative level of advancement of the writer's society at any given time. This absence has dictated that the dialectical engagement with material modernity described by Calinescu should have been at best a tortuous affair. However, the "somewhere else" where the modern is thought to reside for the Spanish American intellectual should not be construed as a discrete place or a concrete set of historical and economic circumstances but rather as what, in effect, it was: a conceptual and rhetorical category. This is why, for instance, when Sarmiento actually visited the United States or Europe, the modern manages to slip away and to acquire substance somewhere else—as Mary Louise Pratt and William Katra have masterfully demonstrated in their studies of his *Viajes*.[54] Sarmiento is but one of a very long list that would include authors such as Bello, Hostos, Avellaneda, Martí, Díaz Rodríguez, Vasconcelos, Henríquez Ureña, and Paz, among many others: writers and intellectuals whose face-to-face confrontation with the modern invariably results in its flight to another location or its identification with an element different from the one with which they started their search. On the other hand, the phantasmatic, displaced existence of the modern "somewhere else" implies that the operative definition of it invoked by each Spanish American author will be acutely predicated on his or her very specific material conditions; that is, the particular configuration of the modern envisioned by each writer will be a projection of the very specific absence of it that is *perceived* in the surrounding context. From this perspective it would be more accurate and useful to speak about the existence of Spanish American *modernities* as opposed to a univocal and homogenizing conception of that experience.[55]

These are the circumstances that determine the specificity of Spanish America's experience of modernity with respect to a conventional conception of Western modernity. Conversely, and as stated earlier, what distinguishes it from the postcolonial discourses of modernity produced by other peripheral areas is the commitment to the deracination of modernity's project and its corrosive critique, with its foreclosure of the past as material for a contestatory posture. Hence, a claim can indeed be made for the specificity of Spanish American modernity—provided that such an affirmation is not used to legitimize essentialist assertions of exclusivity or identity.

The space, the terrain that any postcolonial discourse must negotiate is constructed out of myriad exigencies, openings, and possibilities, all of them shaped as exquisite double binds. The work of Homi Bhabha as a whole engages in a thorough investigation of the difficulties of both the postcolonial discursive situation and those of the critic addressing it. Bhabha, along with other critics such as Gayatri Spivak and T. Niranjana, has attempted to effect a synthesis of poststructuralist positions concerning the instability of the subject's insertion in language and the ideological critique that is at the center of postcolonial studies:[56]

The reason a cultural text or system of meaning cannot be sufficient unto itself is that the act of cultural enunciation—the place of utterance—is crossed by the *différance* of writing. This has less to do with what anthropologists might describe as varying attitudes to symbolic systems within different cultures than with the structure of symbolic representation itself— not the content of the symbol or its social function, but the structure of symbolization. It is this difference in the process of language that is crucial to the production of meaning and ensures, at the same time, that meaning is never simply mimetic and transparent. The linguistic difference that informs any cultural performance is dramatized in the common semiotic account of the disjuncture between the subject of a proposition (énoncé) and the subject of enunciation, which is not represented in the statement but which is the acknowledgment of its discursive embeddedness and address, its cultural positionality, its reference to a present time and a specific space. The pact of interpretation is never simply an act of communication between the I and the You designated in the statement. The production of meaning requires that these two places be mobilized in the passage through a Third Space, which represents both the general conditions of language and the specific implication of the utterance in a performative and institutional strategy of which it cannot "in itself" be conscious. What this unconscious relation introduces is an ambivalence in the act of interpretation. The pronominal I of the proposition cannot be made to address—in its own words—the subject of enunciation, for this is not personable, but remains a spatial relation within the schemata and strategies of discourse. The meaning of the utterance is quite literally neither the one nor the other. This ambivalence is emphasized when we realize that there is no way that the content of the proposition will reveal the structure of its positionality; no way that context can be mimetically read off from the content.[57]

Bhabha's quotation is a description of a problematic that is present in any linguistic utterance, expanded further to encompass the discursive situation of the postcolonial subject. To the poststructuralist ambiguities about the inscription of meaning and subjectivity in language, Bhabha adds the ambiguities that arise from the cultural positionality of the speaker and his or her immersion in an institutional network responsible for the construction of cultural meaning. The significant factor in this other situation, though, is that what Saussure would call the "value" of the sign is not just relative to the other elements in the linguistic system— and therefore identical in every case—but further informed in this instance by a set of hierarchical relations: to the Saussurian horizontal conception of value one must add a vertical dimension that is reflective of the sign's location in the uneven exchange between center and periphery. As is true in the Saussurian model, these relations are always there— inasmuch as their totality contributes to determine the value of the sign (and, by extension, of the individual utterance)—yet they can never be fully articulated or apprehended. The interpreter of cultural discourse is always confronted with a situation in which position—not simply meaning—is always in need of precision and also simultaneously in flight.

In the Spanish American case the natural intensity of this scenario is further heightened by the fact that there has always been a radical ambiguity and ambivalence about the very position of Spanish American culture. This is what has made it possible, for instance, to propose time and again that in order to bring about the culmination of an immanent and privative Spanish American historical development one must, paradoxically, import European or American (choose your product): settlers, technology, philosophical systems, and so on. In most postcolonial situations cultural positionality may not be fully apprehensible to the resisting speaker, as I argued earlier, but in those circumstances any discursive intervention is at least filtered through a model that seeks to invert what used to be the hierarchical colonial state of affairs. By contrast, in Spanish America the problems begin with the difficulties involved in drawing even the most basic distinctions that would allow a subject to attempt a definition—however tenuous—of his or her cultural location.

The distorted and complex specificity of the Spanish American case can also be understood with reference to a fundamental divide that serves, according to Partha Chatterjee, to ground the anticolonial struggle as well as the postindependence period of decolonization. His central argument is summarized in the ensuing quotation:

> Anticolonial nationalism creates its own domain of sovereignty within co-
> lonial society well before it begins its political battle with the imperial
> power. It does this by dividing the world of social institutions and practices
> into two domains—the material and the spiritual. The material is the do-
> main of the "outside," of the economy and of statecraft, of science and
> technology, a domain where the West has proved its superiority and the
> East has succumbed. In this domain, then, Western superiority had to be
> acknowledged and its accomplishments carefully studied and replicated.
> The spiritual, on the other hand, is an "inner" domain bearing the "essen-
> tial" marks of cultural identity. The greater one's success in imitating West-
> ern skills in the material domain, therefore, the greater the need to preserve
> the distinctness of one's spiritual culture. This formula is, I think, a fun-
> damental feature of anticolonial nationalisms in Asia and Africa. (6)[58]

The difficulty in the Spanish American case lies precisely in not being able to articulate clearly the division of the social into the two realms described by Chatterjee. In Spanish America there has been no autoch-thonous sphere that could be configured and opposed overtly to the West as a strategy of containment, since cultural identity has been so inextri-cably bound to modernity. This is why the breach just described is ulti-mately reproduced at another level of discourse, that is, in the text's rhe-torical structure. In fact, my argument could be restated profitably in terms of Chatterjee's proposal: the chasm that according to him organizes the postcolonial world is enacted in the Spanish American text as an in-ternal textual disjunction whose contours I am attempting to delineate. The location of cultural resistance resides in a space created by the text within and against itself rather than in a collectively acknowledged social sphere of contestation. But this circumstance makes exceedingly difficult any determination of the writing subject's position vis-à-vis hegemonic discourse.

Yet positionality is perhaps the most economic term to describe *the* issue, the central concern not only of Spanish American cultural production but of any theory that wishes to give an account of it: the status of Spanish American cultural production and its relation to cultural activity in the metropolitan centers. A few years ago Fredric Jameson was roundly criticized for asserting that all Third World texts were in the final analysis national allegories that invested even the depiction of avowedly private conflicts with a collective charge.[59] Yet I believe that, however awkwardly, Jameson was recognizing and attempting to find a place in his political thought for that dimension that is certainly present in most postcolonial literature, and especially in Spanish American cultural production: the continual need to address the nature of the relationship between the post-colonial nation and the metropolis, to delimit the location of the speaker in a discursive situation that continuously transcends the personal or even the national. Where I believe he may have erred was in reducing this internal exploration of the positionality of postcolonial discourse vis-à-vis metropolitan modernity to an allegorizing intention, therefore leaving his argument open to the sort of reproaches that allegory has consistently evoked since the romantic period.[60] But the reductionism of Jameson's formulation should not obscure his identification of a dynamics that is indeed at the core of all postcolonial discourse. I am referring to the need to demarcate a space, a position from which to speak in the face of an assumed horizon of discursivity that assigns a precarious rhetorical authority to the postcolonial interlocutor. This difficulty becomes even more wrenching in the Spanish American context, since the explicit point of departure for a large segment of Spanish American cultural discourse is the desire to erase the specificity of its location—that is, to argue that its here and now should be the metropolis's there and tomorrow. But this avowed intention cannot ever erase the locational incommensurableness that led to the project in the first place; abolishing the difference that marks the inequity of the exchange does not resolve at all the question of how to shore up a rhetorical situation that is felt as inherently precarious. Discursive authority is necessary, even in order to argue for the erasure of one's specificity.

Jameson's reduction of postcolonial cultural discourse to an allegorical figuration about authority and position may have been limiting, but it is symptomatically accurate. In the specific Spanish American case there is indeed a persistent will to shore up a discursive authority that is felt to be threatened as a result of the rhetorical dynamics that I have described. Nevertheless, this structure does not manifest itself necessarily or uniquely in the form of an allegorical doubling—as Jameson would have it—but as an internal disjunction that can occur in all levels and in all dimensions of the text in question. There is in the Spanish American text a swerve away from itself, a movement that nonetheless also constitutes the foundation of its own rhetorical authority.

This move is reminiscent in its creative potential and its enabling capacity of the Lucretian concept of the *clinamen*: the deviation or swerve from the expected that nonetheless makes possible the beginning of the shaped world.[61] In the Spanish American text this *clinamen* represents both a search for discursive authority *and* the mark of the impossible rhetorical predicament from which it springs. The fact that it is finally impossible to dissociate one characterization from the other makes it exceedingly difficult to advance any concrete formulation about cultural discourse in Spanish America, unless through a critical discourse that endeavors to duplicate within itself the same delicate, fragile balance that characterizes the object it describes.

A Critical Consideration

In order to appreciate how the interpretation of cultural discourse in Spanish America proposed here departs from contemporary critical accounts of it, we must examine the two principal perspectives that have carried the day in dictating our present understanding of the status of discourse in Spanish America. Both of these are cogent and admirable reinterpretations of the Spanish American nineteenth century, since the underlying paradigm for both assumes a genetic predicament coextensive with independence. I begin with what is unquestionably the most influential of these reinterpretations, the critical oeuvre of the late Uruguayan critic Angel Rama.

Anyone whose research centers on the nineteenth century in Spanish America must deal with the reality that—whether one agrees with it or not—Rama's understanding of the period and his characterization of cultural production throughout it configure, by themselves and in their various derivations, the predominant critical discourse of the field. Whether explicitly or covertly, the critical paradigm described by Rama's work on the nineteenth century is invoked by a large number of researchers of the period in their work. I do not mean to underestimate or underplay the fact that there was an evolution in Rama's ideas, something that becomes quite apparent when confronting his essays on *transculturación*, written in the mid-1970s, with *Las máscaras democráticas del modernismo*, a work assembled from manuscripts left unpublished at his death in 1983. But just as surely, there is a Rama *gestalt*, a Rama effect if you will, that has helped to shape the field of nineteenth-century studies as it is configured today. Interestingly, as Mario Vargas Llosa has reminded us in his prologue to *La ciudad letrada*, besides this monograph Rama only wrote one other organic book in his long career: the study on Rubén Darío, whose first edition appeared in 1970. Yet Rama's many essays and compilations have constituted an irrepressible force perhaps *because* of their very dispersion, repetitiveness, and ubiquity. Another factor that must be pointed out in this regard is the obvious predominance of nineteenth-century topics in Rama's work in general. Even in his sweeping *La ciudad letrada* Rama gives short shrift to the colonial period and only considers in detail the first two decades of the present century. In fact, at one point in that book he argues that the Spanish American nineteenth century ended with the Mexican Revolution of 1910.[62]

Few would dispute that Rama's most influential book has been—and justly so—*La ciudad letrada*. In it the Uruguayan critic undertook an ambitious rereading and a thorough reformulation of Spanish American cultural history as anchored on the omnipresent figure of the *letrado*. A Crown bureaucrat during the colonial regime, a state bureaucrat after Independence, a *doctor* during most of the nineteenth century, an autodidact *homme de lettres* toward the fin-de-siècle, an essayist of cultural affairs during the twentieth, the strength and durability of the Spanish American *letrado* always derived—Rama argued persuasively—from his relationship with writing. The written word conveyed to him prestige, an enduring access to power, and an adaptability that determined the survival of the *letrado* even through the most apparently profound social and historical upheavals in the continent's history.

The ultimate significance and the source of the influence of Rama's *La ciudad letrada* lies in that because of its thrust and sweep, it has paved the way for a comprehensive reinterpretation of cultural production in Spanish America. First, by centering his formulations on the figure of the *letrado* and following that figure's diverse avatars throughout time, Rama's work made it possible to read the history of cultural history in Span-

America as an uninterrupted activity that began with the fall of Tenoch-titlán and continues to the present day. In a grand gesture of interpretive appropriation worthy of the most ambitious *letrado*, Rama encompassed five centuries of intellectual activity by positing the *letrado* as the true and lasting agent of that history. This fact manifests itself in Rama's counter-intuitive arguments against the commonly acknowledged significance of epochal events such as the Revolution for Independence, the creation of the national states, or the advent of modernization toward the end of the nineteenth century, since in his view these historical circumstances only amounted to minor disruptions of the *letrado*'s hegemony. In this regard, Rama says the following with respect to the aftermath of the struggle for political autonomy from Spain:

> El gran modelo del comportamiento de la *ciudad letrada* lo ofreció la re-volución emancipadora de 1810, fijando un paradigma que con escasas var-iantes se repetiría en los sucesivos cambios revolucionarios que conoció el continente. . . . Esta curiosa virtud [de la ciudad letrada], diríamos la de ser un "adaptable freno," en nada se vio con mayor fuerza que en la reconver-sión de la *ciudad letrada* al servicio de los nuevos poderosos surgidos de la élite militar, sustituyendo a los antiguos delegados del monarca. Leyes, ed-ictos, reglamentos y, sobre todo, constituciones, antes de acometer los vastos códigos ordenadores, fueron la tarea central de la *ciudad letrada* en su nuevo servicio a los caudillos que se sustituirían en el período pos-revolucionario.[63]

> The best example of the behavior of *la ciudad letrada* was that of the revo-lution for independence in 1810, which established a paradigm that would repeat itself with small variations in the continent's successive revolutions. . . . This curious virtue of being an "adaptable buffer" saw its highest ex-pression in the refashioning of *la ciudad letrada* to serve the interests of the new leaders who arose from the elite military ranks to replace the former representatives of the crown. Laws, edicts, rule books and above all consti-tutions—before undertaking the vast codification of social reality—were the central preoccupation of *la ciudad letrada* in its new service to the strongmen who would succeed one another in the postrevolutionary period.

The enduring activity of the *letrado* and the invariably urban context in which it unfolds became a composite abstraction for which Rama coined the powerful and poetic term *ciudad letrada*. The latter was offered by Rama as the vast, somewhat surreptitious ideological foundation to the material cultural activity of the continent and the everyday life of its cities—that always moving and mutating reality that he referred to as the *ciudad real* and opposed to the seeming permanence of the *ciudad letrada*.

Second, and perhaps more important than the first, Rama's paradigm in *La ciudad letrada* took leave from the Manichaean vision of Spanish American culture which had preceded him and to which he himself had contributed in a number of his earlier essays—that is, that version of Spanish American culture that had always postulated a hell full of traitors to the masses and courters of the continent's oligarchies, as well as its pantheon of popular (and populist) heroes and defenders of the national or continental patrimony. Rama's achievement in *La ciudad letrada* was to put the continent's cultural history beyond good and evil, so to speak, not by suspending the relevance of moral categories, as Nietzsche did, but rather by collapsing the two categories into one: that is, by subsuming *all* writers and intellectuals under the capacious rubric of the *letrado*. In Rama's *ciudad letrada* there are no heroes, only *letrados* who are irrevocably and irremediably tainted—although to a larger or a lesser extent, to be sure—by their contact with the written word. This strategy, which I call perhaps melodramatically the "demonization" of writing, has had, in the context of the long-standing Manichaean interpretation of Spanish American cultural life just mentioned, a salutary influence; for it has opened the way, for example, to the demystified and brazen reconsideration of such figures as José Martí, Eugenio María de Hostos, José Carlos Mariátegui, and many others from perspectives that have already yielded novel and important results.[64]

One also has to measure Rama's contribution in *La ciudad letrada* against the large influence that dependency theory exerted on social and cultural studies in Spanish America in the late 1960s and throughout the 1970s. Under this scheme, the cultural products of Spanish America were regarded as either overt and finally pathetic attempts to copy metropolitan forms or, in the best of situations, as direct reactions against those models through a practice of writing that evinced a resisting intention on the part of the peripheral writer. In either case, the Spanish American producer of culture was posited as simply reacting to stimuli that came from the metropolis, thereby inadvertently putting in check the possibility of a way out of the center/periphery predicament. In the disciplines of the social sciences the critique of this paradigm was swift and effective; one of the achievements of *La ciudad letrada* was to provide a workable exit from this impasse for cultural and literary studies as well. Rama's solution was to propose that the *letrado* was ceaselessly engaged in a scriptural activity that had as its principal and ultimate aim the perpetuation of his power and privilege per se. This coup had two outcomes. First, it postulated an internal, immanent genetic principle for the generation of cultural activity in Spanish America; in other words, above and beyond its specific contents and historical embeddedness, the ultimate purpose of the *letrado*'s agency was to guarantee the survival and continuity of his scriptural activity. Second (an extension of the first), Rama's conception of the *letrado* allowed him to claim for the latter a fairly large degree of autonomy from metropolitan influence, given the fact that the ruling principle of the *letrado*'s activity was the replication and perpetuation of his power. That is, on the surface it may have seemed to many that the *letrado* was merely copying or adapting metropolitan models, but the reality was that through his writerly activity he was nonetheless managing to maintain his prerogatives intact, even while appearing to have surrendered his creative and intellectual will to the prestige of metropolitan forms. Henceforth it would be possible to study the *letrado*'s activity as a self-contained, self-referential activity, without the need to measure it against or relate it to metropolitan models or concerns. This project and the distinct possibilities that it inaugurated have been the major force driving much of recent research on both nineteenth- and twentieth-century cultural studies in Spanish America.

On the other hand, both of the strategies employed by Rama—the demonization of writing and the postulation of the immanent character of the *letrado*'s activity—brought problems of their own. Rama's immanent understanding of the *letrado*'s agency carried with it the danger of subsuming that activity under a mantle of ahistoricity, with the concomitant danger of making every instance of it essentially equivalent to any other. I do not mean by this that Rama's depiction of the *letrado* is static: he indeed describes in his book a succession of changes in the *letrado*'s activity and in his relationship to the social milieu. But the *structural* function and the *locus* of the *letrado* in the history of Spanish American cultural history remain immutable, unaltered. For Rama clearly intended to show in his study the *letrado*'s permanence and survival above and beyond historical change. Remember the quotation cited earlier, in which what is emphasized is the *letrado*'s ability to roll with the historical punches, so to speak. This desire forced him to set up a figural structure to his argument that opposed stasis to change, the *letrado* to history: the *ciudad letrada* as against the *ciudad real*. This is why, when referring to the *letrado* or to his *ciudad letrada*, Rama's vocabulary at times acquires an evidently transcendent tone. Witness, for instance, this assertion:

Las ciudades americanas fueron remitidas desde sus orígenes a una doble vida. La correspondiente al orden físico que, por sensible, material, está sometida a los vaivenes de construcción y de destrucción, de instauración y de renovación, y sobre todo, a los impulsos de la invención circunstancial de individuos y grupos según su momento y situación. Por encima de ella la correspondiente al orden de los signos que actúan en el nivel simbólico, desde antes de cualquier realización, y también durante y después, pues disponen de una inalterabilidad a la que poco conciernen los avatares materiales. (11)

Spanish American cities were relegated from the start to a double life. The first was the physical city, which, on account of its material and sensible nature, was shaped by cycles of construction and demolition, of inaugurations and renovations, and was above all subject to the spontaneous and circumstantial impulses of individuals and groups in their respective historical moments. Above it was the second, the one linked to the order of signs that operate in the symbolic level before but also during and after any material undertaking, since it possesses an immutability unconcerned with material life.

And these are the final words of *La ciudad letrada*, in which history is reduced to an allegorical and seemingly Apocalyptic confrontation between the forces of power and those of the Written Word:

El testimonio de Azuela [in *Los de abajo*] es más crítico del intelectual que del jefe revolucionario, introduciendo un paradigma que tendrá larga descendencia. . . . Esquema dilemático que otros, posteriormente, explicarán con igual criticismo del intelectual por las diferencias de clase, pero que habida cuenta de que ésta es ya una posición intelectual (que confiere la certidumbre histórica a un estrato social) y que bajo otras formas podemos reencontrar el mismo esquema en distintas épocas y situaciones, podemos reinscribirlo en la tradicionalmente difícil conjugación de *las dos espadas, de los dos poderes del mundo*. (171, my emphasis)

Azuela [in *Los de abajo*] is more critical of intellectuals than of revolutionary leaders, therefore introducing a paradigm that will have a long history. . . . A problematic scheme that others later will use to blame intellectuals on account of their class extraction. But when we realize that this is itself an intellectual position (which confers historical truth to a given social group), and that the scheme can be found in different times and situations and under other guises as well, we can reinscribe it in the long and difficult struggle between *the two swords, the two powers of the world*.

The second of Rama's strategies, the demonization of writing, in turn makes *La ciudad letrada* a radically pessimistic and bleak work, a characteristic that Rama never confronted explicitly in his text but that inescapably follows from his premises. For if writing is postulated as an inherently demonized activity that is also the principal vehicle and instrument of the *letrado*'s strength, then there is no way out *from* the *letrado*'s power, just as there is no way out *for* the *letrado*, should he wish to apply his mastery of the written word to an oppositional or contestatory practice within his society.

The pessimistic and inconsolable implications of Rama's book can perhaps be explained as a carryover from the two works that had a major influence in the principal argument of *La ciudad letrada*, even if neither of them is explicitly mentioned in the text. The first of these was Julien Benda's *La trahison des clercs*, a 1927 essay that attempted to explain Europe's malaise after the fin-de-siècle—including the First World War—as the result of the unwarranted and unhealthy involvement by intellectuals in the political life of the continent. The word *clerc* as used by Benda is much closer to Rama's concept of the *letrado* than the standard translation into English of the term as "intellectual" would reveal. The second—and a much more direct influence—was that section of Weber's *Economy and Society* that describes the bureaucrat as an inevitable byproduct of the modern state. For Weber, bureaucracy is what the charismatic authority of the ruler of traditional societies deteriorates and hardens itself into as a result of the increased rationalization of social processes brought about by modernity. Modernity results, then, according to Weber, in a profound sense of the disenchantment of the world—the distinct impression that the world has lost its former auratic quality.[65] Using these insights as a point of departure, Rama rewrote the entire history of Spanish American culture with the *letrado* at the center, as the protagonist of the continent's narrative of cultural history. But the demonization of the *letrado*'s activity condemned Rama's vision of Spanish American cultural history to *ideological* stasis, just as we previously saw that same history mired in a *temporal* paralysis. This can be fully appreciated in the following quotation from *La ciudad letrada*, in which a supposed dialectical opposition within the universe of the *letrado* is described in such a way as to render the dialectic moot:

> Un pensamiento crítico se genera forzosamente dentro de las circunstancias a las que se opone, las que son sus componentes subrepticios y poderosos y al que impregnan por el mismo régimen opositivo que emplea. Las propuestas más antitéticas lo son de los principios que sustentan el estado de cosas contra el cual se formula. Aun las utopías que es capaz de concebir

funcionan como polos positivos marcados por aquellos negativos pre-existentes, de tal modo que en la doctrina nueva que se construye todo el sistema bipolar se prolonga. (128)

A contestatory thought is generated necessarily in the context it opposes, and the latter becomes a powerful and surreptitious component that impregnates it on account of the oppositional strategy deployed. The most antithetic proposals are those that negate the principles that sustain the status quo against which they struggle. Even the utopias that such a thought can concoct act as positive poles for those preexisting negative categories, so that the new doctrine contains the entire bipolar system in itself.

In other words, in *La ciudad letrada* there is no outside to the universe of writing and, accordingly, no possibility of an effective ideological opposition to the universe of the *letrado*. Within the realm of the *letrado* every ideological challenge is defused by the inevitable continuity of the *letrado*'s structural permanence.

Rama's *Ciudad letrada* has been the implicit background—albeit not with uncritical acceptance—for a number of other works that together form the second influential interpretation of Spanish American cultural discourse that I would like to examine. I am referring to those interpretations that are articulated around the study of the so-called state function of literature.[66] Most of these critical works take as the focal point of their analysis the consideration of literature's role in the process that led to the foundation of the modern Spanish American states. In the beginning, in fact, "literature" is not even deemed to exist as such since, given that the state is at that moment an inchoate entity, all social discursive practices are avowedly oriented toward the civilizing needs of the new nations. But as the various Spanish American states become steadily more solidified as political and institutional entities—that is, as the autonomy of the various social spheres becomes increasingly viable—literature slowly arises as an autonomous discourse, one that defines itself as having no utilitarian purpose, as being devoid of instrumentality. This leads to the institutionalization of literature as a paradoxical discourse that is anti-institutional, antispecialization, and antimodern, yet founded on the specialized *technè* of style. In *Desencuentros de la modernidad en América Latina*, Julio Ramos proposes, for instance:

> Hacia las últimas décadas del siglo, la literatura latinoamericana con altos y bajos, comienza a renunciar a la idea de ser expresión o medio. Comienza

a consolidar, incluso, una ética del trabajo y una ideología de la productiv-
idad ligada a la noción de artificio. . . . El estilo es el medio de trabajo que
diferencia al escritor, como el color al pintor, de otras prácticas sociales,
institucionales, que usan la lengua como medio.⁶⁷

Toward the last decades of the century, in varying degrees Latin American
literature begins to renounce the idea of being an expression of something
or a means to an end. It begins to consolidate a work ethic and an ideology
of production linked to the notion of artifice. . . . Style is the medium that
differentiates the writer—like color in the case of a painter—from other
social practices and institutions that use language as a medium.

As in Rama's work, we find in this second proposal on the nature of
Spanish American discourse the projection onto Spanish America of We-
berian notions about modernity's progressive rationalization and auton-
omization of discourses. The essential and quite significant difference
here is that the scheme is now tailored to the Spanish American situation
through the argument that Spanish America's imperfect modernization
has also determined the imperfect enactment, the muddled rendition of
the original paradigm.⁶⁸ Therein resides the explanation for the "state
function" of literature in the Spanish American nineteenth century: the
symptom of literature's lack of autonomy as a rationalized modern discourse in Spanish America lies in that it must find its self-justification
through its direct involvement in the nation-building program of the
modern Spanish American states. It is only later in the century, the argument continues, when a still imperfect and uneven local modernity is
nonetheless more robust, that one can begin to identify the deployment
of strategies that seek to constitute literature into a self-sufficient and
autonomous discourse.

There are three difficulties associated with this otherwise suggestive
and quite seductive interpretation of the period. The first is that the argument necessarily pays little attention to the many significant works
from the first half of the nineteenth century—especially but not limited
to poetry—in which there is an evident and even defiant literary intention.
The second objection is that it assumes that modernity becomes a factor
to contend with in the Spanish American cultural domain only when the
material conditions for modernity begin to obtain in Spanish America—
that is, the last quarter of the nineteenth century—an argument that
misses the fundamentally rhetorical nature of Spanish America's experience of modernity: the fact that one does not have to *be* modern in order

to appropriate discourses deemed "modern"—even if, as I argue, that circumstance has its own set of complications. What does indeed happen in the last decades of the previous century is an intensification of the difficulty that was *always*, from the beginning, a constitutive part of cultural discourse in Spanish America: a heightening of the problematic relationship with modernity dictated paradoxically by what then seemed to be its imminence—in much the same way that a mass will accelerate and heat up as it approaches the dark body under whose gravitational spell it lies.[69]

The third critique is that the ambiguity about the generic, discursive, and functional boundaries of the category of literature is a persistent quality of Spanish American cultural discourse in general and not simply characteristic of its early periods. This ambiguity arises from the fact that the conflicted relationship between modernity and Spanish American discourse summarizes the definition of the category of "literature" as it devolved from its beginnings in the romantic period. It is a widely acknowledged fact that the Western concept of literature arose as a response to the awareness of the experience of modernity toward the end of the eighteenth century.[70] Nonetheless, literature may claim to be profoundly antimodern, but it has also incorporated into itself a version of modernity, something that becomes evident when it is realized, for instance, that the appearance of "literature" was accompanied by the simultaneous surfacing of the demand for originality.[71] This meant at the very least that if the business of literature was going to be to challenge and question modernity, that enterprise would nonetheless be ruled by the requirement of finding ever newer ways of doing so. Hence, from its beginnings literary discourse was constituted around an ambivalence toward modernity that has consistently challenged its oppositional thrust against the latter. This internal split is the same that I have tried to show exists in the Spanish American discursive tradition. More precisely, though, both literature and cultural discourse in Spanish America exist as a simultaneous rejection and affirmation of the modern, but the point of departure for each is the affirmation of what the other assails. For if we give a chronological amplitude and spatial depth to the two rhetorical situations, one could propose that literature and Spanish American cultural rhetoric describe the same movement between opposing poles, but the two start their trajectories from opposite ends, as it were: literature begins with the understanding of itself as engaged in a struggle with the modern and then moves in ways that are inconsistent with that avowed rejection of modernity; in contrast, Spanish American cultural rhetoric takes as its point of departure its identification with modernity and then surreptitiously turns away from that commitment. Each defines an itinerary that is the other's specular opposite, which may help us understand the ambiguous relationship that the Spanish American discourse of cultural specificity has always entertained with the more explicitly literary discursive modalities against which it purports to define itself. In Spanish America literature is not so much a discursive category that serves to delimit the terrain of socially relevant and instrumental discourse by defining its opposite as a specular likeness that confronts that discourse with an inverted image of its unsettled inner self. This dynamic would also explain why Spanish American literature has a very long history—from Bello's *Odas* to *realismo mágico*—of attempting to make a claim to exception for Latin American reality, thereby mimicking the very strategy deployed by the continent's cultural discourse.

Hence, to counter this second perspective it could be argued that literature has been present in Spanish America all along from the start, but under the guise of a rhetorical configuration that enacts a transposed specular double of it. In other words, literature may appear at times to be absent from nineteenth-century cultural discourse in Spanish America, but only because paradoxically it is everywhere. The subsequent institutionalization of literature toward the beginning of the present century is an undeniable fact that would represent the codification of the conditions of possibility of that discourse and of the properties that are deemed to characterize it. More important, it would signal the moment in which the rhetorical structure that is peculiar to the Spanish American discursive circumstance would be established formally as the generative principle for all subsequent aesthetic enterprises.

According to this second critical view, then, the peculiarities of Spanish American cultural discourse would be the result of the latter's uneven modernity, that is, of its inability to deploy the mechanisms and create the institutions that are the hallmarks of the modern rationalized state. In contradistinction to this view, I would contend that the peculiarities, contradictions, and dislocations that are characteristic of Spanish American cultural production arise from the intricate rhetorical situation I have identified. This situation is, to be sure, founded on the historical and economic reality of Spanish America as a neocolonial, peripheral zone, and in that sense there is a point of convergence between this perspective and my own, since the inconsistent modernity of the region is a direct result of its economic subservience to and dependence on the metropolis. But the distinction lies on how to interpret the difference that is characteristic of Spanish American cultural production: is this difference the symptom of an incapacity to fully deploy a given model of development, or is it the trace of an enabling maneuver to negotiate a way out of the strictures imposed by that model? The latter view allows us to consider that perhaps this contradictory and complex rhetorical state of affairs may indeed be Spanish America's own modernity, as opposed to the first option, in which a lingering suspicion about the potential applicability of the concept of modernity to Spanish American circumstance always has to remain. To paraphrase José Martí, our modernity may be a conflicted modernity, but it is our modernity nonetheless; and if we are to study it in all its specificity we must eschew all critical approaches that interpret that complexity as a symptom of deficiency, as a sign of a modernity manqué. In the final analysis, the quality that dictates the outermost limits and limitations of this second critical perspective is a willingness to take cultural discourse at face value, to trust the assertive significance of its formulations. This is not to say that this outlook is not attentive to contradictions and internal dislocation within that discourse—far from it, since the search for contradiction is the sine qua non of ideological critique. But paradox and contradiction in this case are sought as symptoms of the text's *incapacity* to be modern, whereas I would argue that dislocation and contradiction are precisely what *allows* the text to speak in the first place.

The chapters that follow represent an attempt to read a collection of texts from the Spanish American canon in order to identify the presence in their midst of the complex rhetorical structure that I have endeavored to identify in the preceding pages. The larger aim that has guided my efforts throughout has been the desire to arrive at an interpretation of Spanish American cultural production that is neither seduced by the naïveté of autonomy or the dead end of resistance nor overwhelmed and paralyzed by the continent's obvious deference to European models and forms. All of these mutually exclusive and competing interests are present in the Spanish American work: desire for autonomy, subservience to metropolitan paradigms, resistance, epigonality. For this reason, I believe that the most accurate understanding of the phenomenon lies in a perspective that at the very least attempts to give all of these qualities their due, since they themselves all manage to coexist at the heart of the Spanish American work.

My critical itinerary begins with a broad examination of the works of Domingo Faustino Sarmiento, a writer who himself tried to encompass everything in his writing. Nonetheless, the critical view from afar will allow us to detect that dimension in which his gigantic and imposing oeuvre evinces the pressures attendant to the rhetorical predicament I have described.

CHAPTER TWO

Reading Sarmiento
Once More, with Passion

Cualquiera puede corregir lo escrito por él [Sarmiento]; pero nadie puede igualarlo.

———————

Anyone can edit a text written by him (Sarmiento); but no one can match him.

—Jorge Luis Borges, Prologue to *Recuerdos de provincia*

THERE IS PERHAPS no better representative figure of the relentless drive toward modernity in Spanish America than the Argentine writer Domingo Faustino Sarmiento. Conceived, as he claimed in his autobiographical text *Recuerdos de provincia*, in the same year that the struggle for independence from Spain began, Sarmiento's life and writings would seem to mobilize at one moment or another all of the topoi of the modernizing program that in its various manifestations characterized political and cultural life in nineteenth-century Spanish America. He despised the indigenous element in all its variations, branded it "barbarous" and opposed it to a concept of civilization that was firmly anchored in European circumstances and ideology. He read widely from metropolitan sources and used them indiscriminately to analyze Spanish American reality in a dramatic and Procrustean fashion. He espoused incentives to entice European immigrants, whom he thought would transform the Argentine landscape for the better through their habits and ethnic composition. During his tenure as president of Argentina he set in place policies that a few years later would result in the "Campaña del Desierto," a thinly veiled extermination campaign waged against the remaining Indians of the pampas. He was unsparing in his critique of local circumstance, unyielding in his advocacy of the continent's Europeanization, and dithyrambic in his praise for the achievements of a then young United States.

Nonetheless, anyone who has read Sarmiento in a more than casual fashion has probably experienced what I can only describe as a sensation of unsettledness, a moment when one feels that there is something uncanny, something bizarre transpiring before one's eyes—a feeling that some impenetrable and elusive force is at work in the text that is being examined. It begins as a suspicion that Sarmiento's discourse is not governed by the requirements of logic or analysis, that reason and reasonableness may not be the best instruments for moving along its conceptual, tropological, or thematic paths. This impression becomes even more pronounced as one ventures into the vast dimension that comprises the fifty-two volumes of Sarmiento's still incomplete works and encounters fragments such as the following, from a letter written to a friend on learning that his name was being mentioned as a possible presidential candidate:

> Por mi parte, y esto para ti solo, te diré que si me dejan, le haré a la historia americana un hijo. Treinta años de estudios, viajes, experiencias y el espectáculo de otras naciones que aquéllas de aldeas me han enseñado mucho. Si fuera un estúpido, razón tendría todavía de creer que más se me alcanza que a los niños con canas que tienen embrollada la fiesta.[1]

> As far as I'm concerned, and keep this to yourself, if they give me a chance I will get Latin American history pregnant. Thirty years of studies, voyages, experiences and familiarity with nations other than those that just have villages have taught me a great deal. Even if I were a simpleton, I would be right in thinking that I can do it better that than those gray-haired boys that are spoiling the show.

Given the conventions of epistolary writing in the nineteenth century as well as the highness of the office for which he was being regarded as a contender, the text of the letter is a scandal unto itself. Yet the simultaneous aversion and attraction—in short, the amazement—that such a passage elicits in us is a remarkably common experience for a reader of Sarmiento's oeuvre. One could offer as a further illustration the vulgar sublimity of Sarmiento's polemicizing with Alberdi in *Las ciento y una*, in which at different moments he uses the ensuing rhetorical gems to execrate his erstwhile admired antagonist:

> camorrista, charlatán malcriado; truchimán; lechoncito; ratoncito roe papeles; esponja de limpiar muebles; mujer por la voz, conejo por el miedo; sacacallos sublime; eunuco; bodeguero; botarate insignificante; jorobado de la civilización.[2]

troublemaker; ill-mannered charlatan; cheap magician, suckling pig, paper-chewing mouse, furniture duster; a woman on account of his voice, a hare on account of his skittishness; sublime callus remover, eunuch, shopkeeper, insignificant scatterbrain, hunchback of civilization.

In his manner of arguing—Sarmiento will claim in a final rhapsodic torrent of abuse—Alberdi is "like those dogs that walk sideways" [es como los perros que trotan de soslayo], an insult that in its economy and outlandishness is truly one for the ages.[3]

Furthermore, this is a textual universe where contradictions proliferate, inconsistencies flourish, outlandish turns of phrase or metaphors arise unexpectedly, wrongly attributed or incomplete quotations abound, digressions multiply, and tone can shift from the sublime to the maudlin or crass in the space of a single sentence. By the same token, intentions advertised early on are seemingly abandoned after a few pages, the vehemence displayed at any one time is often out of proportion to the subject at hand, and generic expectations are thoroughly thwarted—as it is already commonplace for critics to assert. Specific examples of these qualities abound. There are the notorious metamorphoses in Sarmiento's attitudes regarding the protagonists of his biographies and the targets of his invectives. Facundo Quiroga and Juan Manuel de Rosas are, respectively, widely acknowledged examples of Sarmiento's tendency to rehabilitate enemies on whom he had not so long ago lavished execration and bile (in Quiroga's case, earlier in the same book). Conversely, the list of former allies and friends with whom he later polemicized bitterly would be a who's who of nineteenth-century Argentine history. There is also one of the epigraphs to *Recuerdos de provincia* that mistakenly attributes the provenance of a quotation from *Macbeth* to *Hamlet*—"Es este un cuento que con aspavientos y gritos, refiere un loco y que no significa nada" [This is a tale that with wild gestures and screams is told by a madman, signifying nothing]—in which Shakespeare's original "idiot" is transformed into an outright "madman" by Sarmiento's awkward translation.[4] Along the same vein, another famous instance comes to mind: in *Facundo*, Sarmiento's best-known work, a quotation attributed by Sarmiento to Francis Bond Head really belongs to Alexander von Humboldt's *Tableaux de la nature*. Seemingly aware of this penchant for misquoting and confusing people, Sarmiento writes a letter to the poet Echeverría in which he excuses himself for the many such mistakes that marred his *Viajes*: "Agregue usted eso a la fe de erratas garrafales que he cometido en mis *Viajes*, haciendo almirante a Deffaudis, Maldonado al poeta Hidalgo, y Heredia a Plácido" [Add that to the huge list of errata that I have made in my *Viajes*, in which I made Deffaudis an admiral, confused Maldonado with the poet Hidalgo, and turned Plácido into Heredia.] Yet he never bothered enough to stop the practice.[5] Add to the foregoing the proliferation of dichotomies that can be identified throughout the text of *Facundo* and that, as it is conventional to assert, endlessly fracture the coherence and viability of the work's conceptual scaffolding. Or Sarmiento's last text, *Vida de Dominguito*, a maudlin biography of his only son, killed thirty years earlier, a work whose doleful and almost whimpering sentimentality cannot prevent it from becoming yet another solipsistic discourse on himself. All in all, this writing that we call Sarmiento does not quite make sense, in either the colloquial or the literal meanings of that phrase.

Yet we inevitably struggle to fight off this realization, persist in our interpretive intention, and renew our hermeneutic charge on the text, and by hook or by crook, in the end we manage to produce what we like to refer to as "our reading" of Sarmiento. In the process, contradictions are either disregarded or highlighted as examples of a text that dismantles its own assertions from within (and here I include my own previous work on Sarmiento); inconsistencies become "slippages" or "blanks" that are then used to explain subsequent and divergent readings of Sarmiento's texts, which allows for a reconstruction of the text's reception, or that are claimed to be the signs of a strategic maneuver employed by Sarmiento to control the interpretation of his work;[6] the mercurial unevenness of voice and tone are ascribed to the demands of Sarmiento's polemical newspaper style; or, when all else fails and these problematic qualities are confronted squarely, they are taken to be merely the frail stammerings of a dependent subject writing in a peripheral situation with respect to his metropolitan models. In the finest and most powerful critical readings of Sarmiento, those that have contributed the most to our contemporary and sagacious understanding of him—works by Beatriz Sarlo and Carlos Altamirano, Noé Jitrik, Sylvia Molloy, and others come immediately to mind—an impasse, an unresolved internal difference or contradiction is consistently the teleological terminus of the critical itinerary. But just as consistently, there is always a further effort to subdue, to bring under critical control the unsettledness, the threat entailed by that internal disjunction. There are times, indeed, when one can almost hear the critical gears groaning under the strain demanded by the effort of imposing coherence on Sarmiento's unmanageable writing. For instance, after having identified one such problematic and intractable instance at the very core of *Recuerdos de provincia*, the historian Tulio Halperín Donghi avers the following: "Pero no parece suficiente concluir que Sarmiento se ha resignado a la presencia de un ineliminable elemento de ambigüedad: . . . podría decirse más bien que atesora esa ambigüedad." [It is not enough to conclude that Sarmiento is resigned to the presence of an irreducible element of ambiguity: one could say more accurately that he treasures such ambiguity.] Donghi's statement is a clear effort to tame contradiction and ambiguity by understanding it finally as the mark of an avowedly conscious ideological stratagem.[7]

Yet pretending that finding contradictions, *décalages*, openings, and slippages in Sarmiento is a meaningful hermeneutical discovery is like your being excited about holding the winning lottery ticket when, unbeknownst to you, everybody else chose the same number. It is not that these textual incongruities are not there, scattered about, like easily garnered specimens for a rhetorical teratology; it is rather that there are so many of them that they lose whatever interpretive leverage they might have wielded had they appeared as discrete and isolated instances. Almost every assertion in Sarmiento can be confronted with an opposite opinion, often appearing in the same work, sometimes in the same chapter or page; the most hated character can and does usually become, sometime later, the object of admiration; the grandest pronouncement or universal rule is soon undermined and reduced by its equally important exception. This is why there is always, at least in me, the lingering apprehension that even after we have plied our critical tools on Sarmiento, so very much has been left unaccounted for—that there is an untamable, overwhelming quality to Sarmiento's writing that refuses to be reduced to any category, no matter how capacious or rigorous. I am aware that this incommensurableness of the text with respect to critical discourse on it is, to some degree or another, a circumstance that is attendant to every exegetical enterprise, for interpretation invariably implies an element of willful inattentiveness, of blindness to those aspects of the work that do not quite conform to our chosen critical scheme. But I would also argue that with Sarmiento's works the effort to impose coherence through interpretive closure is always accompanied by the jarring knowledge of its insufficiency, by the glaring awareness of its inadequacy. Sarmiento's discourse never stands still, so to speak, never seems to cohere, and the fixity that interpretation seeks to impose on it always ends up by recognizing its fragility, impermanence, and contingency.

This incommensurable quality of Sarmiento's discourse has been anthropomorphized in his reputation for being a madman, "el loco Sarmiento." This notion seems to have surrounded him throughout his career and has become a leitmotif of biographical writing on him. In one such critical performance, found in Adolfo Prieto's book on autobiography in Argentina, the certainty in the accuracy of the diagnosis is itself a symptom of the patient's universally recognized malady:

> Las confesiones de Sarmiento denuncian una indudable tendencia neurótica, un exacerbado afán de atraer sobre sí la atención y el asentimiento de los demás. Esta tendencia, fortalecida en años posteriores, permite la eclosión de gestos y actitudes que no cuestan ya calificar de claramente neuróticos. . . . La abundancia de anécdotas que recrean ese aspecto de los años de madurez y senectud de Sarmiento, ilustra, sin esfuerzo, la descripción que da Karl Mannheim del *adulto gesticulante*, ese hombre que, durante un período de inseguridad organizada, al no hallar satisfacción inmediata a sus aspiraciones en el terreno del trabajo y el reconocimiento social, sustituye sus objetivos y se satisface con meros gestos y símbolos.
>
> Una neurosis provocada por la frustración total o parcial de las aspiraciones individuales en conflicto con la realidad social, es un fenómeno lo suficientemente común y conocido como para que no escandalice su atribución, aunque sea por vía de hipótesis, a una personalidad que revela tantos síntomas de haberla padecido, como la de Sarmiento.[8]

> ---
>
> Sarmiento's confessions doubtless reveal a clear neurotic tendency, a heightened desire to attract the attention and the approval of others. This tendency, which increased in his later years, revealed itself in gestures and attitudes that can only be classified as clearly neurotic. . . . There is a wealth of anecdotes that show this dimension of Sarmiento's mature and elderly years and illustrate transparently Karl Mannheim's description of the *gesturing adult*: that thoroughly insecure man who substitutes his objectives and consoles himself with mere gestures and symbols, upon discovering that he cannot achieve immediate satisfaction to his aspirations in the realm of social recognition.
>
> A neurosis caused by the total or partial frustration of individual aspirations in conflict with social reality is a sufficiently common and well-known phenomenon for the diagnosis to be considered scandalous, even if only presented as a hypothesis concerning a person who reveals so many symptoms of having suffered from it such as Sarmiento.

One finds consistently that what seem to be physical or psychological accounts of Sarmiento's personality and character are really attempts to describe the unsettled, incongruous quality of his writing. This collapsing together of discursive qualities and physiognomical or psychic traits is abetted, to say the least, by the radically autobiographic dimension of Sarmiento's works; for even if, as has been remarked many times, Sarmiento had a predilection for biographical writing—his accounts of the lives of El Chacho Peñaloza, Padre Aldao, Facundo Quiroga, and Dominguito come immediately to mind—it is no less true that all these presumed works on another are for Sarmiento thinly disguised opportunities to speak about himself. Sarmiento's "being," his "voice" are so thoroughly interwoven with his writing that it is perhaps not surprising that the qualities of the discourse should have finally been attributed to the person.

I offer as examples two verbal portraits of Sarmiento, one of which focuses on the man's physique, the other on his spiritual traits. The first is by the Franco-Argentine man of letters Paul Groussac in his "Artículo fúnebre," written, as the title suggests, upon Sarmiento's death:

> Tal cual se me aparece aún, espaldudo y macizo, rugoso y desarmónico, con su abollada máscara de Sócrates guerrero, cuyos ojos y frente de inspirado dominan una boca y una mandíbula de primitivo, mitad sublime, mitad grotesco, evocando a un tiempo el pórtico de Atenas y el antro del cíclope, queda en pie en mi recuerdo como uno de los seres más extraordinarios que me fue dado contemplar.[9]

> I can still recall him now, broad-shouldered and massive, wrinkled and graceless, with the face of a Socrates at war, whose inspired eyes and forehead are juxtaposed to the mouth and the jaw of a primitive man; half sublime, half grotesque, evoking in turn the portico of Athens and the Cyclops's cave, he remains in my memory one of the most extraordinary beings that I ever had the opportunity to regard.

The second is from Enrique Anderson Imbert's introduction to his 1981 edition of *Recuerdos de provincia*, and it reads as follows:

> Lo cierto es que Sarmiento tenía una complejísima idiosincracia. Era un razonador inteligente, capaz de penetrantes análisis, de ágiles síntesis y de rigurosa dialéctica; pero también era un energúmeno todo estremecido por efluvios de la naturaleza, ramalazos de la subconciencia, golpes de sangre y apetitos urgentes. . . . Era viril pero propenso al llanto; robusto pero delicado y nervioso; agresivo, pero tierno y cortés; intransigente pero comprensivo; sañudo y magnánimo; estudioso e improvisador; truculento y humorista; egocéntrico y excéntrico, con ciclos de euforia y depresión.[10]

> The truth is that Sarmiento had an exceedingly complex personality. He was an intelligent thinker, capable of penetrating analysis, of dazzling syntheses and of rigorous argumentation; but he was also a wild being thoroughly shaken by effluvia of nature, tremors from the unconscious, fits of

violence and peremptory appetites. . . . He was manly but quick to tears; robust but delicate and skittish; aggressive, but tender and polite; intransigent but understanding, spiteful, and generous; a careful researcher and an improviser; somber and humorous; self-centered and outgoing, with cycles of euphoria and depression.

I would argue that the preceding descriptions portray not so much a person as a modality of discourse that exhibits the contradictions and inconsistencies detailed earlier. These incongruities are subsequently ascribed to Sarmiento's character and physical attributes, following a metonymical line of least resistance that travels from the written word to its avowed source, which is presumed to share the same qualities, and which in Sarmiento's particular case is always projecting itself forcefully in the text under a number of guises. But even if we keep in mind that these are, rather, the salient discursive qualities of the writing that we identify as "Sarmiento," the implications of such a characterization remain to be explored. What, for instance, is the status of a writing that does not seem answerable to the customary demands of internal coherence; and, concomitantly, what are the prospects for criticism when one confronts a text that thwarts the usual practice of documenting a critical assertion through the citation of a passage designated as privileged, given that a contrary passage or an opposite conclusion invariably lurks never too far away?

I would like to argue that these incongruous characteristics of Sarmiento's prose can be best accounted for when his writing is conceptualized as discourse in its most naked rendition: discourse as performance, as an *activity* in which intentionality and language intersect in the uninterrupted flow of writing. For discourse in Sarmiento is, more than a disquisition *about* or *toward* something, an act that ultimately finds its justification in its own factualness. Accordingly, there is a certain emergency to Sarmiento's prose, in more than one sense of that word: first, as a writing that positions itself as responsive to the avowed crisis, polemic, offense, situation, or other demanding circumstance that it is purportedly addressing and that provides the stimulus for composition; but also, and especially, as a discourse tied in a radical fashion to the very instant of its *emergence*. This is the reason why Sarmiento's works are persistently reproached for their superficial, unfinished, and spontaneous qualities, as the following quotation by Ezequiel Martínez Estrada amply demonstrates:

[Sarmiento] no ha podido meditar ninguno de los temas que ha expuesto, y de ahí la impresión de que nos ha dejado colosales bosquejos incoherentes de una obra no realizada. Sus ideas brotan espontáneamente . . . sin el cuidado del último retoque. Nada hay en su pensamiento que se proyecte a lo interno ni que surja de complicados laberintos; su pensamiento se parece mucho a los ademanes y los gestos del hombre que habla siempre en voz alta. (164)

Sarmiento has not thought through any of the topics that he expounded on; hence the impression that he has simply left us colossal and incoherent sketches of an unconsummated oeuvre. His ideas sprout spontaneously . . . without the benefit of a finishing touch. There is nothing in his thought that reveals his interiority nor that arises from complexity; his thought resembles greatly the demeanor and the gestures of someone that always vociferates.

Notice, parenthetically, the remarkable coincidence with Prieto's earlier characterization of Sarmiento as an *adulto gesticulador*. Martínez Estrada later adds an oxymoronic observation that, given what has been presented thus far, seems strangely enough to make sense: "Lo más logrado de Sarmiento es lo impremeditado"(177).[11] [Sarmiento's most accomplished work is that which is not planned.] Beatriz Sarlo and Carlos Altamirano echo this impression in their splendid reading of Sarmiento's principal autobiographical work: "*Recuerdos de provincia* conserva todos los rastros del primer trabajo de escritura, todo lo que en la segunda lectura y en la corrección se elimina para alcanzar cierto ideal compositivo limpio de desorden, de repetición, de obsesiones, de idas y de vueltas."[12] [*Recuerdos de provincia* shows all the residues of the first toil of writing, everything that upon a second reading and correcting phase is eliminated in order to achieve a certain rhetorical ideal, free of disorder, repetition, obsessions, and back-and-forth arguing.] Hence, Sarmiento's prose always appears to be a sketch of a still inchoate thought, always moving and unpolished both in its conceptual and stylistic dimensions. It was specifically this quality that led Carlos Alberto Erro to declare that this most idiosyncratic of Spanish American authors nonetheless does not have a style that is recognizably his own:

¿Qué importancia tiene que a veces se empleen mal los gerundios y se cometan tropiezos idiomáticos, si se es capaz de escribir *Facundo* y *Recuerdos de provincia*? Escribe Sarmiento como si su prosa fuera la natural respiración de su espíritu. Nunca se le ve componer, preparar o pulir. . . . Su prosa es . . . el aparato circulatorio de su pensamiento, ramificado canal por donde circula un contenido vivo, cálido, poderoso. Escribe como vive; y sus escritos tienen envión de luchador, filo y fuerza de hacha más que de espada, aliento de pecho ancho, de resuello profundo. Por eso no se le conocen los "tics" que dan sello personal a tantos estilos y que se explican en quienes

tienen que detenerse para volver a empezar. La prosa de Sarmiento sigue
su marcha sin mirar hacia atrás.[13]

Sarmiento writes as if his prose were the natural breathing cycle of his spirit.
You never find him composing, preparing, or polishing. His prose is the
circulatory system of his thought, a series of branching canals through
which a powerful, live, and warm content circulates. He writes the way he
lives, and his writings possess the thrust of the fighter, the sharpness and
strength of an ax rather than an épée, the breath of an expansive chest, the
sound of a profound exhalation. That is why you will not find in him the
"tics" that give a personal cast to so many styles and are to be found in
those who pause in their writing in order to begin anew. Sarmiento's prose
marches on without ever looking back.

In my view, though, these qualities of Sarmiento's writing are not, as these
and many other commentators of his works would have it, reflections of
his lack of deliberation, ideological inconsistency, or shallowness of
mind—qualities that are clearly there but are only symptomatic in character. They are, rather, the result of the way in which Sarmiento projects
his discourse as indistinguishable from the instance, the act of its production. Sarmiento's writing aims to be discourse itself, pure and simple.
It aspires continuously to "represent"—a word I intentionally use here in
its theatrical connotation—the emergence, the coming into being of his
discourse.

Most, if not all, of the critical quotations I have cited allude to that
quality of Sarmiento's writing that recalls the definition of the Kantian
concept of the sublime. Kant ultimately defined the sublime as the mind's
experience of its own capability for thinking the infinite and the simultaneous pleasure and pain derived from comparing that capability with
any sensible experience. Certain objects in nature—mountains, waterfalls,
and so on—are not sublime in themselves, but they instill the feeling of
the sublime in us because their formlessness remind us of that innate
capacity. The mind feels at once attracted and repulsed by these objects;
they produce in us what Kant calls "a negative pleasure" because their
dimensions provoke awe in us, but their boundlessness is expressive of
purposelessness.[14] Such is a fitting description of the feeling induced by
Sarmiento's writing on countless critics of his works, a feeling that is
amply evinced by the astonishment, condescendence, and even contempt
that characterizes their own discourse on Sarmiento.[15]

The explanation for this seemingly monstrous discursive praxis that
characterizes Sarmiento is to be found, I believe, in the larger context of
the foundation of cultural discourse in Spanish America in the nine-

teenth century—that is to say, the rhetorical predicament I outlined in
the first chapter of this book. It is there, I propose, in the conflicted relationship between Spanish American discourse and modernity, that this
contradictory and willful writing that we designate as "Sarmiento" begins to acquire its ultimate significance. For one could construe Sarmiento's discursive posture as a strategy designed to secure a position of
rhetorical legitimacy in the face of the crisis that exists at the core of
Spanish American cultural discourse. Sarmiento's stratagem in his confrontation with this rhetorical circumstance—his "solution" to the rhetorical crisis, so to speak—consists of an attempt to found the authority
of his writing in a conception of discourse as an act that is continuously
being performed before the reader's eyes. In this conception, discourse
has no past and no future, no internal principle of self-consistency or ac-
countability, all of which explains the repeated and seemingly unproblematic presence of incongruities and contradictions in Sarmiento's prose.
Writing in Sarmiento's works becomes simultaneous with the volition of
which it is an expression: discourse is represented as an immediate act of
the will, as a repeated performance of the very moment in which a sub-
jective intentionality avails itself of language for its peremptory needs.
This is why the word that first comes to my mind to describe this writing is *passion*, because in it discourse is depicted as being ultimately ruled
by the relentless, contradictory drives of a desiring subject. This also explains why criticism on Sarmiento is peppered with terms derived from a
theatrical or dramatic lexicon—*gesticulación, volumen, histrionismo, más-
cara*—since there is in his readers the inescapable awareness that, more
than simply reading, they are witnessing a performance of sorts. In the
vocabulary of speech-act theory, the locutionary dimension of Sarmiento's discourse is always on the verge of being overrun by its illocu-
tionary force.[16]

I am fully aware that there is a potential peril in the sort of reading
that I am proposing here: the danger of having Sarmiento's writing retreat
into the opacity of the self-contradictory and the incomprehensible. And
if, as I propose, his rhetorical circumstance is coextensive with Spanish
American discourse in general, there is consequently also a danger of
identifying that entire discursive production with the unintelligible. Nevertheless, I believe that in entertaining this reproach one would indulge
in a more dangerous mystification: that of endowing Western discourse
with an internal consistency and self-centeredness that the most recent
literary and philosophical critiques have irrefutably revealed to be essen-

tially a mirage. What should be emphasized instead is the productive aspect of Sarmiento's rhetorical *clinamen*, the empowerment that it represented for Sarmiento in particular and for the Spanish American discursive circumstance in general. Regardless of its manifest contradictions, Spanish American modernity must be understood as a cultural activity possessing meaning unto itself—that is, as an ongoing process of cultural production that engages in a symbolic appropriation and translation of historical and cultural experience.[17]

On the other hand, given the discursive predicament that I have detailed, one could be tempted to claim that there is something innately heroic about the very existence of Spanish American discourse, given the odds against which it must struggle in order to exist, or that in its underscoring of the inherent incongruity and internal disarticulation of all discourses, the latter is valuable as a critique of hegemonic discursive modalities. The agonistic vision of the universe of discourse entailed by the first of these possibilities (the heroic) must yield nonetheless to Foucault's insight that the mere fact of discourse always implies that the speaker is already immersed in a complex strategic situation that sustains the network of power in a given historical moment. In word, any heroization of creole discourse could only be achieved at the expense of forgetting that such discourse has served in turn to provide ideological legitimacy to creole domination of local subaltern groups. The second one, the critical view, is a more tantalizing possibility but equally problematic: for if we succumb to the temptation of granting a demystifying value to the difference entailed by Latin American discourse, we run the risk of fetishizing that difference, of becoming enamored of the critical opportunities that it affords, thereby drawing attention away from the concrete situation of exploitation and structural peripheralness from which it arises. And the price for engaging in such a critique can become an investment in sustaining the condition of economic and political subjection on which the affirmation of cultural difference is predicated, as well as the acceptance of a marginality that hegemonic cultural discourse is only too willing to confirm in the first place.

Hence, my aim has been not to argue for a recuperation of Sarmiento through tragic pathos or as a fulcrum for critical leverage but to understand the essential qualities of his discourse as they point to the existence in his works of a concrete strategy of rhetorical empowerment. That the questions of authority and voice are at the heart of Sarmiento's writing is substantiated by a recent article by Françoise Pérus in which she summarizes the essential components of the Argentine author's discursive situation. According to her, Sarmiento's writing is split between

> one who observes from the outside, applying notions and value judgments coming from a "universal" and cultured tradition that has still not arrived in Argentina, and one who narrates and recreates from a fundamentally oral tradition, starting from his own experience and his own passions. Without the instability of the subject of enunciation and its displacement from one sphere to the next and from one perspective to another, one could explain neither the linguistic, discursive, and formal heterogeneity of the text, nor the fact that the observed culture can end up acquiring, at least sometimes, the character of a "voice" capable of converting the interpreting culture into the interpreted one (for example, Napoleon or Robespierre seen as "bad gauchos").[18]

What must be emphasized is that "Sarmiento" is a composite of both of those perspectives and that recent attempts to read the second Sarmiento (and, by extension, Spanish American writing in general) as one that unilaterally resists hegemonic discourse—to the exclusion of the first dimension—is a damaging simplification of the gripping predicament in the midst of which he wrote.

Sarmiento's resolute embracing of modernity explains many of the calamitous policies that he pursued when as president he was in a position to translate that commitment to the modern into action. Indeed, in many ways his executive actions and his many texts provided the ideological justification for the genocidal war against the Indians of the pampas unleashed fifteen years later by General Roca and his army. But his writings also betray both the constant discursive peril that accompanied that commitment to modernity and his negotiating of that threat through a continual turning away from modernity's demands for a rational, rhetorically consistent discourse. One could even claim that Sarmiento may have tried to exorcize the resulting ambivalence with respect to modernity in the unusual severity of his official actions, all of which would prove once again that we always despise others—in Sarmiento's case the "barbarian Indian"—who remind us of those weaknesses we cannot bear to recognize in ourselves.

Furthermore, it should be noted that in his peculiar way of disentangling himself from the demands of the modern, Sarmiento's discourse may have arrived nonetheless at a most consummate realization of modernity: writing as an unpremeditated, spontaneous act that knows no past and burns without surcease in the resplendence of the present moment.

It is not simply that Sarmiento consistently endeavored to anchor his writing in the multitudinous affairs of his biography or his season in history; these were simply rhetorical devices and occasions for the mise-en-scène of his discursive performance. Sarmiento's writing attempts to reside perpetually in that point of insertion of the "I," that moment when, as Emile Benveniste phrased it in his now classic work on pronouns, "the speaker takes over all the resources of language for his own behalf," to "effect a conversion of language into discourse" (220).[19] It is hardly surprising, then, to find that one of the most disseminated sobriquets that his enemies consistently brandished against Sarmiento was the revealing nickname Don YO.

Given all of the above, I would like to argue here in favor of what could be called a passionate or pulsional reading of Sarmiento's texts: a reading that is attentive to the power and drive of Sarmiento's discourse, as opposed to circumventing, taming, or overlooking it; a reading that is not oblivious to the aspect of Sarmiento that is alluded to by Martínez Estrada when he identifies in his writings "una oleada de sangre caliente, un calor de tórax abierto como no lo hay parecido en toda nuestra literatura,"[20] [a wave of warm blood, the warmth of an open chest such as there is no other in all of our literature], which he also describes as "una animalidad sublimada."[21] [a distilled animal-like quality.] All these locutions and many more similar ones that could be mentioned here are, I believe, tropological constructions that unknowingly attempt to portray the force, the passion, that is indissolubly coupled to Sarmiento's discourse. No comprehensive account of Sarmiento can fail to address this component of his writing, particularly because it may be, paradoxically, perhaps the single invariant quality that circumscribes its specificity. Moreover, I would contend finally that it is this very aspect of it that keeps beckoning us back, against our own critical best judgment, to the inhospitable morass of Sarmiento's texts.

Indeed, I have often wondered why I, and seemingly everyone who has ever written about Sarmiento, seem unable to leave well enough alone, why we always find ourselves returning to his works: hence the "once more" of my title. Of course, the liminary position that Sarmiento occupies in the development of Spanish American cultural discourse seems a more than reasonable justification. Yet I believe that a more compelling, a more *passionate* reason, shall we say, can also be adduced. I suspect that there is in us a recognition at some level that this writing—the imperious, supple, cajoling, histrionic, contradictory, unfinished, and superficial discourse that we call Sarmiento—discloses the fragile precipice that tempts our own writing at every turn: that of giving ourselves wholly to the pure thrust of discourse, of allowing writing to *be* the force from which discourse always springs, as opposed to being reduced merely to detecting the faint embers of this force in a language that has already been subjected to the strictures and necessities of communication. This should not be construed as a post lapsarian hankering after a discourse that is *truly* ours, one that would reveal the specific imprint of a personality on language, but rather as a desire to dwell, if only briefly, within that dimension of language where, in fact, personality is no longer a significant category. For, as Benjamin has made clear, there is in all linguistic creations, in addition to what is conveyed, something that cannot be communicated, a measure of signifying intention that he refers to as pure language: "In this pure language," he says, "—which no longer means or expresses anything but is, as expressionless and creative Word, that which is meant in all languages—all information, all sense, and all intention finally encounter a stratum in which they are destined to be extinguished."[22] The movement, the pulsion that rules Sarmiento's discourse, discernible in its inattention to internal coherence, harmony, and self-consistency, reminds us that a similar force is at work in our own writing; but it also makes us aware of how far we have gone to suppress it as well, a circumstance that might be encapsulated in Derrida's assertion that criticism is always in the pursuit of structure because "*form* fascinates when one no longer has the force to understand force from within itself."[23] This is precisely why, if we are to write about him at all, we must berate this writing that we have named "Sarmiento" and endlessly denounce it as demented, inconstant, willful, and bizarre.

Yet we always go back to "el loco Sarmiento," perhaps because, paradoxically, we can only come in contact with that dimension of our own writing through the writing of others like him. Indeed, could we not discern in the impetuous, breathless prose of Martí, a man both fascinated and torn by the modern if there was ever one, some of the same qualities that have been identified in Sarmiento's discourse? And conversely, could the carefully parsed, hyperanalytical coolness of Borges be the writing of someone fearful of the profligacy and excess that haunts him as an ever present threat? Maybe this is why Sarmiento is continuously daring us, defying us to stop reading him, or directing us to destroy his pages once we are through with them, as in the blazing introduction to *Recuerdos de provincia*: "Sin placer, como sin zozobra, ofrezco a mis compatriotas estas páginas. . . . Después de leídas, pueden aniquilarlas, pues pertenecen al número de las publicaciones que deben su existencia a circunstancias del momento, pasadas las cuales nadie las comprendería" (3:28). [Without pleasure, but also without sorrow, I offer these pages to my countrymen. . . . After they are read they can be annihilated, since they belong to that species of writing that owes its being to the circumstances of the moment, after which they would not be understood by anyone.] But Sarmiento knows better than that. And the fact that we *do* go back to his works means that *we* also know better—that in spite of all the incongruities and contradictions we have managed to understand him only too well.

The next chapter is devoted to the Cuban antislavery discourse of the first half of the nineteenth century. My aim there will be to show how the rhetorical crisis to which I have alluded manifests itself as a cleavage that rends that textual production and creates a disjunction whose borders coincide with those that presumably guarantee the distinction between fictive and analytical discourses on the subject of slavery.

CHAPTER THREE

Strange Fruit

The Discourse of the Cuban Antislavery Novel

Porque tiene eso de característico la culpa, que, cual ciertas manchas, mientras más se lavan, más clara presentan la haz.

For such is typical of guilt; just as there are certain stains that the more they are washed, the brighter they show themselves.
—Cirilo Villaverde, *Cecilia Valdés*

So its the miscegenation, not the incest, which you can't bear.
—William Faulkner, *Absalom, Absalom!*

THIS CHAPTER IS unconventional in its articulation and rhetorical procedure because the argument that will be presented in it thwarts the customary evidentiary process deployed in critical discourse. Most of what will be adduced here revolves around conveying the existence of a problematics that is exceedingly hard to describe, much less grasp in all its ramifications. But I believe that the object identified and delimited by this critical approach may lead to a novel understanding of one of the most important textual productions of the Spanish American nineteenth century: the Cuban antislavery discourse. I propose that my analysis will allow us to understand, in the end, the peculiar character of Cuban antislavery narrative, a specificity that has been foregrounded by critics from the start—particularly with respect to the North American avatar of the genre—and has been the source of ample speculation throughout the years. But the study of the phenomenon requires advancing through indirection and suggestion rather than through the marshaling of fact and textual quotation. Still, these may be both the ideal approximation as well as the instruments required for the study of works that are themselves structured on ambiguity and ambivalence: texts whose depths are as murky as the genealogies on whose exploration and unveiling they obsessively persevere.

I take as the point of departure for my mediation on the subject the study of the textual production of the antislavery movement as it manifested itself in nonliterary works. I wish to survey the object that is created and refracted in these works—that is, the institution of slavery in its various components—in order to contrast it to the putatively same object that is put forth by the literary texts of that movement, in an effort to understand the forces that guided each of the two projects: forces that I argue are not in as mutual an alignment as one would imagine and as literary historians have proposed throughout the years. The space that opens up as a result of this interpretive maneuver will allow me to identify the mutual imbrication of these two textual registers and forces in the larger context of the antislavery movement's relationship to the modern discourses that provided its philosophical and ideological foundation.

Until very recently, the antislavery project in Cuba has been studied and depicted as a homogeneous enterprise, one in which civic reformers and novelists, intellectuals and mulattoes, slaves and former slaves, poets and white economic aristocrats were united in a common front against the human misery produced by the slavery system. This conception had been sustained to a large degree by the existence and the well-known activities of the so-called del Monte circle, a group in which essayists and literati met to discuss slavery as part of an overarching attempt to define the possible configuration of a future Cuban nationality. The group's philanthropic activities—the buying of freedom for slaves; its sponsorship of mulatto poets such as Gabriel de la Concepción Valdés (Plácido) and Manzano; del Monte's entreaties to others, which led to the writing of antislavery novels and tracts; and his channeling of information to British authorities regarding both slavery and the illegal yet thriving slave trade—have traditionally been taken as signs of the existence of an ample and homogeneous frontal assault against the "peculiar institution" in Cuba. Cuban antislavery discourse has been understood traditionally to reflect the broadness of the common front against the institution that del Monte's group clearly perceived in its activities and in its self-image. And because the group itself has been posited as the ideological core of the antislavery movement in Cuban history, this view has prevailed fundamentally unchallenged during the intervening 150 years. Some recent critical and historical works have tried to provide a more nuanced view by bringing to light, or to the forefront, the signs of ideological dissension and tactical disagreement not only within del Monte's group but in the Cuban intelligentsia of the time in its views regarding blacks, the slave trade, and the plantation system in general.[1] For instance, the highlighting of the questionable mutual loyalties displayed by the principals—whether white, mulatto, or black—when confronted with the repression unleashed by the discovery of the Escalera "conspiracy" of 1844, and the uneven punitive treatment received by them from Spanish authorities, has opened the way for revisiting the seemingly unified and concerted effort tradi-tionally ascribed to the movement. Other critics have underscored the inequalities of power that were always present in the sponsoring and cir-culation by del Monte's *cenáculo* of autobiographical and literary works by slaves or former slaves, shattering from within the illusion of the group's self-proclaimed egalitarian practices and aspirations. Yet whether invoked to corroborate or debunk it, by and large our understanding of the an-tislavery phenomenon in Cuba is still fundamentally mediated by the myth of collective unanimity that lies at the center of this foundational narrative of Cuban nationality. My intent here is to apply a different sort of interpretive pressure, one that will cleave the movement's presumed homogeneity in a novel and productive fashion.

Let me begin by stating unequivocally something that strikes any re-searcher who has spent even a modest amount of time reading the essen-tial tracts of Cuban antislavery prose: the principal goal of antislavery essayistic writing was not, at least not in its innermost core, the denun-ciation of an economic and social system that was regarded as inhuman or unjust. One begins to realize this when one understands that for early-nineteenth-century intellectuals there would be a contradiction in using the adjective "inhuman" to describe a practice that in their view had been so consistently present in human history as slavery; indeed, there seemed to be unanimous agreement that even the most superficial consideration of the institution would show its seemingly universal historical dimension. Cuban intellectuals of the first half of the nineteenth century who none-theless worked to achieve the end of the trade were keenly aware of that fact; for it was that very historical permanence and depth of slavery that José Antonio Saco had exposed to his contemporaries in his painstaking, multivolume study of that social and economic modality, whose original title bespeaks its universalizing intentions: *Historia de la esclavitud desde los tiempos más remotos hasta nuestros días.*[2] Saco's history had as one of its underlying motives the "naturalization" of slavery in history and, further, in its Cuban context; that is, Saco desired to depict the Cuban case merely as the latest installment of an institution that had deep cultural and historical roots. This maneuver had, in turn, two primary and related thrusts: to downplay the historical peculiarities of the Cuban version of the slavery system and to remove moralistic and humanitarian considerations from the study of the phenomenon. Saco's conviction was that in order to arrive at a thorough understanding of slavery in Cuba it was imperative to distance the analysis of that system from the impassioned rhetoric that surrounded the debate on the question. Speaking about Saco's argumentation, Salvador Bueno avers that the great Cuban reformer "no utilizaba argumentos humanitarios, filantrópicos" [he did not use humanitarian or philanthropic arguments], and provides a quotation from Saco to that effect: "Acerca de la moral guardaré silencio; he preferido combatir el interés, pues siendo esta arma la que hiere el corazón, el triunfo es más seguro."[3] [Regarding the moral dimension of the topic I will be silent; I have opted to address self-interest, since this is the weapon closest to the heart and therefore the one that guarantees success.] In fact, what Bueno perceives to be a matter of choice on Saco's part, as well as Saco's stated preference for silence on the moral implications of slavery as opposed to arguments derived from economic considerations, are not simply optative argumentative strategies: I would argue instead that they are an integral aspect of the rhetoric of Cuban antislavery treatises and tracts.

Similarly, in the writings of Domingo del Monte, the ideological mentor of the group baptized with his name, it is surprising to find an almost complete absence of moral allegations or recriminations with respect to the surrounding human spectacle offered by slavery. In a letter written in 1844 to the editor of *El Globo*, del Monte refers with no small amount of pride to this absence of moral considerations in his critique of the institution: "Confesaré a usted, por último, mis opiniones sobre la esclavitud de los negros. Aparte de la natural compasión como filántropo o filósofo humanitario que a todo pecho sensible causan los males del prójimo, nunca he considerado esta cuestión sino bajo un aspecto político y social. Así, poco me he preocupado de la civilización del Africa por medio de la trata, ni de proporcionar mejor suerte a los africanos trayéndolos a nuestros ingenios, bautizándolos y haciéndolos felices."[4] [I will confess to you, finally, my opinion on the bondage of blacks. Aside from the natural compassion as a philanthrope and humanitarian philosopher that the misfortune of our fellow beings cause in every feeling heart, I have never considered this matter except in its political and social ramifications. Hence, I have not cared much about civilizing Africa by means of the slave trade, nor by giving Africans a better life by bringing them to our sugar mills, baptizing them and making them happy.] Here del Monte can be seen repeating, with a sarcastic insinuation, the deliberate side-stepping of the humanitarian consideration of slavery previously seen in Saco's quotation; that is to say, the moral objection against the institution is brought up only to be discarded as a suitable or worthwhile ground for its effective critique. Later in the same text, del Monte makes a statement that allows for no ambiguities about his perspective on the issue:

> Yo no quisiera que en mi patria hubiera esclavos, ni menos que estos es-clavos fuesen negros, es decir, de un ramo tan salvaje de la familia humana. Yo estoy íntimamente convencido, como todos los hombres de corazón y de inteligencia de la isla de Cuba, que nuestros campos pueden ser culti-vados por brazos blancos y libres, y nuestro más ardiente deseo es que la primera de las Antillas escape de la suerte que ha cabido a Haití y a Jamaica, es decir, que no se convierta por nuestra codicia ciega en propiedad de una raza bárbara, cuando puede aspirar a ser un foco de civilización europea en el mundo occidental.
>
> La misión social y política de España en la isla de Cuba es otra, por cierto no menos bella y digna de una gran nación: convertirla en una colonia de una gran nación: convertirla en una colonia *europea*, con población es-clarecida y europea y que sea el más brillante foco de la civilización de la raza caucásica en el mundo hispano americano.[5]

> I wish there were no slaves in Cuba, much less that these slaves were black, that is to say, of such a savage branch of the human tree. I am completely convinced, like all men of good heart and intelligence in Cuba, that our fields can be cultivated by free and white hands, and my most fervent wish is that the largest of the Antilles should escape the misfortune that has befallen Haiti and Jamaica, that is, to become the property of a barbarous race on account of our blind greed, when in fact Cuba can aspire to become a beacon of European civilization in the Western world.
>
> Spain's social and political mission in Cuba is one not less beautiful and dignified and befitting a great nation: to turn her into a European colony, with an enlightened and European population that can be the brightest beacon of Caucasian civilization in the Spanish American world.

This desire to retreat from a humanitarian or moralistic criticism of slavery surfaces repeatedly in Cuban antislavery tracts. As a corollary to this practice, there is an almost total and signal absence in these works of depictions of the horrors and human misery wreaked by the plantation system on its subjects. We find a revealing echo of this hesitation, of these qualms about referring explicitly to the sufferings associated with slavery, in the autobiography that Juan Francisco Manzano composed at the request of del Monte himself. In it, Manzano repeatedly asks for forgiveness for indulging in the description of the punishments and humiliations he suffered during his enslavement. Likewise, at other times Manzano assures the reader that in his account he has often skipped years of his life with the express purpose that his struggle and travails not excessively distract the reader's attention. There is in this text a peculiar modesty about depicting suffering, which is all the more significant since it was commissioned and placed in circulation precisely for its presumed value as a documentary of personal experience and toil. Keenly aware of the need to please his rhetorical masters, Manzano seems to have sensed quite accurately the ambivalent stake that del Monte and his group had on him and his life: to anchor their critique of slavery on real experience, while simultaneously eschewing the concreteness that was afforded by individual perspective. The thrust of the antislavery discourse was toward the generic, a move that foreclosed the only space that would have accommodated Manzano's emphasis on the specificity of his lived experience. The marks of Manzano's negotiation of this predicament in his work are as indelible as those left by the frequent beatings to which he was subjected by his real overlords, the same scars he glosses over to please the current taskmasters—the rhetorical ones—to which he was then beholden.[6]

In examining these quotations from Cuban intellectuals of the period I am not forgetting that being antislavery does not necessarily mean that one is problack, as David T. Haberly has argued for the Brazilian context in his "Abolitionism in Brazil: Anti-Slavery and Anti-Slave."[7] Rather I am interested in establishing the specific nature and source of the arguments being advanced against slavery by Cuban abolitionists. Indeed, if we read carefully the writings produced by the abolitionist intellectuals of the Cuban antislavery movement, we can determine that slavery was execrated above all because it was considered an institution outside the pale of a modernity of which these writers were intent on becoming legitimate and full-fledged participants. The antislavery movement of the 1830s and 1840s in Cuba had its principal source in two historical facts that threatened, each in its own particular fashion, to leave Cuba languishing permanently and without recourse in the periphery of the modern. First, the emancipation of the rest of Spanish America from Spanish hegemony— a process that had come to an official close in 1826—had left the island still attached to a metropolitan enclave that seemed to represent the very negation of modernity. Second (closely tied to the first) there existed among the Cuban intelligentsia the anguish caused by the knowledge of the island's total dependence on slavery and the plantation economy just as the latter system appeared to be in world historical retreat as a viable economic and social paradigm. Already in 1776, Adam Smith had argued in *The Wealth of Nations* that slavery was an anachronism that could never hope to compete successfully with free labor.[8] By the end of the 1820s it was obvious to all concerned that the only tangible effect of Britain's compensation to the Spanish Crown in exchange for the official end of the slave trade in Spanish territories, which had been ratified in 1820, had been to drive a still flourishing market underground.[9] Cuban abolitionists saw themselves caught between the official metropolitan position that alleged the effective demise of the trade and a reality that gave the lie to that claim. Hence, Cuba was not simply beholden to an economic arrangement that was anachronic in nature; historical circumstances were conspiring further to deepen that anachronism by hiding it from view. In this regard, del Monte's exhortation to "cumplir con las necesidades del siglo, poniendo *al orden del día* la cuestión de esclavitud" (1:44–45) [be faithful to the demands of our century, by bringing up-to-date the question of slavery] is exemplary. A few years later, in 1848, del Monte produced an article that is especially relevant because of the transparency with which it evinces his views concerning slavery, the island's colonial predicament, and modernity:

> Opinamos que Cuba hoy no está en términos hábiles para lanzarse a una revolución: que los pueblos, como los hombres, necesitan crecer, robustecerse, instruirse, antes de emanciparse por la fuerza: que Cuba bajo el despotismo, se va desarrollando materialmente poco a poco: que Cuba se va instruyendo, por la experiencia ajena y por su trato con el mundo culto, de los principios que dominan hoy la sociedad humana en las naciones civilizadas: que Cuba se persuadirá, al cabo, que su mal le viene de la esclavitud y de los negros: que ni esta institución abominable, ni esta raza infeliz se avienen con los adelantamientos de la cultura europea: que la tarea, el conato único, el propósito constante de todo cubano de corazón y de noble y santo patriotismo, lo debe cifrar en acabar con la trata primero, y luego en ir suprimiendo insensiblemente la esclavitud, sin sacudimientos ni violencias; y por último, en limpiar a Cuba de la raza africana. Esto es lo que dicta la razón, el interés bien entendido, la política, la religión y la filosofía, de consuno, al patriota cubano. Las vociferaciones contra España y los españoles, los deseos de venganza y de sangre contra éste o aquél tiranuelo

peninsular son miserias que mira con lástima el pensador positivo que se
ha acostumbrado a buscar en los efectos sus causas, y no se deja deslumbrar,
como el vulgo de los apasionados y de los fanáticos, por las alucinaciones
del interés del momento, ni por los arrebatos puramente patológicos de la
sangre. (1:230–31)

We argue that Cuba is not capable at present of launching into a revolution;
that peoples, like men, need to grow, strengthen, and educate themselves
before becoming free through violent means; that under despotism Cuba is
developing materially slowly; that the island is educating itself on the principles that rule human society in civilized nations through the example of
others and through its dealings with the outside world; that Cuba will understand, in the end, that its problems arise from slavery and blacks; that
neither this abominable institution nor this unhappy race are compatible
with the advances of European culture; that the task, the sole desire and
constant purpose, of every true Cuban of noble and saintly patriotism
should be to achieve the end of the slave trade first, and then to bring about
the gradual elimination of slavery, without upheavals or violence, and last,
to cleanse Cuba of the African race. This is what reason, self-interest, politics, religion, and philosophy dictate collectively to the Cuban patriot. The
loud complaints against Spain and Spaniards and the desires of revenge on
this or that peninsular colonial governor are petty thoughts that are regarded with disdain by the positivist philosopher who has trained himself
to find in the effects their causes and who does not allow himself to be
blinded—like the common fanatical and impassioned folk—by the halluci-
nations of the moment or of personal investment nor by the purely path-
ological attacks of passion.

This fragment from del Monte's *idearium* allows us to understand in
all its dimensions the desire for modernity that lies at the heart of his
antislavery enterprise. Del Monte is clearly not concerned with denounc-
ing the injustices produced and sustained by the slave system as such, just
as he is indifferent to—if not outright derisive of—displays of animosity
against Spanish authority. More important, though, the quotation evinces
the fact that for del Monte as well as for the other members of his generation, modernity was also a particular discursive posture and a method;
a procedure of inquiry that should be used to examine, in this case, the
question of slavery but that had universal applicability; a method that
founded its authority and legitimacy in the modernity of its analytical
procedures. The rigor and objectivity of the method removed the writer
from an excessive involvement with the subject under study, which explains del Monte's expressed impatience with arguments against slavery
or colonialism derived from outrage or passion. There are a number of

quotations from del Monte's *Escritos* that indicate his reliance on disciplines of knowledge to which he ascribes a modern value. At one point he refers to the "adelanto de las ciencias morales y políticas" [advances in the moral and political sciences] that in his view have discovered "las leyes eternas de la humana naturaleza" [the eternal laws of human nature]. Like his arguments against slavery, his arguments against colonialism are derived from his contempt for a political arrangement that the modern world had supposedly rendered obsolete. Scoffing at those who would argue for the continuation of Cuba's colonial condition, he avers: "Como si un pueblo civilizado, en fin pudiese ser propiedad, en el siglo XIX y entre naciones libres, de otro pueblo cualquiera."[10] [As if a civilized people could be owned, in the nineteenth century and among free countries, by any other nation whatsoever].

Exactly the same methodological assurance was at work in Saco's monumental and universal *Historia de la esclavitud*, which had as its ulterior goal the creation of a solid historical foundation that would then allow for the systematic study of slavery in the specific Cuban context. The recursive quality of the method can be seen in the flowering in Cuba of the genre of the *memorial* or *memoria*, which purported to be the result of a comprehensive gathering of evidence with respect to whatever subject the researcher decided to examine. By the beginning of the nineteenth century, the word *memoria* had lost its bureaucratic origins in the colonial period as official reports to the Crown or as forensic records of legal proceedings and was used interchangeably with the term *memorial* to denote an investigation whose methodology was the very source of its authority and justification. Indeed, the *Diccionario de Autoridades* of 1732 does not include an acceptation of the words *memorial* or *memoria* that can be related to the way in which either term will be employed toward the end of the eighteenth century by writers in both Spain and Spanish America. Hence, the use of both words is indicative of the modernity that their authors claimed for their analytical study of whatever phenomenon was chosen for examination. Saco's own *Memoria sobre la vagancia en Cuba* and the earlier *Memoria sobre caminos en la isla de Cuba* are excellent examples of this critical modality. The methodological procedure can also be gleaned from titles of other works by Saco, such as "Mi primera pregunta: ¿La abolición del comercio de esclavos africanos arruinará o atrasará la agricultura cubana?" and "Paralelo entre la isla de Cuba y algunas colonias inglesas"[11] ["My First Question: Will the Disappearance of the Slave Trade Bankrupt or Set Back Cuban Agriculture?" and "Parallelism between the Island of

Cuba and Some English Colonies"]. Earlier in the Cuban nineteenth century, the analytical model had also been invoked in Félix Varela's *Memoria sobre la esclavitud* and Francisco Arango y Parreño's several treatises on the condition of agriculture in the Caribbean island.[12] The investigative self-confidence manifested by all of these texts is anchored on the analytical procedures employed by them, which were themselves derived from the deep acquaintance their authors had with the modern disciplines of knowledge that were making their appearance in Europe between the last decades of the eighteenth century and the first half of the nineteenth. Hence, the genre of the *memorial* or *memoria* served as a mediating rhetorical vehicle for the adoption of "modern" instruments of analysis and methodological inquiry. The principal object of investigation for Cuban intellectuals of the times was, of course, the slave system and its extensive ramifications throughout contemporaneous Cuban society. The *memoria* was relied upon to provide an incontestable foundation for the rhetorical authority of its practitioners and to add legitimacy and force to their conclusions as they critically engaged the presence of slavery in their midst.

The epistemological and critical operation of the *memoria*, which yielded a causal explanatory chain, produced also the ideology of *blanqueamiento*, or progressive whitening of the black race, that was propounded by these same Cuban intellectuals. Just as the researcher's activity endeavored to reduce the object under study by forcing it to yield the secrets of its double causality, the repeated and chained seminal intervention of the white race would resolve the problem of the incorporation of blacks into a future Cuban nationality by diluting the race out of existence. A comment by Francisco Arango y Parreño is transparent in this regard:

> Quiero por lo menos, que por sabios artífices se trace el instante, el plan que se debe seguir para blanquear nuestros negros; o sea: para identificar en América a los descendientes de Africa con los descendientes de Europa. Quiero, al propio tiempo, que con prudencia se piense en destruir la esclavitud (para lo cual no hay poco hecho), se trate de lo que no se ha pensado, que es borrar su memoria. La naturaleza misma nos indica el más fácil y más seguro rumbo que hay que seguir en esto. Ella nos muestra que el color negro cede al blanco, y que desaparece si se repiten las mezclas de ambas razas; y entonces también observamos la inclinación decidida que los frutos de esas mezclas tienen a la gente blanca.[13]

I want to see at least the discussion by wise statesmen of the timing and the plan that must be followed to whiten our negroes; that is, to blend in

America the descendants of Africa with the descendants of Europe. I want, simultaneously, to start thinking prudently about the destruction of slavery (to which end much has been done already), to discuss something that has not been entertained, that is, the erasure of its memory. Nature itself points to the easiest and safest direction to follow on this matter. It shows that the color black yields to white, and that it disappears if the mixtures of the two races are repeated; and we should also point out the decided good disposition that the fruits of such mixtures have toward white people.

Hence, in *blanqueamiento* the researcher's goal of arriving at a causal explanatory paradigm of critical mastery became metamorphosed into a genealogical scheme of racial mastery that projected to the nation's future an equally reassuring outcome for the handling of its black quandary.

Nonetheless, the adoption of discursive modalities associated with modernity was an enterprise that was conflicted and fraught with hazards for Cuban intellectuals, as was also the case, I am proposing in this book, for their counterparts in the larger Spanish American continental milieu. In the Cuban antislavery discourse one finds as well the deployment of a rhetorical stratagem whose purpose is to buttress the text's authority by moving away from the presuppositions of its chosen discursive model. In the specific case of the antislavery discourse, this turning away from modernity, this surreptitious rejection of the modern, is—I will argue in the remainder of this chapter—the maneuver that produces the antislavery novel. Or, in other words, within antislavery writing, antislavery *literature* is that rhetorical displacement that represents that radical questioning of modernity's appropriateness for the examination of Spanish American circumstance. In the chasm that opens up between antislavery discourse and its literary offshoot one can identify the essential components of that problematics that in my view characterizes Spanish American discourse in general. As we saw earlier, in the works of del Monte, Saco, Arango, and other intellectuals of the period, slavery is regarded as an object of study that could be managed and reduced through the use of an analytical method derived from discursive models associated with modernity. But if, as Foucault has shown to us conclusively, modern knowledge is founded in a genealogical paradigm of interpretation, the antislavery novel will oppose to that conception of slavery an object that is refractory to that epistemological conceit.[14] The object I refer to is the portrait of slavery that arises from the works that compose the genre of Cuban antislavery literature.

I am not arguing for a moment that antislavery literature does not share and reflect the modernizing project that links its texts to the wider antislavery discourse. This dimension of it can be easily appreciated in many levels and qualities of these works: the long and frequent digressions that describe the slave trade, the plantation system, and its infernal machines; textual tangents that are always in danger of collapsing narrative continuity; the vehement proselytizing against the ills brought about by slavery; the editorializing that purports to envision a future configuration of Cuban nationality. They are all vivid reminders of the reformist enterprise to which these novels understood themselves to be contributing and which they have in common with other antislavery tracts. I am referring to the fact that, despite that common finality, the antislavery novel is engaged in the construction and circulation of a discourse on slavery that is founded on the categories of strangeness, perversion, and opaqueness.

I would like to think that this characterization will not be disputed by anyone who has even a passing acquaintance with these works. The Cuban antislavery novel presents us with a textual universe teeming with insinuations of the bizarre, of the dark, of the *uncanny*.[15] One could point out as examples a number of instances that traverse various levels of textual depth and significance. There is the fact that Cirilo Villaverde named the protagonist of his novel *Cecilia Valdés*—a female character for whom he feels an evident ambivalence—using his own initials. One could also mention the compounding of genotypical and phenotypical characteristics of all sorts that are invoked to construct the principal mulatto characters of these novels and that render them into teratological figures. Take, for instance the description of Sab in Gómez de Avellaneda's novel of the same name:

> Era el recién llegado un joven de alta estatura y regulares proporciones, pero de una fisonomía particular. No parecía un criollo blanco, tampoco era negro ni podía creérsele descendiente de los primeros habitadores de las Antillas. Su rostro presentaba un compuesto singular en que se descubría el cruzamiento de dos razas diversas, y en que se amalgamaban, por decirlo así, los rasgos de la casta africana con los de la europea, sin ser no obstante un mulato perfecto. Era su color de un blanco amarillento con cierto fondo oscuro; su ancha frente se veía medio cubierta con mechones desiguales de un pelo negro y lustroso como las alas del cuervo; su nariz era aguileña pero sus labios gruesos y amoratados denotaban su procedencia africana.[16]

The character that had just arrived was a young man of tall height and regular proportions but of a peculiar physiognomy. He did not look entirely like a white Creole; neither was he black, nor could he be thought to be a descendant of the first inhabitants of the Antilles. His face presented a peculiar composite in which one could discover the crossing of two different races, and which amalgamated to put it that way, the traits of the African race with the European one, without being nevertheless a perfect mulatto. His color was yellowish white with a certain dark background; his wide forehead was half covered by uneven locks of hair, black and shiny as a crow; his nose was aquiline, but his thick and purplish lips betrayed his African descendance.

One could also cite in this regard the by now obsessively inventoried peculiarities of Manzano's autobiographical narrative—its grammatical and syntactical dislocations, indeed, everything that has been corrected or erased from Manzano's text throughout the years—all that has been cast off or explained away so that the slave's work could speak with a voice consistent with itself.[17] Sylvia Molloy's essay on Manzano's work succinctly summarizes this aspect of his work. She concludes, "The *Autobiografía* as Manzano wrote it, with its run-on sentences, breathless paragraphs, dislocated syntax and idiosyncratic misspellings, vividly portrays that quandary—an anxiety of origins ever renewed, that provides the text with the stubborn, uncontrolled energy that is possibly its major achievement. The writing, *in itself*, is the best self-portrait we have of Manzano as well as his greatest contribution to literature; at the same time, it is what translators, editors and critics cannot tolerate."[18] There are also those passages that betray the disturbing feelings of affection that Manzano had for his sadistic mistress, the perversely (and uncannily) named Marquesa de Prado Ameno [Marchioness of the Pleasant Meadow].[19] But my intention here is to underscore the most salient instance of this syllogistic of the outrageous (to paraphrase Lezama) that is the Cuban antislavery novel: the constant and disquieting presence of sexuality and incest at the very core of this novelistic production, itself perhaps the most important element contributing to the unusual specificity of Cuban antislavery literary texts.

In her *Literatura y esclavitud en la novela cubana del siglo XIX*, Mercedes Rivas observes quite accurately,

"Las relaciones sexuales en la narrativa antiesclavista, desde *Petrona y Rosalía* hasta *Cecilia Valdés*, son el eje temático y estructural del relato. El planteamiento y desenlace de estas relaciones deciden el comienzo y el final de cada novela, y su desarrollo articula el núcleo de su trama. Gradualmente constituyen un paradigma que arranca en la simplicidad de *Petrona y Rosalía*, regulan *Sab, Francisco* y *El negro Francisco*, y se diversifica y completa en *Cecilia Valdés*."[20]

In antislavery narrative, sexual relations, from *Petrona y Rosalía* to *Cecilia Valdés*, are the thematic and structural axis of the story. The depiction and denouement of these relations decide the beginning and end of each novel, and their development articulates the nucleus of the plot. Gradually these relations configure a paradigm that begins with simplicity in *Petrona y Rosalía*, regulates *Sab, Francisco*, and *El negro Francisco*, and diversifies and completes itself in *Cecilia Valdés*.

What has not been sufficiently emphasized is that this emphasis on sexuality radically distinguishes the antislavery novel from the traditional romantic plot of ill-fated, impossible, or unconsummated love—even if there is by now a well-established critical habit of subsuming these novels under the romantic modality. In other words, the erotic/incestuous narrative mainspring of the antislavery novel has very little in common with the one that generates, for instance, novels such as *Amalia* or *María*, true exemplars of the genre. One might also add that this quality also sharply distinguishes the Cuban antislavery novel from its American counterpart. Carolyn L. Karcher has summarized the sociological factors that in her view determined the specific configuration of the North American antislavery novel. The characteristics of the novelistic texts that they produced allow us to see starkly the differences between them and the Cuban antislavery works:

> As a genre largely shaped by middle-class white women, it reflects the complex relationship between the patriarchal system that victimized women and the racial slave system that victimized blacks. At the same time, the conventions of antislavery fiction delimit the parameters within which women had to confine their exploration of slavery and their attempts to imagine alternative social orders. By dictating a romance plot involving refined heroines, by proscribing frank treatment of sexuality and violence, and by imposing a white middle-class code of values as the ideal toward which all were to aspire, anti-slavery fiction reproduces and may well have reinforced the ideological assumptions that marginalized the masses of American blacks and circumscribed the freedom of white women.[21]

Furthermore, it is the presence of sexuality as a central element in Cuban antislavery works that creates the possibility for their exploration of the sadistic, the sensual, and the perverse.

This dimension of the novels reaches its most distilled expression in the theme of incest that is such an integral part of the genre. I refer to the fact that in general the plot of most of these works revolves, indirectly or explicitly, around the possibility of an incestuous relationship, a potentiality that exists because the protagonists are not aware of the blood ties that connect them. Again one can see clearly a point of divergence with the parallel literary production in the United States. The first recorded American antislavery novel, William Hill Brown's *The Power of Sympathy* (1789), mobilized the topic of incest in the figure of two lovers who are not aware of the fact that they are half-siblings;[22] but given that the subject is hardly present in antebellum literary texts against slavery after this liminal instance, one must conclude that the theme was not regarded as particularly productive from a discursive point of view in the American context. By contrast, the possibility of incest is the principal narrative element on Félix Tanco Bosmeniel's *Petrona y Rosalía* and Villaverde's *Cecilia Valdés*. In Villaverde's novel there are also clear allusions to the incestuous attraction between Leonardo and his legitimate sister Adela. In Avellaneda's *Sab*, Sab and Carlota have been raised together, and they are referred to as being linked by filial love. In *Cecilia Valdés*, *Francisco*, and *El negro Francisco* there are also intimations about the excessive attraction felt by the mothers for their sexually promiscuous yet weak sons. In the preface to his parodic rewriting of *Cecilia Valdés*, Reinaldo Arenas argues that the original text of Villaverde is the accumulation of "una suerte de incestos sucesivos. . . . Porque la trama de *Cecilia Valdés* no se limita a las relaciones amorosas entre los medio hermanos Cecilia y Leonardo, sino que toda la novela está permeada por incesantes ramificaciones incestuosas hábilmente insinuadas"[23] [a series of successive incests. . . . Because the plot of *Cecilia Valdés* does not limit itself to the depiction of the love relations between the half-siblings Cecilia and Leonardo; rather, the entire novel is permeated by incessant incestuous ramifications cannily insinuated throughout]. This genealogical disorder and confusion is the figure that paradoxically generates the textual order of the antislavery novel.

In its literary rendition, then, slavery is depicted as a system capable of fusing and therefore confusing the genealogical and phenotypic taxonomies that provided the foundation for the Cuban nineteenth-century social order. If a number of these works depict the lives of at least two generations of a family, it is precisely in order to show how genealogy is thwarted by the intrusion of endogamy in what should be an exogamous arrangement. That is to say, this plot characteristic exists to expose the existence of repetition in a sequence that should be ruled by linearity and difference. In *Petrona y Rosalía* and *Cecilia Valdés*, for instance, the incestuous son is depicted as repeating structurally a triangular relationship earlier entertained by his father with a black mistress, which underscores the fact that regardless of the linear descent from father to son, repetition has managed to bring the genealogical order to a halt. It is not surprising, then, that the antislavery novel would also end up undermining the ideology of *blanqueamiento* that, as we saw, was an ethnic project founded on the same epistemological assurance that undergirded the analytical formula of the *memoria*. For even if it did not address the issue directly, *blanqueamiento* was obviously predicated on the orderly succession of sexual unions between white men and progressively whiter black women in order to achieve its ultimate goal. But these novels reveal the nightmare that unrestricted availability of such women to white men could become by underscoring the incommensurability of desire and social institutions. For what they show time and again is not simply that such an arrangement could probabilistically lead to an endogamous pairing, but that men would in fact be propelled by the unappealable laws of desire to seek women with whom they shared consanguinity.

From the perspective of my larger argument, the literary characterization of slavery is problematic in turn because it also places in check the legitimacy of the critical knowledge that founded the epistemological authority of the antislavery discourse. As portrayed by the literary text, slavery resided in a space of genealogical confusion and stagnation that was inaccesible to that knowledge, since the latter presupposed an object of study transparently linked in a genealogical fashion both to its causes and to its ramifications, and all of them configuring a chain that the researcher could traverse in both directions at will in order to arrive at a final understanding of the subject under scrutiny. The novels about slavery refract instead an object that by its very nature is located outside the margins of the antislavery discourse itself and, by extension, outside the pale of the discourse of modernity that the latter purported to appropriate. The genealogical upheaval and confusion that characterizes the antislavery novel—founded as it is on the imminence and inevitability of incest—is indicative of a desire to keep modernity at bay by configuring a textual space that represents the limits of modernity's knowledge. One could even argue that slavery may have become an obsessive theme in Cuban cultural production precisely on account of its irrepressible anachronistic and retrograde nature, a quality that nevertheless guaranteed its irreducibility to modern categories of knowledge and understanding.

This interpretation of antislavery literature may help us understand the persistent longevity of a black thematics in the history of Cuban literature. For it must be stressed that the literary representation of slavery outlasted by many years the disappearance of the institution whose execration was supposed to justify the existence and social pertinence of those texts that engaged in it.[24] One could say about the discursive machine that produced the writing of antislavery novels what Antonio Benítez Rojo has said about the economic system of the Plantation against which they inveighed: "The machinery of the sugar mill, once installed and set in motion, soon becomes almost indestructible since, even after it is partially dismantled, its transformative impact will survive it for many years and its mark will be inscribed within nature itself, in the climate and the demographic, political, social, economic, and cultural structures of the society to which it was once joined."[25] Indeed, works that have slaves or slavery as a theme configure a chain that extends from the beginnings of an avowedly Cuban literature almost to the present. The novels that were coeval with the slave system were succeeded by others of a naturalist slant that revisited the topic, then by historical novels that attempted to resurrect the slavery period, later by the various manifestations of the Afro-Cuban movement (among which one would have to include Carpentier's *realismo maravilloso* and the anthropological studies of Fernando Ortiz and Lydia Cabrera) and, finally, contemporary works that have attempted to reconstruct the historical presence of the black from within the testimonial or recuperative framework provided by the Cuban Revolution (Miguel Barnet and César Leante are exemplary in this respect). In my view, all the works that constitute this very long list can be subsumed under the rhetorical maneuver that was instituted by the antislavery novel and that each of them recapitulates in its own peculiar way: to turn the black into a site of resistance to modernity that signals the impossibility of submitting Cuban reality to the coordinates of the modern. But that strategy also provided a foundation for the rhetorical authority of Cuban intellectuals and writers, who turned their discourse into a surreptitious and persistent claim of radical difference vis-à-vis modernity. This realization may yet prove to be the most conclusive confirmation of the central role played by blacks in a comprehensive history of Cuban cultural production.

Our next chapter addresses Lucio V. Mansilla's remarkable text *Una excursión a los indios Ranqueles*. We will see how in Mansilla's writings the appeal to modernity is confounded through the projection onto Argentine history of a tropological figure founded on the family romance. The discussion will also allow us to revisit Sarmiento, the subject of our first chapter, from Mansilla's contemporaneous perspective.

CHAPTER FOUR

Oedipus in the Pampas

Lucio Mansilla's *Una excursión a los indios Ranqueles*

> *Death of the Father would deprive literature of many of its pleasures. If there is no longer a Father, why tell stories? Doesn't every narrative lead back to Oedipus? Isn't storytelling always a way of searching for one's origin, speaking one's conflict with the Law, entering into the dialectic of tenderness and hatred. . . . As fiction, Oedipus was at least good for something: to make good novels, to tell good stories.*
>
> —Roland Barthes, *The Pleasure of the Text*

> *¿Y quien es ese general Mansilla? le preguntaba yo. Un pituco del siglo XIX que tenía mucha facilidad de palabra, me contestaba el Profesor. Un dandy de quien puede decirse que hizo, de su vida toda, una sola y gran digresión.*
>
> And who was that General Mansilla? I asked him. A well-spoken nineteenth-century fop, the Professor answered. A dandy who made of his life, one could say, a single and long digression.
>
> —Ricardo Piglia, *Respiración artificial*

As a CULTURAL MOVEMENT, romanticism manifested itself in Spanish America primarily as a multifaceted enterprise to express a nature that was understood to be in need of articulation, a nature that was alternately and variously conceived in linguistic, geographic, historical, or literary terms. But this need did not arise from the perception that this was a suppressed essence with roots in a remote past—as was the case in European romanticism—but rather from the understanding (and the conceit) that this essence was thoroughly new and distinct. Spanish American intellectuals and writers of the nineteenth century embraced romanticism because they (mis)interpreted it as constituting a quintessentially modern phenomenon, and not especially or necessarily on account of the specific programs or ideological constructs advanced by that movement. The construal of romanticism as a European novelty, its selective involvement in the unmediated present of political action, and its break with traditional literary rhetoric convinced them that romanticism was the perfect vehicle for the expression of that modernity that they judged to be consubstantial with Spanish America. In other words, the *newness* of romanticism as a cultural and literary phenomenon was mistakenly taken as an incontrovertible sign of its *modernity*, thereby becoming for a larger part of the Spanish American nineteenth century the privileged formula for the expression of that thoroughly modern essence. This explains why the heated and protracted polemics surrounding romanticism in the first half of the nineteenth century throughout the Spanish American continent exhibit what can only be regarded as a facile awareness of the essential characteristics of the movement; it also accounts for why, regardless of this superficiality of understanding, romanticism soundly and almost invariably carried the day, and why until recently there has existed the commonplace critical notion that Spanish American literature has a determinedly romantic character.[1]

The adoption of romanticism in Spanish America from within this cultural paradigm of essential identification with modernity managed to obscure the fundamentally antimodern, backward-looking dimension of romanticism—the fact, for instance, that if European romantics spoke and fought for nationalistic crusades, it was because these movements longed to actualize primeval essences and forms, constitutive of the "nation" or "race" in question, that had either been suppressed by a foreign oppressor (person or country) or had otherwise not been allowed to manifest themselves. That such a conservative ideology should have paradoxically become virtually undistinguishable from political liberalism in nineteenth-century Spanish America attests to the overriding fascination with modernity that has been the persistent hallmark of the continent's cultural production. In an important recent book, Derek Flitter has studied the introduction of romantic ideas in Spain and shown how in that very different context romanticism was consistently understood and appreciated—from Böhl de Faber to Fernán Caballero—for its *conservative* implications instead.[2] With customary insight, Claudio Véliz in turn has referred to the Spanish American rendition of romanticism as a

> truncated, incomplete romanticism, usually found in the company of much rebellious fury, excessive ardor, and even more self-indulgence, but none of the pensive, somber moods, the brooding, nostalgic evocation of ancient roots, the intense sense of the past, and the feeling for the sublime in nature that are definitive characteristics of the romantic moment. These absences

were particularly important during the formative decades of the republics spawned in the distant Indies by the Napoleonic onslaught. The newly constituted entities were unlikely to find inspiration or solace in a past dominated by the hated Spanish oppressor but even less inclined to bring about a profound cultural transformation of society that would result in entirely different patterns of behavior.[3]

Hence, the cultural foundation of the new republics was based on a double act of willful suppression and forgetfulness of the past, a repressive operation demanded by the enthrallment with the modern that characterizes their founding moment: first, a rejection of the autochthonous Indian presence that predated the Spanish conquest of the Americas; and second, a forsaking of the Spanish colonial past that preceded the advent of the "new" continent. But as I have argued earlier, given the material social and economic conditions of Spanish America, the adoption of the discourse of modernity could only result in a most profound rhetorical crisis, since the authority of the Spanish American writing subjects was effectively challenged and undermined by the very discourse they endeavored to wield. In order to stave off this possibility of rhetorical disenfranchisement, one can identify in the more significant texts of this tradition a moment when a claim to exception is made for Spanish America vis-à-vis the modern—a moment when Spanish America is proposed to be incommensurable with modernity, even if the work explicitly and simultaneously advances programs and formulas meant to hasten the continent's participation in the modern. In the larger context already described, this surreptitious turning away from modernity can be identified in a turn, a troping toward that which had been suppressed on account of its presumed incompatibility with the modern. Hence, during the remainder of the nineteenth century and beyond, Spanish American writers will engage in various attempts to recuperate two of the most significant elements that had been forsworn in the rush to embrace the modern: the indigenous past and the Spanish legacy. The recovery of the autochthonous element will become the driving force behind the advent of *indigenista* literature: works such as Clorinda Matto de Turner's *Aves sin nido* and Juan Zorrilla de San Martín's *Tabaré*; the rehabilitation of the Spanish past explains the sporadic attempts to reaffirm the links with a larger Hispanic tradition that Hostos's *La peregrinación de Bayoán* exemplifies most saliently.[4] Lucio Mansilla's *Una excursión a los indios Ranqueles* is unquestionably among the most important and enduring instances of the first of these two enterprises.

Still, for a long time the book did not receive any rigorous critical attention, so until quite recently it remained largely neglected, substantiating Martínez Estrada's claim that *Una excursión a los indios Ranqueles* is one of the most badly read works of the Spanish American nineteenth century.[5] The principal reason for this neglect is, I would venture, the text's generic indeterminacy and intractability, a trait that it shares with many other works of the period in Spanish America, but most notably with Sarmiento's *Facundo*. As is the case with its more famous predecessor, *Una excursión a los indios Ranqueles* evinces a protean nature, the result of the seemingly indiscriminate collapsing together of several genres and discursive modes: autobiography, travelogue, adventure novel, sociological treatise, geographical survey, and ethnographic document. This quality placed Mansilla's work from the outset in a discursive no-man's-land, where no one discipline could convincingly and exclusively lay claim to it. One suspects that if *Facundo* has not suffered a similar fate, it is because its multifarious nature proved reducible to the powerful dialectical scheme of civilization versus barbarism—a formula that henceforth acquired a life of its own within Spanish American intellectual circles, and turned Sarmiento's work into an unavoidable cultural icon. Nonetheless, the blurring of the boundaries between the disciplines that has obtained in the last decades has made us more comfortable with works such as *Una excursión a los indios Ranqueles* that occupy an interstitial space between the genres and discourses sanctioned by those various disciplines, when not questioning them outright. It is in that fashion that we have come to understand the possibility of rhetorically analyzing works that claimed to derive their authority from their inscription within the disciplinary confines of the emerging natural or social sciences, as well as the possibility of contemplating, conversely, the ways in which more "traditional" literary texts availed themselves of the discursive possibilities inaugurated by those very disciplines.

But there is perhaps a more telling explanation for the abandonment suffered by Mansilla's text, for the easy disdain that *Una excursión a los indios Ranqueles*—and, indeed, everything else he penned—seems to have evoked from the moment it appeared. It has to do with the public persona that Mansilla carefully constructed for himself as a dandy, as a flâneur who ambulated through the boulevards of a fin-de-siècle Buenos Aires that was very conscious of being the most modern city in Spanish America.[6] Mansilla's insertion in the modern took the shape of the adoption of the identity of the cosmopolitan flâneur, a deracinated and decontextualized inhabitant of the modern city who could feel equally at home in whichever urban landscape he happened to stroll by, whether in Europe or in the Southern Cone. His image as consummate clubman and dandy determined to a large extent not just the redaction but also the reception of his works as *pièces d'occasion*, as superficial compositions that were irremediably contaminated by their author's effeteness and ultimate lack of seriousness. Mansilla's desire to participate in the modern by donning the mask of the flâneur seems to have generated that negative interpretive reception; but it also created the persona that according to most critics has come to exemplify most saliently Argentina's so-called "generación del '80," paradoxically endowing him in that fashion with the weight of being an archetypal figure for fleetingness and superficiality. Mansilla's insouciant works and raffiné personal style represent nonetheless a deliberate pose, a remarkably consistent personal project to inscribe the self in the ever changing landscape of urban life and to derive its identity—or, more precisely, its anonymity and therefore its insubstantiality—from that association. As such, his persona constitutes yet another version of the commitment to modernity that is the founding conceit for Spanish American culture.

Yet I will argue that if Mansilla's self-fashioning as a flâneur bespeaks his identification with the modern, one can also trace in some of his works the existence of another plot—another stage, as Freud would have it—one in which self-constitution is founded not on the nonidentity conferred by the modern city to the dandy but, quite the opposite, on the singularity and irrevocableness of family relations, and their projection in Mansilla's writing to a personal past perceived as a premodern, banished time. We shall see how this dimension of Mansilla's works will almost seem to thematize the ahistoricity of the unconscious, thereby posing an unresolvable challenge to his carefully constructed self-inscription into the maelstrom of modernity. Our itinerary begins with Mansilla's *Una excursión a los indios Ranqueles*, a work whose examination will allow us to begin to tease out the essential elements of this alternate plot.

Although the details surrounding the subject and the composition of *Una excursión a los indios Ranqueles* are well-known, I will recapitulate them briefly here. In 1870, from March 30 to April 17, Colonel Lucio Mansilla undertook an expedition from the outermost fort in the frontier to the encampment of the Ranqueles Indians, deep in what was then called Tierra Adentro or, in its more general contemporaneous appellation, "el desierto.''[7] Accompanied by only ten men and two priests, he traveled through largely unexplored territory in order to meet with the chieftain of the Ranqueles, a cunning and feared man. The principal objective of the journey was not to sign a peace treaty with the Indians, as is widely recounted in the critical literature, since the terms of the treaty had been agreed upon by both parties in an earlier meeting when the leader of the Ranqueles had sent an embassy to the fort where Mansilla was stationed.[8] The need for his expedition arose, as Mansilla explains in his work, from the fact that the treaty would not be legally binding until the Argentine National Congress had discussed and ratified it. Mansilla's task, he argues, was to explain this parliamentary technicality to the Ranqueles in such a way as to not jeopardize their original favorable disposition toward the pact. The necessity of conveying to the Indians the legalities involved in the ratification of the treaty in terms that would be culturally meaningful and understandable to them continually forces Mansilla into a position of cultural relativism and eccentricity from his own culture. This allows him, in turn, to discern the continuities between his world and that of the Ranqueles, a circumstance that produces at times some of the most sympathetic and demystified consideration of the Indian to be found in any text of the Spanish American nineteenth century and beyond. After spending two weeks with the Ranqueles, Mansilla returned to his frontier outpost, only to find that in his absence he had been relieved of his military post and its attendant prerogatives pending the result of an earlier preliminary investigation surrounding the execution of a soldier under his command. Thus separated from his duties, Mansilla returned to Buenos Aires, where in the newspaper *La Tribuna* he published, from May 20 through September 7 of the same year, a serial account of his recently completed journey. Later that year, as was customary at the time, the first edition of *Una excursión a los indios Ranqueles* appeared in book form, the first of a large number of subsequent printings.

Puzzlingly enough, however, the historical record shows that the reasons Mansilla gave for having undertaken his expedition were not accurate in any degree. Although it is indeed true that Congress had seen fit to renegotiate some of the terms of the treaty with the Ranqueles, the latter had accepted the emendations and the pact had been ratified by the Argentine Congress in February of the same year Mansilla set out toward the Indian encampment—that is, a full month and a half before his voyage. Hence, Mansilla's sally into the pampas could not have had as its object the explanation of statutory technicalities associated with the approval of a treaty that was already ratified, contrary to what he claims in the following passage:

> Expliqué lo que antes le había explicado . . . , lo que es el Presidente de la República, el Congreso y el Presupuesto de la Nación. Les dije que el Gobierno no podía entregar inmediatamente lo convenido, porque necesitaba que el Congreso le diera la plata para comprarlo, y que éste antes de darle la plata, tenía que ver si el tratado convenía o no. Eso era lo que en cumplimiento de órdenes recibidas debía yo explicar, como si fuera tan fácil hacerles entender a bárbaros lo que es nuestra complicada máquina constitucional.[9]

> I explained to him what I had explained previously: what is a president of the republic, a legislature, and the nation's budget. I told them that the government could not hand out immediately what had been agreed upon because it needed funds from the Legislature to purchase it, and that before disbursing any money the latter had to first determine the treaty's worthiness. That is what I had been instructed to explain, as if it were so easy to make savages understand our complex constitutional apparatus.

Given what we can ascertain from historical sources, witnesses, and contemporaneous official documents, the explanation advanced by Mansilla for his excursion has to be regarded as a spurious justification.[10] I would like to propose that we may perhaps glean from the difficult personal circumstances surrounding Mansilla at the time of his voyage some insight into a more plausible or at least more interesting motivation for his expedition.

As I stated earlier, when Mansilla returned to the garrison from his journey he found that he had been severed from his command and duties. This disciplinary action stemmed from the investigation of a charge that had been levied against him, whereby he was accused of ordering the execution of a deserter without due process. An anonymous accusatory notice that denounced the arbitrariness of Mansilla's action had been published in the Buenos Aires newspaper *La Nación* on January 15, 1870.[11] The anonymous note identified the victim's name and the event's date erroneously, but the essential charge was correct: the soldier, a man by the name of Avelino Acosta, had been summarily executed on May 30, 1869, following Mansilla's orders. As a result of a general offensive, the army had successfully advanced the frontier to the Río Quinto, whereupon there was a sudden rash of desertions, probably owing to opportunity and the increased vulnerability of the advancing forces. In his defense, Mansilla claimed that he had chosen Acosta, a repeat offender, in order to set an example for the rest of the troop.

Feeling compelled to act after the accusation was so publicly made, the president of the Argentine Republic had ordered a preliminary inquest on the matter in February 1870, scarcely a month before Mansilla embarked on his journey. Hence, it was while this official investigation was taking place that Mansilla decided to set forth on his expedition to the domains of the Ranqueles. While in the pampas, Mansilla was removed from his command pending the result of the formal trial that was recommended by the preliminary inquest. Eight days after returning to Buenos Aires, the first installment of *Una excursión a los indios ranqueles* was published. On June 3, the day the ninth chapter of Mansilla's serial appeared, the president found Mansilla guilty of the crime for which he was tried and sentenced him to a dishonorable discharge from the army. The president of the Republic, the man who had ordered the investigation that would cast such a pall over Mansilla's future, was Domingo Faustino Sarmiento.

Una excursión a los indios Ranqueles is clearly modeled on the scientific travelogues that were so commonplace during the nineteenth century in Latin America. Indeed, in 1875, five years after its initial serial publication, Mansilla's work received a prize from the Congrès Géographique International de Paris. The wealth of topographical and ethnographic details in the book is indeed impressive, and Mansilla manages to convey these details in a narrative that is as engaging and full of wonder as those produced by other European travelers of the last century in Latin America. Yet it also seems readily evident that in the specific Argentine context in which it circulated originally, a text lurks in the background of Mansilla's work without detracting for that reason from its uniqueness and originality: Sarmiento's very own *Facundo, o civilización y barbarie*. The existence of manifestly pointed passages such as the following leave little room for doubt:

El aire libre, el ejercicio varonil del caballo, los campos abiertos como el mar, las montañas empinadas hasta las nubes, la lucha, el combate diario, la ignorancia, la pobreza, la privación de la dulce libertad, el respeto por la fuerza; la aspiración inconsciente de una suerte mejor—la contemplación del panorama físico y social de esta patria—, produce un tipo generoso [el gaucho], que nuestros políticos han perseguido y estigmatizado, que nuestros bardos no han tenido el valor de cantar, sino para hacer su caricatura. (156)

The open air, the manly handling of horses, the fields as wide as the sea, the mountains that rise to the clouds, fighting, the daily struggle, ignorance, poverty, the curtailment of sweet freedom, the respect for strength, the unconscious desire for a better lot, the contemplation of the physical and

social panorama of this country; all of these factors have produced a generous individual (the gaucho) that our politicians have persecuted and stig-
matized, and our poets have not had the courage to take up except to create
its caricature.

Any reader of Sarmiento's *Facundo* will recognize in this assertion an unmistakable polemicizing with its author. In it, Mansilla reproduces Sarmiento's essential argument regarding the determination of the gaucho's
moral and social constitution by the geographic milieu, but Mansilla finds
the final product to be undeserving of the opprobrium with which Sarmiento had judged him. Furthermore, there are at least twelve instances
throughout *Una excursión a los indios Ranqueles* where Sarmiento's formula
of "civilización y barbarie" is explicitly invoked by Mansilla—for example:
"Es indudable que la civilización tiene sus ventajas sobre la barbarie; pero
no tantas como aseguran los que se dicen civilizados" (49); or "La civilización y la barbarie se dan la mano; la humanidad se salvará porque los
extremos se tocan" (115); or "Alguien ha dicho que nuestra pretendida
civilización no es muchas veces más que un estado de barbarie refinada"
(180). [It is a fact that civilization has a number of advantages over barbarism; but not as many as it is thought by those who consider themselves
civilized. . . . Civilization and barbarism shake hands; humanity will be
saved because opposites finally come together. . . . Someone said that our
so-called civilization is nothing more that a state of refined barbarism.]
Many more similar instances could be easily produced.[12] There is, in fact,
very little reason to doubt Emilio Carilla's assertion that "*Una excursión*
es—como muchos contemporáneos vieron al aparecer los volúmenes de
la obra—un alegato velado contra 'la civilización', encarnada en ciertos
hombres (sobre todo Sarmiento). Lo que ocurre es que su prédica aparece
hoy oculta o desvanecida frente a otros aspectos de la obra" (41). [*Una
excursión* is—and this was readily seen by many of its readers—a veiled
indictment of "civilization" as represented by some men (above all Sarmiento). The difficulty lies in that its argument seems nowadays hidden
or diffused by other aspects of the work.] The presence of Sarmiento's
reductive shibboleth for Argentine reality in Mansilla's text is, nonetheless, only a surface manifestation of a more concealed and therefore more
significant inscription of Sarmiento in *Una excursión a los indios Ranqueles*.
The clues to this subtext will begin to emerge from a reading of Mansilla's
unfinished autobiography, a volume entitled *Mis memorias*, published in
1904. I would like to propose that an examination of *Mis memorias* will
allow us to perceive that in *Una excursión a los indios Ranqueles* Mansilla

used Sarmiento's formulation of a presumed conflict between civilization and barbarism as a vehicle to give expression to what could be construed as an extended family romance, as a narrative where a cultural and historical conflict that supposedly summarized nineteenth-century Argentina acquires all the trappings of an Oedipal mise-en-scène.[13]

The first of these textual instances refers to the dictator Juan Manuel de Rosas, Mansilla's uncle on his mother's side, and the ruler whose regime Sarmiento vehemently attacked in his *Facundo* from his exile in Santiago de Chile. In it, Mansilla recollects a season spent as a child in Rosas's country retreat in the outskirts of Buenos Aires with his aunt and uncle. But what is remarkable about the fragment is that it occurs at the precise moment in which Mansilla announces his intention to offer the reader of his autobiography a portrait not of his famous aunt and uncle but of his own parents:

> Mejor será que primero me detenga un momento a esbozar cómo eran física y moralmente mis padres, que veo fotografiados al través de tres momentos de mi vida distintos y distantes; la edad madura, la adolescencia, la infancia.
>
> Mi memoria es feliz, muy feliz, particularmente en lo que a la primera edad se refiere, tan feliz que recuerdo, ahora, en este mismísimo instante ni más ni menos que si de algo de ayer se tratara, que cuando tenía apenas cuatro años mi tía Encarnación Ezcurra de Rozas me llevó a la estancia del Pino.
>
> En una cama muy ancha, entre ella y mi tío Juan Manuel dormía yo el sueño de la inocencia. (¡que no dure más!).
>
> Una noche sentí que me sacaban del medio.... (117–18)

> I should first offer a physical and moral description of my parents, whom I see pictured in my mind on three distinct periods of my life: adulthood, adolescence, and childhood. My recollections are happy, very happy, especially about my early childhood; so happy that I can still remember now as if it happened just yesterday that when I was not yet four my aunt Encarnación Ezcurra de Rozas took me to her house in El Pino. In a very ample bed, between her and my uncle Juan Manuel, I slept with a child's innocence. (May it not last!) One night, I felt that they were moving me from between them....

I do not think it would be audacious to suggest that this episode can be interpreted as a displaced primal scene, one where Mansilla's powerful and authoritarian uncle has usurped the place of his biological father and where the awareness of sexual relations between the parents is clearly intimated. The displacement of his parents from the position they should have occupied in the narration, and their substitution by his masterly uncle and aunt, are simply a textual rendition of the substitution effected by the *content* of the recollection when considered as the child's primal scene: the parents are replaced in the plot of Mansilla's autobiographical account in much the same way they are supplanted in the Oedipal scenario by the aunt/uncle pair. Indeed, there are a number of passages in Mansilla's writings that attest to the patriarchal authority that his uncle had in the affairs of his extended family: moments in which Rosas's figure appear as a deus ex machina in order to settle definitely even seemingly inconsequential family affairs.[14] By the same token, on at least two occasions Mansilla informs us that his own mother used to call her brother Juan Manuel "Tatita," an affectionate appellation commonly used invariably to address a father, a practice that further underscores the ambiguity of his parents' status vis-à-vis the powerful uncle.[15] The importance and centrality of the experience related by Mansilla in this fragment is signaled by the fact that it is immediately followed by a meditation in which the author comments on the indelible trace left by it in his memory:

> La facultad biológica de la retroactividad mnemónica, o sea el fenómeno de una imagen más neta de lo que pasó hace muchos años—visión casi luminosa—, comparada con el recuerdo vago y confuso de escenas posteriores . . . debe provenir de que, en la primera edad, las impresiones se localizan dentro de un radio limitado, siendo reducidas en número y el cerebro más apto para estamparlas en sus celdas misteriosas a la manera de signos eléctricos en la cinta Morse o en un disco fonético. (118)

> The biological faculty of mnemonic recollection, that is, the possession of a most clear image of something that occurred many years ago—an almost luminous vision of that event—as compared with the vague and confused remembrance of later scenes, must arise from the fact that in early childhood impressions arise within a limited context, and therefore are fewer and more apt to be stored by the brain in its mysterious cells not unlike electrical signals in a Morse strip or in a phonetic disk.

The conjunction of the displaced primal scene and the discussion that immediately follows it, with its metaphors of engraving and codifying, constitute an uncannily condensed formulation of that instance that Lacan has identified as instituting the Law of the Father—the psychic imprinting that marks the passage from the Imaginary to the symbolic realm of language through the structuring and fixating presence of paternal authority. Nevertheless, one could say that the Lacanian scenario in this instance represents a moment of accession to the order of history rather than merely to the symbolic order of the social. For in Mansilla's narrative the substituted paternal figure of the powerful uncle provides access not only to experiencing Argentine history as a familial (and therefore familiar) narrative but also to the possibility of inscribing Mansilla's own writing performance within it. Mansilla may have complained on a number of occasions about the difficulties undergone by him and his family on account of his genealogical ties to Rosas after the dictator's defeat in Caseros and his subsequent flight to England (1852). But conversely, most of his works will derive their subject matter, their interest, and finally their authority from the privileged perspective afforded him by this very closeness—because of closeness of kin—to the deposed ruler and his world. Sylvia Molloy has already noted the refraction of Mansilla's remembrances in *Mis memorias* through the prism of Argentine history: "La mayoría de los recuerdos del Mansilla niño . . . surgen ligados al acontecer histórico, imbricados en él" (1980: 750). [Most of Mansilla's recollections as a child . . . are linked and embedded in the flow of history.] My argument in the remainder of this chapter will be that in Mansilla's rendition of the rhetorical *clinamen* whose presence in Spanish American discourse I trace in this book, history is projected in Mansilla's texts as a family affair, as reducible and reduced to the emotional coordinates of the familial. Mansilla's purposeless sally into the pampas will be seen to provide a figural anticipation of the aimless walking through the urban landscape of the flâneur he would become. On the other hand, his ordering of the uncharted geographic expanse of the desert through the imposition of an oedipal itinerary onto it will serve also proleptic notice of the historical/familial counternarrative that he will articulate in order to contest the deracinating implications of modernity.

Mansilla does devote eventually some attention to a characterization of his mother and father, a description that is cut short when Mansilla makes a descriptive verbal parcours of the house where he spent his childhood. The verbal wandering throughout the house takes him to his parents' bedroom, at which point Mansilla jumps chronologically and narratively into a long excursus regarding the adjacent room, his mother's "famous" sewing parlor.[16] Surprisingly enough, this passage consists wholly of an incident involving Sarmiento and a flag that Mansilla's mother had reluctantly hung from that particular room after Rosas's fall:

Al decir famoso no pondero. En él estaba la bandera que, por decreto del entusiasmo libertador, se había ordenado a todo el mundo enarbolar, le gustara o no la caída del tirano. . . .

El júbilo ostensible de los vencidos debía durar tres días. Mi madre no tenía más banderas que las patrias federales, es decir, las que habían reemplazado el celeste por el rojo. Esas puso, y las menos candilejas y fanales posibles.

   Sarmiento . . . acertó a pasar por allí. Una de las banderas tenía un agujero en el sitio mismo donde en la verdadera bandera nacional debe estar el sol. El agujero aquel, y sin que en ello se mezclara para nada el sentimiento patriótico, ni el que la casa fuera la de la hermana de Rozas, circunstancia que el viandante ignoraba, ejerció en su retina una impresión magnética y mecánicamente metió en el círculo, destrozando el trapo, la espada envainada que, por comodidad, no llevaba al cinto. (128–29)

When I say famous I do not exaggerate. From it hung the flag that the decree of liberation had ordered everyone to fly, whether they took pleasure in the tyrant's fall or not. . . . The enforced glee of the losers was meant to last three days. My mother had no other flags than the Federalist ones, the ones that had replaced blue with red. She hung those, as well as the least number of gas lamps and candles possible. Sarmiento . . . happened to stroll by. One of the flags had a hole in the very place in which the true national flag would have its sun. That hole—and not on account of patriotic feelings, and unrelated to the fact that the house was that of Rozas's sister since the stroller was unaware of that fact—exerted in his retina a magnetic impression, and he unthinkingly penetrated the hole and ripped the flag with his sword, which he was not wearing on his belt out of comfort.

Mansilla goes on to narrate how some months later, while they were fellow travelers on a ship, Mansilla confronted Sarmiento, accused him of having besmirched his mother's honor through this act, and demanded an apology:

Apreté el paso, a poco andar lo divisé a Sarmiento. En un abrir y cerrar de ojos estaba a su lado. . . .
—¡Caballero!
—¿Qué hay?
—Usted me debe una satisfacción por haberle faltado el respeto a mi madre.
—¿Yo?
—Sí (y nervioso y brevemente referí el caso). (130–31)[17]

I hurried my step until I saw Sarmiento. In an instant I was next to him. . . .
—Sir!
—Yes?
—You owe me an apology for besmirching my mother's honor.
—I?
—Yes! (and nervously I recounted quickly the event)

Mansilla's interpretation of Sarmiento's defilement of the flag as an affront to his mother only serves to vouch for the evidently sexual connotation of the latter's act in Mansilla's unconscious understanding of it. Through an erotic association in which Sarmiento is construed as exerting phallic violence over his mother when he penetrates the flag with his sword, Mansilla places Sarmiento in an oedipal triangle where the latter occupies, structurally at least, the place of the paternal figure. This scene serves as counterpart to the earlier one in which his parents had been swiftly substituted by his aunt and uncle, inasmuch as—regardless of the violence of the last scene—they are both figurations of a family romance: as Freud defined the term, the expression of a desire to be the child of a different set of parents than one's own. What further allows us to make this interpretive claim is that without any reasonable transition, Mansilla then engages in a recollection of the death of Sarmiento's ill-fated only son, Dominguito, in the third fragment from *Mis memorias* that I would like to examine.

As chance would have it (if chance has anything to do with such matters), the young Mansilla was the best friend of Sarmiento's son, with whom he had collaborated in a translation of *París en América* by the French writer Pierre Laboulaye. In 1866, during the disastrous war with Paraguay, Dominguito fell mortally wounded in the calamitous attack against the fortifications of Curupaití. Mansilla's haunting re-creation of this incident in his memoirs must be read as complementary to the one cited earlier:

> [Dominguito] cayó mortalmente herido en la retirada. . . . El recuerdo inefable de aquel niño, que era una esperanza para la patria, está en mi corazón. *En el amor fraternal que le profesaba hay un misterio* . . . y si, como dice Michelet, "la historia es una resurrección," no sería maravilla que en lo que me propongo escribir una vez terminadas estas páginas preparatorias, se alzaran algunas sombras a las que trataré de darles cuerpo, alma y animación para que digan algunas verdades, a no dudarlo provechosas, en todo caso confirmatorias de que no hay culpa sin castigo mediato o inmediato acá o allá. (131–32, my emphasis)

> [Dominguito] fell mortally wounded in the retreat. . . . The indescribable memory of that child, who was a future hope for the nation, is in my heart. In the fraternal love that I felt for him there is a mystery . . . and if—as Michelet says—"history is a resurrection," it would not be surprising if in what I aim to write once I finish these preparatory pages there would arise some shadows to which I will endeavor to give body, soul, and energy so that they may speak some truths; truths that will be undoubtedly useful, and which in any event will confirm that there is no guilt without punishment, be it swift or long in coming, be it here or there.

As the passage makes explicit, Mansilla perceives an enigma surrounding his fraternal affection for Dominguito, a conundrum that is accompanied by an undefined yet keenly felt sense of guilt over his death. I would argue that the entire passage is suggestive of a desire to assume the role, to take over the place of Sarmiento's son, pointing as it does to the existence of a "mysterious" fraternal rivalry between them—a rivalry that would be terribly decided in Mansilla's favor by the random catastrophes of war.[18] As if to play into Mansilla's family romance, following Dominguito's death Sarmiento sent Mansilla a missive from the United States in which he makes his son's best friend the offer to extend to him the mantle of his paternal protection, "ofreciéndole lo que un padre puede ofrecer al amigo, compañero y jefe del hijo malogrado" (*Obras*, 49:272) [offering what a father can offer to the friend, companion, and superior of his ill-fated son]. A few months later, Mansilla corresponded in kind by effectively becoming the principal sponsor of Sarmiento's successful candidacy for the Argentine presidency in 1868.

Disaffection between "father" and "son" probably began when Sarmiento did not appoint Mansilla to a ministerial position that the latter thought he deserved for his political efforts in Sarmiento's behalf. Full of disappointment, Mansilla wrote the following to a confidant: "En este momento de mi vida represento el papel de un concurrente que no halla lugar, ni de pie, en la gran representación política que el mismo ha organizado."[19] [At this moment in my life I am like the participant who cannot find a place—not even standing—in the great political spectacle that he himself has organized.] But bitterness erupted in full when Mansilla's military career was clouded by the accusation that he had executed a deserter in an evident abuse of his authority—that is, toward the beginning of 1870, the year in which Mansilla undertook his expedition to the pampas. In January of that year, Mansilla began publishing notices in a Buenos Aires newspaper complaining about changes that Sarmiento had seen fit to make to the peace treaty that Mansilla had agreed upon with the Ranqueles before submitting it to the approval of Congress, changes that Mansilla claimed would ruin the pact. On February 15, a month and a half before Mansilla sallied into the pampas, Sarmiento sent him a stern communiqué ordering him to desist in his criticism of the president's policies. At the end of his letter, Sarmiento reiterates the offer he had made two years earlier to become a paternal figure to his son's best friend: "Como le prometí desde los Estados Unidos en mi primera carta, *quiero servirle de padre*, y en ese concepto le diré a Vd. que no tiene quien lo desfavorezca sino Vd. mismo" (*Obras*, 50:318–19, my emphasis). [As I promised you from the United States in my first letter, *I want to be as your father*, and I tell you that there is no one who can change that determination but yourself.]

I would argue that all the fragments reproduced here attest to the existence of a peculiar psychohistorical paradigm that underlies Mansilla's formulation of his autobiographical narrative. Mansilla's genealogical ties to Rosas allowed him to project onto Argentine history the design of an extended family romance of an intensely oedipal nature, of investing both history as he lived it—and especially as he recollected it—with a profound familial intensity. In this oedipal family romance, Mansilla portrayed himself as a child choosing between two surrogate and mutually exclusive paternal figures: Rosas and Sarmiento. I am not endeavoring to identify the ultimate roots of these fragments in some privileged psychological register; rather, my intention is to establish their presence in Mansilla's autobiographical text in order to reveal the oedipal masterplot that subtends Mansilla's account of lived history, a masterplot on which the authority of the narrator of Mansilla's oeuvre is founded. More important, I would like to locate the echo of the plot these scenes configure in the text of *Una excursión a los indios Ranqueles*. For if we reconstruct the narrative logic that determines the inclusion of these fragments in Mansilla's autobiography, we may begin to discern a possible motivation behind the author's otherwise puzzling journey to the Ranqueles.

Mansilla's *Excursión* begins, if not literally in earnest, with what is truly a displaced reenactment of the crime for which he had been indicted by a military court—the execution of a soldier—and an equally circuitous attempt at self-defense from the accusation. This occurs in the guise of the first of a number of fireside stories (*cuentos de fogón*) that are told throughout *Una excursión a los indios Ranqueles*: the tale of Cabo Gómez, a soldier that had presumably served under Mansilla during the war with Paraguay (21–41). This man had mistakenly killed a shopkeeper while attempting to avenge a personal affront by a military superior who had slapped him in public. Mansilla believes in the man's innocence and becomes his defender and suggests that a miscarriage of justice has taken place after Gómez is finally condemned by a military tribunal to be executed on the basis of purely circumstantial evidence. But after the sentencing Gómez privately confesses to the killing, explaining to Mansilla that he had denied committing the murder because he thought he had killed the man that had insulted him earlier, not a civilian.

The extenuating circumstances that muddle the issues of innocence versus guilt in Gómez's case, and the fact that both incidents occur during the hardships of a military campaign, make this narrative significant as a thinly veiled allusion to Mansilla's own legal predicament during his voyage to the Ranqueles. This becomes apparent when we compare Mansilla's tale of Cabo Gómez with a present-day historian's account of Mansilla's troubles at the time:

> No podemos dejar de mencionar un suceso luctuoso acaecido a los pocos días de establecido el ejército en la nueva frontera [Río Quinto], y que influyó ulteriormente en la foja de servicios del coronel Mansilla. Si bien las fuerzas expedicionarias coronaron con todo éxito su cometido, debieron enseguida afrontar una deserción de características graves. Para impedirla, debieron los mandos tomar medidas en extremo rígidas, pero contempladas en la ordenanza militar. En consecuencia, el soldado Avelino Acosta, reincidente en el delito de deserción, fue fusilado el 30 de mayo de 1869, contra las barrancas del río Quinto, en cumplimiento de una orden emanada de la jefatura de frontera. Quiso con ello Mansilla aplicar un castigo, ejemplar, para cortar de raíz el cáncer que raleaba los batallones. Si en verdad lo consiguió, la omisión de un trámite administrativo le produjo, meses después, la mayor pesadumbre de su carrera militar, como fue su destitución del cargo de comandante de frontera el año siguiente. (Mayol, 93)

> We cannot avoid mentioning a tragic event that occurred a few days after the army had established itself in the new frontier (Rio Quinto), and which reflected itself subsequently in Colonel Mansilla's military record. If it is true that the expeditionary forces saw their efforts succeed, they also had to face immediately a serious rash of desertions. To counter it, the officers had to take measures that were extreme, yet in accord with the military code. As a result, Private Avelino Acosta, a repeat deserter, was executed by firing squad on May 30, 1869, in Rio Quinto, following orders—that came from frontier headquarters. With this act, Mansilla wanted to effect an exemplary punishment that would go to the root of the problem that was plaguing the battalion. Although he was successful, his omission of an administrative technicality caused him some months later the biggest misfortune in his military career: his removal from the post of frontier commander the next year.

In this account, Mansilla's punishment was unfair, since his "crime" amounted to not following proper bureaucratic procedure before executing the deserter—an act nonetheless sanctioned by military law. Likewise, Mansilla, who at the time of his writing considered himself the victim of a military tribunal, circuitously argues for his innocence through the story of Cabo Gómez, a story that collapses together both his supposed crime, the execution of a soldier, and what he believe to be his plight: being the unfair victim of martial justice and national ingratitude. In a metaphorical reversal that is typical of much dream work, Mansilla's innocence is argued for by means of his partial identification with his victim, the executed soldier. The result is the confused but richly suggestive story of Cabo Gómez: an inharmonious narrative that evoked sympathy for the soldier while acknowledging simultaneously that he had committed a most serious crime. Like Mansilla, Gómez is a persecuted victim, but on the other hand, the soldier Mansilla executed deserved his lot because he was, in fact, guilty of the desertion for which Mansilla condemned him to death. Gómez's bitter last words before his execution could have been uttered by Mansilla himself, even if Gómez is nonetheless portrayed as a man deservedly condemned by the law: "¡Compañeros: así paga la Patria a los que saben morir por ella!" (37). [Friends: this is how the Fatherland repays those who are willing to die for it!] The liminary position occupied by this revealing anecdote in *Una excursión a los indios Ranqueles* is indicative of the crisis that enveloped Mansilla during both his voyage and his subsequent composition of his work as a result of his arbitrary act. More important, its prominent placement allows us, to my mind, to understand Mansilla's impulsive expedition as a response to that very crisis, as a reply articulated in the context of the oedipal narrative paradigm proposed earlier.

Faced by the paternal injunction and threat represented by the official inquest initiated at Sarmiento's behest, Mansilla retorted by appropriating the Father's enabling discursive gesture in the *Facundo*, yet he carried it out in space rather than as a rhetorical maneuver. Hence, Mansilla's excursion to the pampas can be read as a reenactment of the beginning of Sarmiento's *Facundo*, where Sarmiento had effected an imaginary survey of Argentine geography in an operation that legitimized the authority of his discourse on national history and political reality. Nonetheless, the outcome of this internment in the country's vast geographical expanse is quite different this time around. Mansilla, in a hallucinatory dream in the middle of the pampas, aligns himself with the forces of barbarism and leads them to vanquish civilization:

> Yo era emperador de los ranqueles. . . . Mi nombre llenaba el desierto preconizado por las cien lenguas de la fama. Me habían erigido un gran arco triunfal. Representaba un coloso como el de Rodas. Tenía un pie en la soberbia cordillera de los Andes, otro en las márgenes del Plata. Con una mano empuñaba una pluma deforme de ganso. . . . Con la otra blandía una

espada de inconmensurable largor. . . . Por debajo de aquel monumento . . .
desfilaba como el rayo, tirada por veinte yuntas de yeguas chúcaras una
carreta tucumana, cubierta de penachos, de crines caballares de varios co-
lores y en cuyo lecho se alzaba un dosel de pieles de carnero. En él iba
sentado un mancebo de rostro pintado con carmín. ¡Era yo! Mi traje con-
sistía en un cuero de jaguar; los brazos del animal formaban las mangas, las
piernas, los calzones, lo demás lo cubría el cuerpo y, por fin, la cabeza con
sus colmillos agudos adornaba y cubría mi frente a manera de antiguo ca-
pacete. . . .

Una escolta formada en zigzags, me precedía, cubriéndome la retaguar-
dia. Indígenas de todas las castas australes se veían allí: ranqueles, puelches,
pehuenches, piscunches, patagones y araucanos. Los unos iban en potros
bravos, los otros en mansos caballos, éstos en guanacos, aquéllos en aves-
truces, muchos a pie, varios montados en cañas, infinitos en alados cóndores.
Sus armas eran lanzas y bolas. . . . Yo marchaba a la conquista de una ciudad
poderosa. . . . Me había hecho aclamar y coronar por aquellas gentes sen-
cillas, había superado ya algunos obstáculos de mi vida; ¿Por qué no había
de tentar la empresa de luchar y vencer una civilización decrépita? (175–
76)[20]

I was emperor of the Ranqueles. . . . My name filled the desert, shouted by
the hundred mouths of fame. They had erected a great triumphal arch in
my name that depicted a colossus like the one in Rhodes. It had a foot in
the proud range of the Andes and another in the shores of the River Plate.
In one hand it had a misshapen goose feather. . . . The other sported the
longest sword. . . . Under the monument . . . a Tucuman wagon sped by,
pulled by twenty teams of tailless mares and covered with feathered hats
and horse manes of various colors. In it there was a sheepskin canopy, and
underneath it a young man with red face paint. It was I! I was dressed with
a jaguar's skin. The skin's front legs were my sleeves, its hind legs my pants,
and the rest was hidden by my body. Its head with its sharp teeth covered
my forehead like a helmet of old. . . . An entourage that moved zigzag followed, protecting my back. Indians from all the southern tribes could be
seen there: Ranqueles, Puelches, Pehuenches, Piscunes, Patagones and Ar-
aucanians. Some rode wild horses, others tamed ones; some rode ostriches,
others were on foot; some rode in bamboo stretchers and countless others
in winged condors. Their weapons were spears and bolas. . . . I was riding
to the conquest of a powerful city. . . . I had convinced these simple people
to crown and pay homage to me, and had already surmounted several obstacles in my life; why would not I attempt to do battle with and vanquish
a worn-out civilization?

Mansilla's tiger skin will remind any reader of Sarmiento's *Civilización y
barbarie* of Facundo Quiroga, whose popular appellation "el tigre de los
llanos" had been craftily invoked by Sarmiento in order to begin his bi-

ography of the Argentine caudillo.²¹ In his dream, like a Conde don Julián *avant la lettre*, Mansilla depicts himself staging the eradication of civilization by the combined forces of barbarism united under his command. Given the explicit dialogue with Sarmiento's work that obtains throughout *Una excursión a los indios Ranqueles*, Mansilla's dream must be interpreted as a violent repudiation of Sarmiento through the former's identification with barbarism, the category the latter excoriated in his dichotomous yet influential analysis of Argentine reality.

But if we interpret civilization and barbarism to be allegorical abstractions for Sarmiento and Rosas, respectively (in a substitutive operation that had already been at the core of Sarmiento's text all along), in Mansilla's dream of identification with a triumphant barbarism we can discern a choice between the two powerful paternal figures of Mansilla's family romance that is ultimately decided in Rosas's favor. In his journey to the Ranqueles and his subsequent written account of it, Mansilla engaged in an enterprise that was a phantasmatic playing out of a family romance of historical proportions—a fantasy in which the desiring subject rejects a paternal figure (Sarmiento) while simultaneously embracing its antithetical, antagonic rival (Rosas). This displacement away from Sarmiento and the simultaneous movement toward Rosas are metaphorically incorporated in *Una excursión a los indios Ranqueles* in the geographic trajectory described by Mansilla in his work. For Mansilla's point of departure, the outermost enclave of civilization from which he sallied into the pampas, had received the name Fuerte Sarmiento from him a year earlier, in honor of the nation's president: "En un respiro del viaje, contemplando el futuro promisorio que esperaba a aquellos campos ubérrimos, [Mansilla] resolvió bautizar con el nombre del presidente de la República al fuerte que se estaba levantando contiguo al paso de las Arganas."²² [In a respite from the journey, and envisioning the bright future of those bountiful plains, (Mansilla) decided to christen the fortification that was being built next to the Arganas pass with the name of the nation's president.] And conversely, the person whom Mansilla had set out to encounter, the feared chief of the Ranqueles, had been captured as a boy, christened, and partially schooled by white men before he had escaped back to his tribe. His Christian name was Mariano Rosas, and his godfather had been Juan Manuel de Rosas, Mansilla's later exiled and disgraced uncle. In his book on Rosas's amorous entanglements, Pineda Yánez suggests that Mariano Rosas, the Indian leader, was in reality Rosas's son, conceived when the latter visited the Ranqueles during his famous 1833 campaign against the Indians.[23] And in *Una excursión a los indios Ranqueles* Mansilla reports the following words by Mariano Rosas concerning his "godfather" Juan Manuel de Rosas: "Mariano Rosas conserva el más grato recuerdo de veneración por su padrino; hablaba de él con el mayor respeto, dice que cuanto es y sabe se lo debe a él; *que después de Dios no ha tenido otro padre mejor*" (180, my emphasis). [Mariano Rosas has a most endearing remembrance and veneration for his godfather. He speaks with the highest respect for him, saying that everything he is and all he knows he owes to him, and that after God he has not had a better father.] Hence, in Mansilla's journey from the Río Quinto to Tierra Adentro, from civilization to barbarism, there is also a toponymic displacement from "Sarmiento" to "Rosas" that signals the resolution of Mansilla's conflictive filial romance through a final identification with the figure of his powerful uncle. This denouement would mark Mansilla's subsequent literary production as well. From this moment on, Sarmiento will reappear periodically in Mansilla's later works, but always as an uncomfortable and reproached figure,[24] while a progressively more vindicated Rosas—and especially the Argentine history lived by Mansilla as his nephew—will be the subject of the majority of his subsequent writings. Indeed, his most significant book before the appearance in 1904 of *Mis memorias* is devoted exclusively to the character of Juan Manuel de Rosas.

Rozas: ensayo histórico psicológico (1898) is a long monographic study in which Mansilla endeavored to explain, if not outright rehabilitate, the historical persona of his uncle Juan Manuel.[25] Curiously, throughout this work Mansilla writes the name Rosas consistently as Rozas, with an intervocalic *z*. This, he explains in a prominent footnote to the title of the book, was the real family name of don Juan Manuel, which he later arbitrarily changed in his youth to Ro*s*as with an *s*: "Repetiremos aquí lo que otras veces hemos hecho notar a los que insisten en escribir Rozas con *s*. Viene este nombre patronímico de *rozar*. Los Rozas argentinos, es decir, los hijos de don León Ortiz de Rozas y de doña Agustina López de Osornio fueron tres, que se firmaban así: Juan Manuel de Rosas, con *s*; Prudencio Ortiz de Rozas y Gervasio Rozas con *z*: singularidades que se explicarán en el cuerpo de la obra."[26] [I repeat here what I have at other times remarked to those who insist in writing Rozas with an *s*. The name comes from *rozar*. The Rozas from Argentina, that is, the three sons of don León Ortiz de Rozas and doña Agustina López de Osornio, used to sign their name as follows: Juan Manuel de Rosas, with an *s*; Prudencio Ortiz de Rozas and Gervasio Rozas with a *z*. These differences will be accounted for in what follows.] Mansilla's account of the genesis of this graphemic transformation is, I would argue, significant.

On one occasion the young Rosas had been punished for disobedience by his parents, who had sentenced him to bread and water and to incarceration in his room. That night the youngster escaped from his prison, leaving a defiant note behind:

> Todos dormían . . . falseó la cerradura, escribió con lápiz en papel que puso en sitio visible unas palabras, se desnudó y casi como Adán salió a la calle yendo a casa de sus primos los Anchorena para vestirse y conchabarse. Al día siguiente, cuando fueron a llevarle el pan y el agua, hallaron el susodicho papel, el cual rezaba esto: "Dejo todo lo que no es mío, Juan Manuel de Rosas" con *s*. Y este fue su primer acto de rebelión contra toda otra autoridad que no fuera su voluntad. Y de ahí que en lo sucesivo se firmara como no debía, puesto que su verdadero nombre patronímico era Juan Manuel Ortiz de Rozas, Rozas con *z* y no con *s*. (25)

> Everyone slept . . . he picked the lock, pencilled some words in a piece of paper that he left in a prominent place, undressed himself, and like a new Adam took to the streets in the direction of his cousins' house, the Anchorenas, in order to get new clothes and to conspire with them. The next day, when they went to take bread and water to him they found the piece of paper, in which he had written the following: "I leave behind everything that does not belong to me, Juan Manuel de Rosas, with an *s*." And this was his first act of rebellion against any authority that did not arise from him. This is why in the future he would sign his name incorrectly, since his true surname was Juan Manuel Ortiz de Rozas, Rozas with a *z* and not an *s*.

As is obvious from this passage, Mansilla regards Rosas's willful graphemic transformation as the beginning of the latter's historical persona, the moment when Rosas breaks with his personal past in order to become a decisive protagonist of Argentine history. Yet though Mansilla is concerned in his biography with "Rosas" the historical figure—the Ro*s*as with an *s*—throughout his biography he consistently writes the dictator's name with a *z*: Ro*z*as. Should this be interpreted merely as evincing a penchant for onomastic accuracy, as Mansilla tries to explain in his opening footnote and in other writings? Possibly. But given that the change in spelling is the mark of a rebellion against paternal authority, could we not also perceive in Mansilla's suppression of the *s*, the *s* of Sarmiento, in Rosas's name a synthetic formulation of the latent narrative content of the oedipal romance that I have tried to identify at the core of *Una ex-*

cursión a los indios Ranqueles? Mansilla's anecdote regarding Rosas's patronymical change is also meaningful because it establishes the association between the act of writing and rebellion that can also be seen at work in the antagonistic relationship between *Una excursión a los indios Ranqueles* and Sarmiento's *Facundo*. For the composition of Mansilla's account can be viewed as an attempt to use writing to defy the rhetorical authority of his text, and of Sarmiento's presidential dominion as well.

But if Mansilla's filial rebellion against Sarmiento is expressed through a simultaneous choice for Rosas—the other paternal figure in this family romance—then Mansilla always remained within the clutch of his filial role, "choosing" to linger forever in the grip of the oedipal thrall dictated by the content of the psychohistorical fable that we have been examining. In his figuration of history as a family romance, Mansilla found both a justification and a perspective from which to narrate authoritatively: the role of the ephebe, which endowed his writing with the prestige derived from being close to the main protagonists of nineteenth-century Argentine history, without being one himself. What Mansilla did not—perhaps could not—realize was that the part he carved for himself in this historical/psychological scene relegated him also to the inconstancy and impotence demanded by his chosen role: that is, condemned him to live and write through the persona of the perpetual adolescent. Sylvia Molloy has spoken about the difficulties faced by any reader of Mansilla's oeuvre who expects to encounter in his pages a coherent narrative voice, since Mansilla's depiction of himself is "un derrumbe, una falta de composición básica de la voz que enuncia, un notable desencuentro" (1980: 753) [a collapse, an elementary lack of composition in the enunciating voice, a remarkable disjunction]. And she adds a comment that proves significant from the perspective I have tried to elucidate: "Es tarea inútil intentar recomponer a un yo que por fin no quiere componerse: que prefiere—no como un *dandy* sino como un adolescente—mantenerse en la indecisión" (757).[27] [It is useless to attempt to recompose an I that in the end is not interested in achieving cohesion: an I that prefers—not like a dandy but like an adolescent—to remain indecisive.] Mansilla's writings reveal the vanity and assurance of one who can speak because the historical events reported occurred to protagonical figures with whom he was intimate; but his chosen role in the structure of feeling he projected onto history also determined that his oeuvre would be the inchoate, indecisive, and contradictory text that it is. It also explains Mansilla's seeming destiny to be the perennially expendable and expedient man, the subaltern who waited in vain to be called from the wings of the historical stage by the powerful protagonists whose careers and ambitions he helped in turn to promote: Urquiza, Mitre, Sarmiento, Avellaneda, Roca, Juárez Celman.[28]

In the opening chapter of this book I referred to the problematic character of modernity in Spanish America and to the rhetorical crisis that it represented to the intellectuals and writers of the continent. I also proposed that this crisis was dealt with by means of a contradictory turning away from modernity that manifested itself in a variety of ways in the works that compose this textual tradition. In Mansilla's case, this crisis of discursive authority was addressed through the assumption of a rhetorical mask in a drama based on the most traditional and conservative of institutions: the family. Luiz Costa Lima has argued that one of the symptoms of a troubled modernity in Latin America has been the predominant role played by the family in the social sphere. According to him, "the conditions were lacking for the modern experience of public opinion. And this lack, I repeat, is associated with the enduring presence of the family as the paramount means of socialization. In other words, the absence of a public, a fact noted by many observers, had to do both with the absence of middle classes and with the preservation of a *family-centered* conduct that was inconsistent with bourgeois rationality."[29] For as we have seen, Mansilla endeavored to warrant the validity of his writing by exercising prerogatives engendered in the fusion of history and the emotional landscape of the familial.[30] During his life Mansilla did his best to live the persona of that Baudelairean icon of modernity, the dandy. In fact, the entire *generación del ochenta* with which he is customarily identified is considered the first to have fully achieved a consciousness of the country's participation in the modern. But in the end, one could argue that Mansilla—ardent follower of European fashion, flamboyant Parisian flâneur, and consummate traveler—never truly left home, rhetorically speaking.

Our next chapter addresses the works of the Uruguayan author Horacio Quiroga, whose stories, written during the first forty years of this century, defined the genre of the modern short story in Spanish America. We will examine how Quiroga's understanding of modernity is intertwined with his poetics of the short story and how this conjunction results in the undermining of his declared principles of literary composition.

CHAPTER FIVE

Death and Resurrections
Horacio Quiroga's Poetics of the Short Story

Death is the most proper or literal of meanings, and literal meaning partakes of death.
—Harold Bloom, *Poetry and Repression: Revisionism from Blake to Stevens*

Artistic vision presents us with the whole hero, measured in full and added up in every detail; there must be no secrets for us in the hero with respect to meaning. . . . From the very outset, we must experience all of him, deal with the whole of him: in respect to meaning he must be dead for us, formally dead.
—Mikhail Bakhtin, "Author and Hero in Aesthetic Activity"

Transgression carries the limit right to the limit of its being. Transgression forces the limit to face the fact of its imminent disappearance, to find itself in what it excludes (perhaps, to be more exact, to recognize itself for the first time) to experience its positive truth in its downward fall.
—Michel Foucault, "Preface to Transgression"

ONE OF THE MOST PERSISTENT THEMES over time in the critical literature on Horacio Quiroga's oeuvre has been the constant and overwhelming presence of death, both in the Uruguayan writer's personal life and in his work. With regard to his literary production, it would be difficult to disagree with Jaime Alazraki when he notes that "de frente o de soslayo el tema de la muerte entra en casi todos los cuentos de Horacio Quiroga"[1] [directly or indirectly the theme of death enters into almost all of Horacio Quiroga's stories]. Noé Jitrik has also stated that "hay una predilección [en Quiroga] por los temas relacionados con la muerte y, aún más, que la muerte es la variante y cauce en el que se resuelve la mayor parte de las situaciones que describe"[2] [there is a predilection (in Quiroga) for themes related to death, and, moreover, death is the outcome and the direction in which most of the situations that he describes are resolved]. It is equally clear that in Quiroga's disastrous life, death hovers solicitously from very early on. The devastating series of tragic events that seems to accompany every step of his stormy existence is outlined with meticulous economy in the following excerpt by the Argentine critic H. A. Murena:

> Primero fue su padre quien se hirió de muerte involuntariamente en una partida de caza; luego es su hermano mayor el que perece también en forma accidental. El tercer golpe es siniestro: su padrastro, que había quedado casi del todo paralítico, acciona mediante el dedo de un pie el disparador de una escopeta cuyo cañón tenía apoyado contra el rostro, y cae destrozado frente a su hijastro. El cuarto resulta el más absurdo, el más desgarrador, porque es Quiroga mismo quien, en vísperas de un duelo, da muerte a un amigo querido mientras examina una pistola. Y cuando se piensa, además, en el súbito deceso de la primera mujer del artista, en Misiones, y en el de él en un hospital de Buenos Aires, se acaba por vislumbrar una secreta elección, se siente como un símbolo esa persistencia oscura y aterradora de la muerte.[3]

> First it was his father who was accidentally killed in a hunting party; then it was his older brother who also perished accidentally. The third blow is sinister: his stepfather, who had been left almost completely paralyzed, used his toe to pull the trigger of a rifle, the barrel of which was resting against his face, and fell in front of his stepson, destroyed. The fourth instance is the most absurd, the most heart-rending, because it was Quiroga himself who, on the eve of a duel, killed a dear friend while examining a pistol. And when one considers as well the sudden demise in Misiones of the artist's first wife, and his own decease in a Buenos Aires hospital, a secret election begins to become apparent; it is as if that dark and terrifying persistence of death were a symbol.

Some of the particulars of Murena's enumeration are not exact, but the accounting accomplishes its purpose: to provide evidence of the events that fundamentally shaped the writer's turbulent and star-crossed biography. We should also add to the list the suicides of Eglé (1938) and Darío (1951), children by Quiroga's first marriage: although they occurred after Quiroga's death in 1937, they necessarily fall within the framework of his biography—particularly since they repeat their parents' gesture of self-inflicted death. It is therefore understandable that critics should almost ritualistically invoke this long bloody destiny as the origin and source of the undeniable fascination with death saliently present in the majority of the Uruguayan's stories.[4]

Yet we must delve more deeply into this aspect of Quiroga's work, which is evident to any reader and is confirmed time and again by the surprising unanimity of selection shown by all the various attempts to anthologize his most representative works: the most striking narrative pieces of his oeuvre, those consistently considered most noteworthy, are invariably and fundamentally related to death. In his early and important study to which we alluded earlier, Jitrik had already formulated the pertinent questions with his usual precision and perspicacity: "¿Qué buscaba Quiroga al recaer constantemente en temas de muerte? ¿Por qué en esos temas es cuando obtiene sus mejores obras? ¿Por qué es allí que su estilo es el más personal y más limpio de influencias?" (126). [What was Quiroga searching for as he constantly returned to death themes? Why are his best works those that treat these themes? Why is it that when handling these themes his style is at its most personal and is most free of influences?] Jitrik concludes that the repeated representation of death in Quiroga's stories reflects the attempt to exorcize that other death—the existential, biographical one. For Jitrik, Quiroga "se ve muerto aun antes de morir como dándose una última oportunidad. Si logra expulsar esa imagen [de la muerte] de su vista o de su cerebro quizás no muera. La única manera que se le ocurre para expulsarla es escribirse muerto, única arma con que cuenta para conjurar y deshacer la imagen que lo atemoriza y cohíbe" (126) [sees himself as dead, even before his death, as if he were giving himself one last chance. If he can manage to expel that image (of death) from his sight or from his mind, perhaps he will not die. The only way he can conjure up to expel it is by writing himself as dead, as if it were the only weapon at his disposal to exorcize and destroy the image that terrifies and restrains him]. Nevertheless, Jitrik's proposal coincides with the general tendency of critics to see in the thematics of the Quiroguian oeuvre a direct manifestation of his personal anxiety in the face of death, a view according to which the presence of death in Quiroga's stories would be a reflection of that biographical narrative of death that has for so long been a part of the critical folklore of Latin American literature. In this chapter, I would like to move to another hermeneutical space from which to attempt a response to the questions so clearly posed by Jitrik, questions that to my mind address the most essential dimension of Quiroga's writings. That is, I propose to study the presence of death in his work not as a thematic occurrence but rather as an element closely related to both the discursive practices engaged in and the poetics of the short story espoused by the Uruguayan writer. This will finally allow us to suggest the existence of a connection between Quiroga's literary praxis and the larger phenomenon of the experience of modernity in Spanish America.

It will hardly surprise anyone if we affirm that in Horacio Quiroga's texts the end of the narrative is the axis around which the short story as a literary form revolves. In the various statements about the essence and composition of the short story produced by Quiroga throughout his life, there is a recurring and even obsessive preoccupation with the story's end.[5] Let us review some of these statements.

In his famous "Decálogo del perfecto cuentista"—his epigrammatic list of suggestions for the writing apprentice determined to cultivate the short story—Quiroga sets forth as the fifth commandment the following: "No empieces a escribir sin saber desde la primera palabra adónde vas. En un cuento bien logrado, las tres primeras líneas tienen casi la importancia de las tres últimas" (87). [Do not begin writing without knowing from the very first word where you are going. In a well-written story, the first three lines are almost as important as the last three.] Exactly the same idea is found in an article written by Quiroga two years earlier ("Manual del perfecto cuentista"), in which he stated that "la primera palabra de un cuento . . . debe ya estar escrita con miras al final" (62). [The first word of a story . . . should be written with an eye already toward the end.] Significantly, in this essay Quiroga *begins* his reflections on the short story with a paradox that reveals the importance he ascribed to the denouement in his conception of the story: "Comenzaremos por el final. Me he convencido de que del mismo modo que en el soneto, el cuento empieza por el final" (61). [We shall begin with the end. I have become convinced that, just as with the sonnet, a short story begins from the end.]

Quiroga's insistence on the end of the story is merely the most visible aspect of a poetics of the short story that he articulated throughout his work and that is easily extracted from his various and several writings on the rhetoric of that literary form. Numerous passages in Quiroga's precepts immediately come to mind, beginning with the seventh commandment of the "Decálogo del perfecto cuentista": "No adjectives sin necesidad. Inútiles serán cuantas colas de color adhieras a un sustantivo débil. Si hallas el que es preciso, él sólo tendrá un color incomparable. Pero hay que hallarlo" (87). [Do not use adjectives unnecessarily. No matter how many colored tails you attach to a noun, if it is a weak noun they will be useless. If you find the right one, by itself it will have an incomparable

color. But you must find it first.] The sixth commandment is also pertinent to our discussion: "Si quieres expresar con exactitud esta circunstancia: 'desde el río soplaba un viento frío,' no hay en lengua humana más
palabras que las apuntadas para expresarla" (87). [If you want to express
exactly the following situation: "a cold wind was blowing from the river,"
there are no other words in any human language better than those to
express it.] Later, in the late 1920s and early 1930s, when Quiroga saw
his star decline in the stormy and mutable Argentine literary firmament,
he wrote another well-known essay that from its title—"Ante el tribunal"—reveals the self-defensive maneuvering that prompted him to write
it. Here Quiroga depicts himself as confronting his detractors, addressing
them as though they were judges, and his argument is transformed imperceptibly into a theory of the short story as the author attempts to
exonerate himself from all charges by demonstrating that he has always
written with a resolutely conscious mastery of his métier. In his argument
Quiroga proposes the following:

> Luché porque el cuento . . . tuviera una sola línea, trazada por una mano
> sin temblor desde el principio al fin. Ningún obstáculo, ningún adorno o
> digresión, debía acudir o aflojar la tensión de su hilo. El cuento era, para
> el fin que le es intrínseco, una flecha que, cuidadosamente apuntada, parte
> del arco para ir a dar directamente en el blanco. Cuantas mariposas trataran
> de posarse sobre ella para adornar su vuelo, no conseguirán sino entorpe-
> cerlo. (137)
>
> ———————
>
> I struggled that the story . . . have a single line, traced with an unwavering
> hand from beginning to end. No obstacle, no embellishment or digression,
> should come to the aid of or weaken the tension of the narrative thread. In
> order to accomplish its intrinsic purpose, the story was to be like an arrow
> which, carefully aimed, is shot from the bow and goes directly to its target.
> No matter how many butterflies might try to perch on it to adorn its flight,
> they would only impede it.

It is often stated—as indicated by Quiroga himself—that the extreme
economy of his stories had its origins in his early literary contributions
to the journal *Caras y Caretas.* The editor of the literary supplement, Luis
Pardo, was, according to the author, "quien exigió al cuento breve hasta
un grado inaudito de severidad" [the one who required that the short
story have an unheard-of degree of sparseness] and who was responsible
for "el destrozo de muchos cuentos por falta de extensión, pero . . . también en gran parte el mérito de los que han resistido" (95–96) [the destruction of many stories because of excessive length, but . . . also to a

large extent for the merits of those that have survived.] Quiroga then notes, not without a little pride, the severe strictures that Pardo imposed on all his pieces that appeared in the journal:

> El cuento no debía pasar entonces de una página, incluyendo la ilustración correspondiente. Todo lo que quedaba al cuentista para caracterizar a sus personajes, colocarlos en ambiente, arrancar al lector de su desgano habitual, interesarlo, impresionarlo y sacudirlo, era una sola y estrecha página. Mejor aún: 1256 palabras. . . . Tal disciplina, impuesta aún a los artículos, inflexible y brutal, fue sin embargo utilísima para los escritores nóveles, siempre propensos a diluir la frase por inexperiencia y por cobardía; y para los cuentistas, obvio es decirlo, fue aquello una piedra de toque, que no todos pudieron resistir. (95–96)

> The story, then, had to be no longer than one page, including the accompanying illustration. In one single, narrow page the author had to create characterizations, situate his characters in an appropriate setting, draw the reader out of his habitual inertia, interest him, impress him, seduce him. Even more exactly: 1,256 words. . . . Such inflexible and brutal discipline, imposed even on articles, was nevertheless extremely useful for novice writers, with their propensity to dilute sentences because of inexperience or cowardice; and for some of them, naturally, that limit was a stricture that not all of them could survive.

Notwithstanding its indisputable anecdotal value, this statement by the author is ingenuous when offered as an explanation of a lesson that Quiroga had in fact already learned from Poe's commentaries on the poetics of the short story, which in turn summarized romantic ideas about the organicity of the literary work and of the experience of literature. The emphasis that Quiroga places on the sense of economy that should govern a story's structure had been set forth much earlier in Poe's famous review-essay of Hawthorne's *Twice-Told Tales*: "A skillful literary artist has constructed a tale. . . . Having conceived, with deliberate care, a certain unique or single *effect* to be wrought out, he then invents such incidents—he then combines such events as may best aid him in establishing this preconceived effect."[6] And in words reminiscent of some of Quiroga's statements cited earlier, Poe continues: "If his very initial sentence tends not to the outbringing of this effect, then he has failed in his first step. In the whole composition there should be no word written, of which the tendency, direct or indirect, is not to the one pre-established design" (136).

For Poe as well as Quiroga, the short story was based on a total rhetorical economy that is articulated around the denouement. The rhetoric of the short story gleaned from Quiroga's statements doubtless has its roots in Poe's theories, and it would be useless for us to claim for Quiroga an originality that Quiroga himself would never have asserted.[7] Quiroga's lack of anxiety about literary epigonality is expressed in the first of the commandments in his "Decálogo" to the aspiring writer of short stories: "Cree en un maestro—Poe, Maupassant, Kipling, Chejov—como en Dios mismo" (86). [Believe in a master—Poe, Maupassant, Kipling, Chekhov— as in God Himself.] Rather, Quiroga's intentions were precisely the opposite: to make a claim of dutiful *apprenticeship*; to aver that his praxis of the short story was predicated on the knowledge of a métier and of a technique that made him a truly modern and foundational writer, a knowledge that he had distilled from his reading of the works and the criticism of Poe, Maupassant, Kipling, and others. Many of Quiroga's writings on the short story attest to this emphasis on his possession and control of a technique essential for the successful composition of a short story. Some of the titles of these pieces leave little room for doubt: "El manual del perfecto cuentista," "Los trucs del perfecto cuentista," "Decálogo del perfecto cuentista," and "La retórica del cuento." In many ways—and as a number of critics have already noted—Quiroga's concept of the writer as a technician was a reflection of the increased professionalization of the writer in fin-de-siècle Spanish America, a process that was perhaps at its most advanced stage in the Southern Cone. Nonetheless, the new and multiple opportunities then offered by the surge in the number of outlets for literary production—reviews, newspapers, magazines, and so on—also meant the subjection of the writer to the rules of a market that was perceived as arbitrary and fickle. In response, a conception of literature as a craft arose in order to define it as a kind of writing exempt from the laws of the market. Through his formulation of a poetics of the short story founded in the praxis and theories of major European and American masters, Quiroga sought to establish a claim to a knowledge about his métier that was objective and verifiable and therefore placed the absolute worth of literary writing above the vagaries of the print market. This technification of his craft is the source of the many articles written by him with such words as "trucs," "decálogo," and "retórica" in their titles; in these articles Quiroga attempted to reduce to formulas and lists of instructions the production of the short story as a genre. Yet this distilling of literary creation to a scheme would also seem to entail the danger of turning the writing of short stories into a recipe repeatable and ultimately accessible to anyone, which would also go counter to the criterion of originality that supposedly determined value in the literary market. This is why, irrespective of his emphasis on technique, and in a thoroughly antithetical gesture, Quiroga does not ever abandon completely the idea of a personal literary gift or genius. Quiroga's many writings on literature and on the poetics of the short story are rent by this contradiction, but the latter should not distract us from the fact that his essential stratagem was to institute the authority of his writing in a knowledge acquired from "modern" metropolitan writers and their meditations on their craft. The received critical notion of Quiroga as the founder of the modern Spanish American short story attests to the final efficacy and success of this strategy.

In a study entitled *La imaginación técnica: sueños modernos de la cultura argentina*, Beatriz Sarlo advances an argument concerning Quiroga (and principally the Argentine author Roberto Arlt) that might help explain further the nature of Quiroga's writings on the short story. Sarlo sees the Uruguayan writer as exemplifying a paradigmatic figure of modernity that arose after 1910 in the River Plate region: the amateur technologist and inventor. She argues that the praxis of this peculiar individual was founded on an alternative kind of knowledge opposed to the codified knowledge of universities and official institutes, one that was based on an ethics of bricolage and tinkering. This amateur inventor subscribed to technical how-to magazines and newsletters, built prototype apparatuses from scratch in makeshift home shops, and was driven by the desire to invent items and processes that could be patented and marketed for profit. His was a practical knowledge based on know-how, but interestingly, it was also a knowledge that allowed for the spark of genius and innovation that would lead to an invention that would make him both famous and wealthy. Sarlo examines biographical works on Quiroga that attest to his fascination with new technologies such as home radio and film, his subscriptions to publications dealing with the latter, his contributing of articles to daily newspapers on the topic, and his lifelong tinkering and various failed attempts to arrive at new processes for everything from distilling orange liqueur to making coal. She also points to several of his stories that deal with individuals obsessed with experimentation and inventing, all of which leads her to propose that Quiroga was imbued with the mentality of the amateur technologist of his time.

Surprisingly, Sarlo makes no attempt to relate this significant characterization of Quiroga to his poetics of the short story, a link that I would argue can lead to a more complete understanding of the latter. For one could easily see Quiroga's many writings on the poetics of the genre as conforming to the format of the instruction manual and how-to columns of the technical magazines of which he was both a contributor and an avid consumer. The lists of "trucs" and his reductions of the literary craft to recipes and formulas reveal this connection clearly. Even Quiroga's affirmation of literary genius can be understood as his projection onto the literary métier of his belief in the gift of the inventor/craftsman, who, as Edison would have it, still needed that 1 percent of inspiration in order to turn the other 99 percent of perspiration into real technological marvels. Hence, Quiroga's poetics of the short story was an expression of modernity both in its desire to follow the dictates of the modern European masters of the genre and in its internalization of an ethics of writing derived from modes of consumption and reproduction of knowledge that were unequivocally aligned with a modernist perspective.

The concept of the short story as built on a textual economy organized around the ending in turn presupposes a particular understanding of the experience of reading: the end of the story is conceived as a moment in which the reader can comprehend in an instantaneous revelation the singular economy that has generated the story just read. In other words, what would have been until that moment the temporal and successive experience of reading is resolved in the denouement into a stasis that allows the reader to experience the total organicity of the story; that is, the way in which the story has been structured in its entirety as a function of the ending that has just been read. Given the fact that this teleological and economic concept of the story has been attributed to the modern avatar of the genre from its origins, it becomes clear that the various precepts regarding the short story that have been expounded here conspire to promote a poetics based on surprise and shock: the end of the story must be surprising because it combines the *maximum* of the desired effect on the reader with the *total* comprehension of the rhetorical economy that organizes the story. Hence, the surprise occurs on two levels: the psychological and the aesthetic. An analysis of Quiroga's various comments on the composition of the short story demonstrates that his poetics of the genre is based on this transcendent conceptualization of the denouement. By the same token, in their narrative processes many of his stories—including even the early ones—fully illustrate Quiroga's knowledge and mastery of this requirement inherent in the modern genre, which he had intuited from his principal literary models, Poe and Mau-passant.[8]

However, although the facts just stated are hardly disputable, there is nevertheless a dimension of Quiroga's work that is paradoxical in light of his avowed rhetoric of the short narrative: in many of his stories Quiroga deliberately provides the reader *from the very beginning* with overt clues—if not the actual events depicted at the end of the plot that he or she is about to witness. This device ranges from entitling a story "El hombre muerto" when the conclusion and culmination to the story are the pro-tagonist's death, to the feeling of inevitability and absolute fatalism that is so familiar after a while to any of reader of Quiroga's works. Such a tactic could be interpreted as the expression of a certain hubris in a writer aware of being in full possession of his or her creative capabilities: how indeed could a writer, having already revealed the end of the plot, sustain the necessary suspense and intensity to make the story effective? This was indeed a challenge that Quiroga was to set for himself again and again, as if in a perpetual dare: keeping the reader's attention despite having revealed the terminus of his literary itinerary. In fact, Quiroga alludes to the challenge implied in this technique in a letter to a friend in which he explains that, although stories with surprising endings are more popular, it is also "bastante más difícil meter un final que el lector ha adivinado ya"[9] [a great deal more difficult to introduce an ending that the reader has already guessed]; and I would add that it is particularly more difficult when the reader has hardly had to guess at all, since the author has already presented the end itself beforehand. However, these conjectures cannot resolve the scandal, the conundrum that this practice of writing represents when considered in the context of Quiroga's own rhetorical precepts and exigencies of the short story.

If we take into account the intensification of the teleology that for Quiroga is consubstantial to the genre of the short story, it becomes evident that this circumstance that Quiroga constantly confronts—wrought by his own hand—is laden with danger and risk. Revealing the end of the story in its initial lines creates a situation that contains the danger of redundance, the possibility that writing will close in on itself from the very first sentence. From a rhetorical perspective, this tactic is the equivalent of threatening the act of writing with nothingness, with the indifferent and absolute homogeneity of silence. Thus, in the context of the Quiroguian theory of the short story, such a writing practice implies a mortal challenge in which—metaphorically, of course—the existence of not only the text but also the author as such are placed in the balance. It could be said that in each one of these stories, Quiroga flirts openly with the possibility of his own disappearance as a writer.

In addition, this daredevil rhetorical balancing act is complemented by Quiroga's odd repertoire of story endings. I am referring to the fact that in many of his tales Quiroga also radically departs from the exigencies of his own poetics regarding the exceptional character of the denouement. In the instances in which this happens, the rhetorical economy that supposedly should be centered on the conclusion is adulterated by the addition of a supplement, a kind of coda that is appended at the end before the closing of the narrative. The enigmatic conclusion of "El almohadón de pluma," one of Quiroga's best-known stories, clearly demonstrates this procedure. Here it takes the form of an annotation in which the apparently fantastic and unlikely nature of the situation described in the story is explained away by a statement that seems to be reaching for the rhetorical authority of scientific discourse.[10] The narrative presents the story of young newlyweds whose ambiguous married life is interrupted by the wife's mysterious debilitating disease. After her death a maid discovers in the pillow the woman had been using a gigantic insect that had suctioned all the woman's blood. The final revelation is described as follows:

> Sobre el fondo, entre las plumas, moviendo lentamente las patas velludas, había un animal monstruoso, una bola hirviente y viscosa. Estaba tan hinchado que apenas se le pronunciaba la boca.
>
> Noche a noche, desde que había caído en cama, había aplicado sigilosamente su boca—su trompa, mejor dicho—a las sienes de aquélla, chupándole la sangre. En cinco días, en cinco noches, había vaciado a Alicia.
>
> Estos parásitos de aves, diminutos en el medio habitual, llegan a adquirir, en ciertas condiciones, proporciones enormes. La sangre humana parece serles particularmente favorable, y no es raro hallarlos en los almohadones de pluma.[11]

> In the background, among the feathers, slowly moving its hairy legs, was a monstrous animal, a boiling and viscous ball. It was so swollen that its mouth could hardly be discerned.
>
> Night after night, ever since the woman had been reduced to lying in bed, it had stealthily employed its mouth—its trunk, rather—on her temples, sucking her blood. In five days and nights, it had emptied out Alicia.
>
> These bird parasites, minute in their normal habitat, under certain other conditions can grow to enormous proportions. Human blood seems to be

particularly favorable to them, and it is not unusual to find them in feather pillows.

Exactly the same narrative procedure is found in the story entitled "La miel silvestre," which recounts the death of a young man who innocently goes into the woods to hunt, with the epic idea of man's confrontation with nature in mind. The misguided protagonist is devoured by an army of carnivorous ants—*la corrección*—that finds him lying on the ground after he is paralyzed by the narcotic effect of a particular variety of wild honey that he has ingested. As frequently occurs in Quiroga, the fortuitous nature of a series of circumstances in the middle of the jungle leads to the character's death.[12] The story concludes as follows:

> Su padrino halló por fin, dos días después, y sin la menor partícula de carne, el esqueleto cubierto de ropa de Benincasa. La corrección que merodeaba aún por allí, y las bolsitas de cera, lo iluminaron suficientemente.
>
> No es común que la miel silvestre tenga esas propiedades narcóticas o paralizantes, pero se la halla. Las flores con igual carácter abundan en el trópico, y ya el sabor de la miel denuncia en la mayoría de los casos su condición; tal el dejo a resina de eucaliptus que creyó sentir Benincasa. (1: 199)

> Two days later his godfather finally found, without a particle of flesh on it, the skeleton covered with Benincasa's clothes. The army of ants that was still marauding around there, along with the little wax honey sacs, were sufficient for him to guess the rest.
>
> It is not common for wild honey to have these narcotic and paralyzing properties, but such honey can indeed be found. Flowers with identical properties abound in the Tropics, and the mere taste of the honey will in most cases indicate its nature; such was the slight taste of eucalyptus resin that Benincasa thought he had detected.

No serious reader of these two stories can overlook the incongruity between the closing paragraphs and the narrative that has unfolded until that moment. The final statements give their respective stories a somewhat trivial finish, since they seem to stem from a truculent and sensationalist desire to impress on the reader not only that the experience just recounted is actually plausible but that the same lot could befall him or her. The narrative disjunction that these additional paragraphs represent is the result of a combination of at least three rhetorical reverses. For one, the conclusion breaks with the discursive uniformity characteristic of the story up to that point, installing in its place a rhetorical model derived from pseudoscientific language. Moreover, in both instances there is an undeniable attempt to void the specificity of the events narrated in the story and to inscribe them instead in a wider experiential context so that the narrated events suddenly acquire an aura of universal applicability. But above all, the concluding paragraphs of both stories constitute unnecessary and transgressive additions in light of the rhetorical economy of the short story espoused by Quiroga. Their supplementary quality vis-à-vis his narrative theory is without a doubt the most notable and disturbing aspect of these passages. The subversion and infringement that this rhetorical practice represents is even more surprising when we observe the regularity with which it occurs in Quiroga.[13]

We have established the presence of two writing practices that transgress the exigencies of Quiroga's own articulation of the poetics of the short story in his critical essays: on the one hand, the proleptic revelation of the story's ending is in direct opposition to the teleological importance of the conclusion that is argued in his essays. On the other, closing the story with what is patently a footnote, a supplementary addition to the obvious end of the narrative, is a practice that transcends—and therefore places in check—the rhetorical economy so often emphasized by Quiroga. Interestingly, these two transgressive swerves from his own poetics of the genre come together in a text that Quiroga wrote toward the end of his literary career entitled "Las moscas: réplica de 'El hombre muerto.' "[14] A brief analysis will allow us to explore in more depth the significance of this rhetorical catachresis that often makes its presence felt in Quiroga's work.

The very title—"Las moscas: réplica de 'El hombre muerto' "—proclaims its relationship with the story "El hombre muerto," to which we have already alluded and which had been published thirteen years earlier.[15] Critics who have addressed this text have interpreted the word *réplica* as "copy" or "tracing," based on the many similarities between the two narratives. Indeed, the plot of "Las moscas" is undeniably similar to that of its predecessor: whereas in "El hombre muerto" the protagonist awaits death after having tripped and fallen on his machete in the first few lines, in "Las moscas" the man slips on a piece of wet bark and falls with a broken spine. A summary comparison clearly reveals even stylistic similarities between the two stories: "El hombre intentó mover la cabeza, en vano. Echó una mirada de reojo a la empuñadura del machete, húmeda aún del sudor de su mano. Apreció mentalmente la extensión y la trayectoria del machete dentro de su vientre, y adquirió, fría, matemática e inexorablemente, la seguridad de que acababa de llegar el término de su existencia" (2:551). [The man tried to move his head, in vain. He looked out of the corner of his eye at the handle of the machete, still wet from the sweat of his hand. He estimated mentally the expanse and trajectory of the machete inside his abdomen and reached the cold, mathematical, inexorable certainty that he had come to the end of his existence.] In "Las moscas," in turn, we find the following passage: "Clarísima y capital, adquiero desde este instante mismo la certidumbre de que a ras del suelo mi vida está aguardando la instantaneidad de unos segundos para extinguirse de una vez" (2:605). [From this precise moment I reach the very clear and fundamental certainty that lying on the ground my life is waiting for the fleetingness of a few seconds to be extinguished once and for all.] In spite of the clear similarities, I would argue that the word "réplica" is appropriate in its second meaning of "response" or "reply," rather than "copy," as a description of the relationship between the two texts. "Las moscas" is as much a "response" to "El hombre muerto" as anything else, because the later narrative represents an alternate version—a reply— to the conclusion of the earlier story. The reader will remember that "El hombre muerto" ends with the description of the protagonist's actual death:

> Puede aún alejarse con la mente, si quiere: puede si quiere abandonar un instante su cuerpo y ver desde el tajamar por él construido, el trivial paisaje de siempre: el pedregullo volcánico con gramas rígidas; el bananal y su arena roja; el alambrado empequeñecido en la pendiente, que se acoda hacia el camino. Y más lejos aún parece ver el potrero, obra sola de sus manos. Y al pie de un poste descascarado, echado sobre el costado derecho y las piernas recogidas, exactamente como todos los días, puede verse a él mismo, como un pequeño bulto asoleado sobre la gramilla, descansando porque está muy cansado . . .
>
> Pero el caballo rayado de sudor, e inmóvil de cautela ante el esquinado del alambrado, ve también al hombre en el suelo y no se atreve a costear el bananal, como desearía. Ante las voces que ya están próximas—¡Piapiá!—, vuelve un largo rato las orejas inmóviles al bulto: y tranquilizado al fin, se decide a pasar entre el poste y el hombre tendido, que ya ha descansado.
> (2:553)

He can still mentally distance himself if he wishes: if he wishes he can abandon for an instant his body and from the dam that he built, he can see the same trivial landscape as always: the volcanic rocky land with its rigid grass; the banana grove with its red sand; the wire fence, dwarfed by the slope, that leans toward the road. And even farther away, can make out the ranch, all of it the work of his hands alone. And at the foot of the post stripped of its bark, thrown on his right side with his legs pulled up, exactly like other days, he can see himself like a small sun-drenched bundle on the grass, resting because he is very tired . . .

But the horse, streaked with sweat and standing cautiously still by the barbed fence, also sees the man on the ground and does not dare go near the banana grove, as he would like to do. As he hears the voices that are already near—"Piapiá"—he pricks his immobile ears toward the bundle for a long while; and finally reassured, he decides to pass between the post and the man lying down, who has already rested.

The relationship between the two works is easier to discern when we examine the end of "Las moscas," which is without a doubt a polemical rewriting of the denouement just cited:

Amodorradas en el monte por el ámbito de fuego, las moscas han tenido, no sé cómo, conocimiento de una presa segura en la vecindad. Han olido ya la próxima descomposición del hombre sentado, por caracteres inapreciables para nosotros—tal vez en la exhalación a través de la carne de la médula espina cortada. Han acudido sin demora y revolotean sin prisa, midiendo con los ojos las proporciones del nido que la suerte acaba de deparar a sus huevos. . . .

Mas he aquí que esta ansia desesperada de resistir se aplaca y cede el paso a una beata imponderabilidad. No me siento ya un punto fijo en la tierra, arraigado a ella por gravísima tortura. Siento que fluye de mí como la vida misma, la ligereza del vaho ambiente, la luz del sol, la fecundidad de la hora. Libre del espacio y el tiempo, puedo ir aquí, allá a este árbol, a aquella liana. Puedo ver, lejanísimo ya, como un recuerdo de remoto existir, puedo todavía ver, al pie de un tronco, un muñeco de ojos sin parpadeo, un espantapájaros de mirar vidrioso y piernas rígidas. Del seno de esta expansión, que el sol dilata desmenuzando mi conciencia en un billón de partículas, puedo alzarme y volar, volar . . .

Y vuelo, y me poso con mis compañeras sobre el tronco caído, a los rayos del sol que prestan su fuego a nuestra obra de renovación vital. (2: 606–607)

Drowsy because of the fiery atmosphere, the flies have discovered—I do not know how—a sure prey in the vicinity. They have already smelled, through signs incomprehensible to us, the impending decomposition of the sitting man—perhaps because of the spinal fluid escaping through the skin. They have gathered without delay and are flying around unhurriedly, measuring with their eyes the size of the nest for their eggs that chance has just provided them. . . .

Yet I notice that this desperate yearning to resist becalms and gives way to a blessed imponderable thought. I no longer feel like a fixed point on the ground, rooted there by a most grave torture. I feel that like life itself, the lightness of the atmospheric vapor, the sunlight, the hour's fecundity, everything is flowing from me. Freed from space and time, I can go here, there, to this tree, to that vine. I can see, very far away now, like a memory of a remote existence, a doll with unblinking eyes at the foot of a tree trunk, a scarecrow with glass eyes and rigid legs. From this expanse, which the sun magnifies, splintering my conscience into a billion particles, I can rise and fly, fly . . .

And I fly, and I perch with my comrades on the fallen trunk, under the sunlight that lends its fire to our work of vital renewal.

The death with which "El hombre muerto" ended appeared to be de-scribed—and the redundancy is appropriate here—as the end of existence. The unfettered and flying imagination of the character in the first story only serve to give a more pathetic cast to his vulnerability and impotence in the face of death. At the same time, the shift of narrative attention to the horse confirms the man's expiration through the description of the horse's challenging of an authority that the man, while alive, had exercised over the animal. In contrast, in "Las moscas" the protagonist's decease is presented simply as a transition: consciousness has the ability to transcend the end of bodily life, transferring itself to a fly that, in what the narrator calls an "act of vital renewal," is about to feed and eventually feed its larvae alongside its companions on the fallen man's cadaver. The story thus projects a kind of materialistic pantheism that points to a survival of the spirit based on the indestructibility of matter even as it decomposes. In the writing of "Las moscas" Quiroga uses multiple changes in the narrative point of view precisely to underscore that fluidity in the meta-morphosis of both matter and conscience. Nevertheless, the story is not particularly remarkable or original, either as eschatological philosophy or as a literary creation. In spite of that, I would like to propose that in the transformation that it evinces in its conception of death, a transformation that obtains in a work that presents itself explicitly as the rewriting of an earlier text, there is a key to the fundamental question of inconsistency noted earlier between Quiroga's literary praxis and his rhetoric of the short story.

In the writing of "Las moscas" the two practices that transgress Qui-roga's narrative poetics come together: proleptic knowledge of the de-nouement, on the one hand, and superfluous supplementarity to the end-ing, on the other. That is, "Las moscas: réplica de 'El hombre muerto' " denies from its inception its sui generis nature, its organic and particular economy, announcing from its very title that it is nothing more than a simple facsimile, a "réplica" or copy of an earlier model. Additionally, because it is the re-elaboration of a preceding text, it calls into question the presumed completeness and organicity of the original story. Moreover, this double infraction occurs in a narrative whose express purpose is to formulate explicitly an argument against death understood as the extinction of the personality. In other words, in the space between "El hombre muerto" and "Las moscas" Quiroga transgressed the fundamental principles of his own narrative theory; but in that same space the author represents—in the dramatic sense of the word—the possibility of transcending individual death, that event which in the earlier story had been described as the absolute limit of existence. Hence, the writing of "Las moscas" simultaneously effects two operations: a reformulation of the concept of death, on the one hand, but through a transgression of Quiroga's rhetorical precepts, on the other. This conclusion will allow us to begin to understand the inconsistencies that I have shown between Quiroga's narrative theories and his literary praxis.

The characterization of the ending of the story as the narrative's absolute telos led Quiroga to identify death as the essential component of his narrative craft. Quiroga intuited early on that death represented a narrative device perfectly suited to the economic and teleological requirements of his poetics—a perfect trope to be used in the economic structuring of the story. This is why the demise of many of his protagonists coincides with the end of the narrative, or the story is sometimes radically condensed until it becomes solely the description of a process that leads inexorably to death. This also explains Quiroga's decision to move to the barely colonized region of Misiones, not in search of atmosphere and themes for a nativist praxis of literature, as some have suggested, but rather to create a narrative universe and a literary mask fraught with the constant and unexpected possibility of death.[16] Quiroga's self-internment in the jungle was more a rhetorical than a geographic journey, a voyage through the textual realms of literature and poetics rather than a displacement from the city to its savage antithesis.[17] Paradoxically, Quiroga's project to found a modern practice of writing led him to assume the persona of a man engaged in a primeval and premodern struggle with an unyielding and unforgiving nature.

Quiroga understood his literary modernity as a practice of literature founded on the knowledge of the poetics of the modern short story—a knowledge that he had acquired from the study of his acknowledged metropolitan master, as well as through his acquaintance with modes of knowledge derived from the existence of modern technological objects. One can also see this penchant for the modern in his spirited and early defense of film at a time in which the medium was being written off by most of his contemporaries as devoid of artistic possibilities.[18] But true to the dialectics that I have endeavored to identify in this book, Quiroga's formulation of a rhetoric of the short story—his undertaking to become a modern writer—was accompanied by a simultaneous distancing from the demands and strictures of a poetics singularly identified with the modern. This retreat from modernity manifests itself as those instances in which Quiroga openly takes leave from the requirements of the poetics of the short story as he had formulated them in his rhetorical prescriptions for the genre. The result is narratives that may have forsaken their exemplarity, their adherence to a poetics, but that nonetheless derive their considerable power from the impossible rhetorical struggle being waged in their midst. The intensity of Quiroga's short stories may be attributable in the final analysis to the internal rhetorical conflict around which they are articulated, a conflict in which there is a sort of death perennially lurching: the death that comes with the threat of being an echo of someone else's voice.

Indeed, the question of authority lies at the heart of Quiroga's paradoxical and discordant praxis of the short story. To understand this statement fully, one only has to consider the following insightful comment by Ross Chambers on the nature of narrative in general:

> To the extent that the act of narration is a process of disclosure in which the information that forms the source of narrative authority is transmitted to the narratee, the narrator gives up the basis of his or her authority in the very act of exercising it. This is not unlike the well-known paradox of the teacher, who, to the extent that he or she is successful in educating the young, thereby renders them independent of the need of education and hence less likely to accord their educator the authorization to teach. There is no need to insist in the various well-known "tricks of the trade," used by teacher and by narrator, to "maintain interest," as it is called: divulgence is never complete, the telling of the ultimate secret is indefinitely deferred—and it most often transpires, in art as in education, that there *is* no ultimate secret. The fact does remain, however, that at the end of a "successful" narration, the interest that authorized the act of narration has been destroyed.[19]

In the narrative power game described by Chambers, the narrator's authority is sustained by holding back the final revelation of the secret from the reader in order to impel him or her to persevere until the end. But within the situation envisioned by that game, could it not be said that Quiroga's continual revelation of his narrative endings evinces a subjectivity that understands itself as located beyond questions of authority or impugnation? Is this a narrator whose dominion places him in a position of uncontested and incontestable control? In this game, the real winner would be the person who would not have to play the game at all.[20]

In sum, the dynamics of attraction and distancing from the modern that I am tracing here played itself out in Quiroga as the concurrent espousal and abandonment of his poetics of the short story, a poetics that revolved around death as a structuring device. Yet if we recall the details of Quiroga's startling biography, the articulation of his literary practice around the concept of death could not have been sensed by him as anything other than a conflictive and troubling circumstance. In this biographical register Quiroga's disregard of the dictates of his own poetics acquires a different significance, but one as compelling as the one identified earlier; for through this transgressive literary practice Quiroga sought to transcend the total annihilation to which he otherwise condemned his characters. The specificity of the two transgressive procedures in Quiroga's work becomes absolutely transparent from this perspective. We had observed earlier how Quiroga threatened his story—and, by extension, himself—with death when he revealed the story's ending at the beginning—that ending toward which any effective story should be unerringly directed, according to his theory. But clearly, this is a death whose defeat is represented again and again by the very materiality of writing: by simply existing, the story itself gives testimony of the author's victory over the precipice with which he himself has threatened his own rhetorical existence and that of his work. The second transgressive practice, articulated as an addendum that serves as a coda to what is in effect the story's conclusion, infringes on the required nec plus ultra quality of the ending; yet by its very supplementary nature, the statement that closes the story indicates a transcendence of the final silence and the narrative stasis of the end. Thus, while in his stories Quiroga depicted situations that revolve around death or that lead inevitably to it, he also repeatedly dramatized in them the spectacle of the author's death and resurrection. The disjunction that exists between Quiroga's poetics of short narrative and his practice of writing opens up in his work a rhetorical space in which an eschatological drama is being staged time and again. In his repeated violation of the dictates of his own narrative theory, Quiroga continually sacrifices himself and is reborn in a salvific rite of his own creation. Death is exorcized in Quiroga's work through the violent rhetorical stratagem analyzed here, a stratagem that results in the existence of an unbridgeable abyss in his literary praxis, and not—as critics have maintained for many years—through its obsessive representation in his works.

In the context of all of the above, the almost total abandonment of the literary métier that characterized Quiroga's last years (preceded by an unfruitful attempt to return to obsolete *modernista* formulas) could be seen in an entirely different light. If, as I have proposed, Quiroga used writing metaphorically to keep death at bay, then his eventual suicide would constitute not the closing of a life cycle but rather a corroboration—redundant as any verification necessarily is—of a death that had already occurred years earlier. But perhaps this is where Quiroga's final triumph lies: his biological death was merely an addendum, a superfluous coda to that other death—the real one perhaps—the one he had forged and summoned to himself earlier in renouncing writing altogether.

The Peruvian author Mario Vargas Llosa is the subject of our next chapter. In a variation of the predicament we have seen in Quiroga, in Vargas Llosa's fiction we shall examine the way in which the espousal of an ideology of literature that is identified with modernity—in this case literary postmodernity—is countered by a persistent and invariant recourse to an antithetical performance of textual form.

CHAPTER SIX

The Elementary Structure of Kinship
Vargas Llosa's *La tía Julia y el escribidor*

We have invented the creation of forms: and that is why everything that falls
from our weary and despairing hands must always be incomplete.
          —Georg Lukács, *The Theory of the Novel*

LA TIA JULIA Y EL ESCRIBIDOR is widely regarded to be representative of a significant transformation that occurred in Vargas Llosa's literary production—a shift that purportedly had begun with the author's previous novel, *Pantaleón y las visitadoras*, published in 1973.[1] This "new" phase of Vargas Llosa's novelistic production is considered as having marked the inflection in his works of some of the qualities and concerns that are understood to be characteristic of literary postmodernism: humor, the literary exploration and exploitation of low cultural discourses, the undermining of the novelistic subject as an organizing principle, the radical questioning of ideological commitment, and so on. The transformation in Vargas Llosa's writing is seen as having also occurred, around the same time, in the works of most of the writers of the so-called Spanish American boom: Gabriel García Márquez, Julio Cortázar, Carlos Fuentes, José Donoso, and others. Indeed, on the surface it seems difficult to posit a continuity between Fuentes's *La muerte de Artemio Cruz* and *La cabeza de la hidra*; between García Marquez's *Cien años de soledad* and *Crónica de una muerte anunciada*; or between Donoso's *El obsceno pájaro de la noche* and *El jardín de al lado*. Making the necessary adjustments, the qualities that I have already enumerated provide an adequate summary of the modifications registered in the writing of these authors. Those changes have served in turn as a context in which to understand and appreciate the production of other upcoming authors whose mode of writing was from the beginning inscribed in the new sensibility—Sarduy, Puig, Valenzuela,

Arenas—or to find a place for completely heterodoxal, sui generis texts such as Roa Bastos's *Yo el Supremo*. Perhaps predictably, the critical label "postboom" was coined and received wide circulation as a means to describe and encompass the various manifestations of the phenomenon.

The interpretation of the postboom as equivalent to the literary postmodernity of metropolitan circles is by now well entrenched in our discipline. For instance, Roberto González Echevarría's book *La ruta de Severo Sarduy* ends with a consideration of this very topic that begins as follows: "Pero antes, y para ver el fenómeno del post-Boom en un contexto que lo aclare un poco, consideramos los rasgos de un movimiento del que sin duda forma parte: el postmodernismo, o la literatura postmoderna. Veremos el postmodernismo a través de lo propuesto por el gran novelista norteamericano John Barth y el teórico francés Jean-François Lyotard."[2] [But first, and in order to see the phenomenon of the post-boom in a context that clarifies it, we shall consider the characteristics of a movement of which it is doubtless a part: postmodernism, or postmodern literature. We shall examine postmodernism through the writings of the great American novelist John Barth and the French theoretician Jean-François Lyotard.] The rubric "postboom" serves, then, not merely as a chronological marker, as a way to express that the literary production that it designates follows the boom in time; it is meant to convey as well the fact that this period is presumed to be the Spanish American rendition of literary postmodernity. Further, the argument has been taken backward to its logical conclusion, proposing an equivalence also between Anglo-American modernism and the literature of the boom.[3] This double periodization is taken almost as an article of faith in critical commentaries now, and several books and countless articles have been written that take it as their unquestioned point of departure.[4]

Nonetheless, I would like to interrogate the analogy that maps Spanish American postboom literary production onto metropolitan literary postmodernism through a close reading of one of the avowed exemplars of the postboom modality. My discussion of Vargas Llosa's *La tía Julia y el escribidor* will argue that while the author may have indeed proposed to inscribe his writing in a "postmodern" literary universe, the novel retreats in a surreptitious and significant fashion from the full implications of that stance. I am not concerned at this point with the issue of whether there is a Spanish American postmodernity or what its attributes may be: that subject will be confronted squarely in the next chapter. My interest here is to understand what results when a postmodern scriptural praxis is identified by a Spanish American author as a discursive paradigm to replicate on account of its presumed modernity. In this regard, literary postmodernism can be considered the latest acceptation of modernity for Spanish America and can therefore be seen to be implicated in the rhetorical crisis that I am examining in this work.

Most critical considerations of Vargas Llosa's *La tía Julia y el escribidor* converge on the work's manifestly dual nature, that is, on the very conspicuous fact that the novel consists of two well-defined tracts or textual divides. The first of these comprises an account of the narrator's secret affair with, and subsequent matrimony to, a divorced aunt by marriage twelve years his senior; the vicissitudes that befall the couple during their elopement; and the familial scandal that the union precipitates. The other register is a textual rendition of the essential story lines of a number of radio soap operas produced by the *escribidor* in the novel's title, a remarkable, driven man by the name of Pedro Camacho. These begin as discrete narratives, only to deteriorate subsequently into a chaotic mélange of characters and plots. In a desperate attempt to wipe the slate clean, Camacho proceeds to concoct outlandish situations that somehow allow him to bring his characters together, just to have them perish in the midst of the most improbable and apocalyptic cataclysms. The novel's concluding installment serves as a coda to the events depicted in earlier chapters: many years later the narrator has become a successful and established writer who lives in Europe, has divorced his older aunt, and has remarried, this time to a younger cousin. During a visit to his country there is a chance meeting with Camacho; the erstwhile prolific scribbler is now reduced to the condition of simple gofer for a third-rate sensationalist rag in Lima.

Yet what is perhaps most singularly striking about these two textual levels is that despite the strict parallelistic structure of the novel, they seem on the surface not to have too much in common. Some critics have endeavored to resolve this perplexing circumstance by pointing to the fact that after a while the adolescent's affair with his aunt begins to take all the trappings of one of Camacho's melodramatic and passionate plots, a resemblance that is in fact commented on by a number of the novel's characters, including Aunt Julia herself: " 'Los amores de un bebe y una anciana que además es algo así como su tía,—me dijo una noche la tía Julia, mientras cruzábamos el Parque Central. 'Cabalito para un radioteatro de Pedro Camacho.' " ['The love affair of a baby and an old lady who's also more or less his aunt,' Aunt Julia said to me one night as we were crossing the Parque Central. 'A perfect subject for one of Pedro Camacho's serials.']⁵ In this way, the presumably self-evident distinction between autobiographical account of experience and formulaic soap opera model is shaken and overturned. This commingling would seem to point to the inevitable reduction of experience through emplotment or, conversely, to the realization that there is no such thing as a personal experience that is not already perceived from within a framework provided by autobiographical plot. The novel would appear to suggest that for all our pretensions, the plots that we use to make sense of our lives (or our recollections of them) are finally not that different from Camacho's bizarre creations. Furthermore, given the high culture/popular culture dichotomy evidently at work in the novel—as represented by the sort of writer that Varguitas eventually becomes versus the writer as embodied by Camacho and his tempestuous inventions—there would seem to be in the text a deliberate attempt to question the very tenability of that distinction, since the narrative mechanisms at work in both scriptural modalities can be shown to be analogous once they are reduced to their essential components. In this respect *La tía Julia y el escribidor* could be read as an example of a more general tendency within postmodern literature that seeks to explode the chasm between high and low cultures through the use of popular forms and discourses for the production of objects that can ostensibly claim to belong to high literary culture.⁶

But even though such an interpretation of the relationship between the two levels of the narrative may indeed be practicable, I would like to argue that this connection can be more profitably examined in the context delimited by what I believe to be the story at the heart of *La tía Julia y el escribidor*: the story about the coming to being of a writer; about how Varguitas, the young fledgling artist, becomes Vargas Llosa, the established and successful creator who makes his appearance in the last pages of the novel.⁷ For whatever examination there may be of the formal and discursive issues mentioned earlier, there is also in *La tía Julia y el escribidor* an exploration of the requirements of writing and storytelling: the unstinting commitment to one's work, the techniques that make for an effective story, the elements that advance the action and keep the reader's interest engaged.⁸ Camacho's soap opera plots are indeed hackneyed and predictable, but therein lies their strength as well, since they operate at the most essential level of continuity, expectation, and readerly satisfaction; they work as narratives precisely because they remain at this basic stratum of story-crafting. Furthermore, Camacho is also an example of how being a writer is an activity—a consuming passion and an obsessive engaging in the act of writing. These are perhaps the most important lessons learned by the aspiring writer Varguitas, who is seen throughout the novel posing as a writer rather than writing, and concocting the most intricate stories that finally amount to nothing because he has not yet learned the elementary principle of storytelling: that the reader's attention has to be captured and sustained if the work is going to be read at all.

But from this same perspective *La tía Julia y el escribidor* would also have to be interpreted as a cautionary tale. For though Camacho is at first a model of effective composition (with respect to productivity, not necessarily quality) and of consummate commitment to his métier, the novel also chronicles just as carefully his gradual coming apart as a writer, a process that culminates in his total mental collapse and his complete abandonment of writing as an endeavor. Hence, at another level Camacho seems to operate as a counterexample, as a case study of how a writer can self-destruct by allowing his personal demons to take over his productive life. The desire to address this ambivalence in the novel's depiction of Camacho's writing activity is one of the motivations for this study. My overarching aim, though, is to analyze in some detail Vargas Llosa's parable of how a writer is formed, as a means of conceptualizing in a novel fashion the juxtaposition of the two planes whose exact alternation results in the text that concerns us. Simply stated, my reading would like to account for the relationship of mutual implication and supplementarity between the two seemingly unrelated stories told in the novel, a relationship that is heralded from the outset by the title, *La tía Julia Y el escribidor*. My point of departure is another text by Vargas Llosa that shows the unmistakable signs of repression at work in his own discourse on the novel.

In an interview granted shortly before the publication of *La tía Julia y el escribidor*, Vargas Llosa found an opportunity to speak at length about his recently completed work. Some of his remarks regarding the novel are of interest not because they afford any especially penetrating insights into it but rather because of the very superficiality with which the author refers to his text. The first of these, which is reproduced here at length for reasons that will become obvious later, concerns the inspiration for the character of Pedro Camacho as represented in *La tía Julia y el escribidor*:

Vargas Llosa: Well, it took shape, like almost everything I've written, from my old memories. In this case, memories of the year that I worked for Radio Panamericana in Lima, that is, 1953, or '54. I've always remembered this period as linked to a man who used to work, not for Radio Panamericana where I was in charge of news bulletins, but for a neighboring radio station, Radio Central, which was also owned by the owners of Radio Panamericana. This fellow was quite a colorful person who wrote all the scripts for the soap operas which were the highlight of Radio Central programming. He was a Bolivian, and had been brought to Lima by the proprietors of the radio station, the Delgado Parker brothers, because in Bolivia he was an "ace" in all that concerned soap operas and melodramatic theater. He was in charge of all the soap operas at the radio station, not only writing the scripts but also directing and acting the male leads. He was truly a picturesque character who worked like a slave, who had an extraordinary sense of professional responsibility, and who was very absorbed by his role as writer and performer. But at the same time, judging him from a literary perspective, shall we say, he was a sort of parody or caricature, a pedestrian, twisted and somewhat pathetic version of a "writer." Still, the man was truly quite popular. I understand that his soap operas were a real success on Radio Central. . . . Well, something happened to Raúl Salmón, something between the comic and the tragic: he went insane. But the way in which his insanity was revealed was rather amusing, because it happened through his listeners. One day, Radio Central began to receive letters, telephone calls, and all sorts of protests from listeners of the soap operas who were discovering gross incongruities and incoherences in the scripts: soap opera characters would change names or professions or would even skip around from one soap opera to another. And so, because enormously bizarre and extravagant things began to happen in Raúl Salmón's scripts, the owners of the radio station discovered that he was undergoing some sort of crisis. They spoke to him about it. As a result, Salmón nervously started to conjure up in his scripts a series of catastrophes designed to kill off the characters he could no longer keep separate in his mind, so that he could begin anew with a clean slate. But in the end there was no way out: Raúl Salmón had to go off to a hospital to recuperate. His story always stuck with me and I kept thinking that I would some day write something related to it. *Actually that tale is the most remote origin of this novel. Naturally, that entire story is quite transformed in my book, where it can only be discerned as a sort of embryonic vestige.* (Oviedo, "A conversation," 154–56, my emphasis)

Any reader of *La tía Julia y el escribidor* will realize immediately that Vargas Llosa's closing statement is inaccurate to the point of being outright interesting. For what precedes it, contrary to the author's final assertion, is a perfect summary of the novel's depiction of Pedro Camacho and his misfortunes. And yet he feels compelled to clarify, seemingly as an afterthought, that there is hardly any relationship between this story and the one detailed in the novel because the original anecdote has been radically changed. He proposes that the earlier tale only serves in reality as a "remote" source that can be likened to the undifferentiated matter of an embryo when compared to the final version recounted in the text. Likewise, Vargas Llosa's account of the other story told by *La tía Julia y el escribidor*, that of Varguitas's romance with his aunt, is couched in the same absolute terms, but this time with the intention of alleging the existence of a perfect consonance between autobiographical experience and novelistic account:

> Vargas Llosa: After giving it a great deal of thought—because this novel has been a project of mine, like I told you, for a long time—when I began to try to shape it, to give form to the story, it occurred to me that in order for it not to be excessively abstract, for it not to take place in a realm of purely mental games, of delirious fantasy, it might be balanced by a realistic story, that is, by a more ordinary, more direct one; a story more of lived experience than of fantasy or imagination. Then I thought of this: why couldn't the story of Raúl Salmón be combined with a story born of personal experience? The Raúl Salmón story happened during a very important time in my life because, in the first place, it was at that time that after feeling the urge for years, my vocation was decided, although until then I had not dared to pursue it totally. Secondly, it was then that I got married for the first time, and that marriage was in certain ways a very daring act, because I was only 18, and also because it caused me many practical and even family problems. *Then it occurred to me that the delirious stories of the protagonist who writes melodramas and who has a disturbed imagination could perhaps be intertwined with a story which was precisely the opposite, something absolutely objective and absolutely true.* I would narrate *exactly* some episodes of my own life that would cover several months. (Oviedo, "A Conversation," 156, my emphasis)

Vargas Llosa's assertion here of absolute objectivity in his retelling of the *affaire d'amour* with his aunt is an affirmation that, because of its insistence and formulaic nature, sounds more like a protestation of truthfulness than a statement of fact: "something absolutely objective and absolutely true." One could immediately question this claim by simply pointing to the existence of another version of the affair, written by Vargas Llosa's first wife, which sought to correct and amplify on the facts as depicted by the author in his novel and which carried the obviously contestatory title of *Lo que Varguitas no dijo* [*What Varguitas Forgot to Say*].[9] Furthermore, and

more significant still, the belief on which the declaration is predicated—
the presumed possibility of a perfectly objective and accurate account of
experience—is one whose naïveté is especially surprising, considering that
Vargas Llosa's novelistic production and critical oeuvre could be said to
be a continual and relentless undermining of the very assurance displayed
by that phrase. One has only to think of the experiments with narrative
fragmentation and perspectivism in the earlier novels that have culmi-
nated in the constructivist outlook on history and experience that is advanced by *La verdadera historia de Mayta*, *¿Quién mató a Palomino Molero?*,
and *La guerra del fin del mundo*, or to consider Vargas Llosa's numerous
critical essays on literature in which the novel is characterized as an un-
repentant purveyor of falsehoods. Therefore, in Vargas Llosa's characterization of Camacho's story we have the assertion that there is nothing
in common between biographical experience and literary creation except
in the incongruous form of a synopsis of that "original" story that only
manages to repeat down to its most minute details the account produced
by the text.[10] By the same token, regarding Aunt Julia's tale it could be
argued that the "absolute objectivity" that the author would claim for his
literary depiction of it is rendered problematic not only by the existence
of a contrasting and competing version but also because the simple con-
cordance between lived experience and text that Vargas Llosa invokes is
denounced as simplistic by the remainder of his own literary and critical
production.

One can infer from these two contradictory and tortuous rhetorical
maneuvers that the distinction that Vargas Llosa's statement is trying to
establish—the *fabricated* story of the scriptwriter versus the *objective*, truthful account of the affair with Aunt Julia—is, in fact, an attempt to suppress
a more essential resemblance between them: a similarity that is not, however, related to the degree of accuracy or fictionality that is supposedly
intrinsic to each plot. In my view the two stories appear alongside one
another in the novel not because they strike a balance between fiction
and reality as Vargas Llosa would have it but rather because *together* they
weave the real story, the surreptitious subject of *La tía Julia y el escribidor*—
the account of a writer's coming into being. That is to say, the copula of
the title denotes a mutual imbrication of the two stories, as opposed to
being reflective of their parallel yet separate presence in the novel. This
is why these two dissimilar stories are nonetheless presented in the novel
as beginning and ending at precisely the same time: "Recuerdo muy bien
el día que me habló del fenómeno radiofónico porque ese mismo día, a

la hora de almuerzo, vi a la tía Julia por primera vez" (16). [I remember very well the day he spoke to me of the genius of the airwaves [Camacho], because that very day, at lunchtime, I saw Aunt Julia for the first time (7).] And it is also why their coevalness is continuously underscored: "En nuestras andanzas nocturnas, la tía Julia me resumía a veces algunos episodios que la habían impresionado y yo le contaba mis conversaciones con el escriba, de modo que, insensiblemente, Pedro Camacho pasó a ser un componente de nuestro romance" (113). [During our nocturnal rambles, Aunt Julia sometimes gave me a résumé of certain episodes that had impressed her, and I in turn gave her a rundown of my conversations with the scriptwriter, and thus, little by little, Pedro Camacho became a constituent element in our romance (91).] Hence, the narration of Camacho's travails and the tale of Marito's affair with his aunt should be read concurrently, as complements of one another. The specific nature of that convergence and what it intimates about Vargas Llosa's ideology of literature will be addressed later. My discussion borrows its form from the novel's strictly sustained alternation between the two stories.

The Scriptwriter

What is, finally, the story told by the even-numbered chapters of *La tía Julia y el escribidor*? Each one of the nine episodes begins anew with a different tale altogether, as if to settle from the outset that whatever continuity may exist between them does not reside at the level of plot. In this way, the reader is immediately thrust into a critical frame of mind where stylistic, linguistic, and psychological constants become more noticeable, on account of the realization that what is being read are repeated opening instances of an identical discursive performance. This deemphasizing of *histoire* and the concomitant displacement of attention to the particularities of *récit* advances the proposition that in the final analysis the "protagonist" of the story told by the even chapters of the novel is Camacho himself, the anchoring figure for the discursive traits thus underscored. But if that is the case it must also be concluded that the "plot," the meaning of this tale, is the progressive deterioration of Camacho's authorial capabilities: from being a creator in full control of his exacting métier to becoming a desperate writer whose only hope of regaining command lies in the painstaking destruction of everything he has begotten.

Now, I would argue that however one might interpret the decline of Camacho's powers or whatever lessons one might wish to draw from it, there is in the text a correlation between the scriptwriter's collapse and the first-person narrator's rise to a position of discursive authority.[11] If we consider that Camacho's first action in the novel is to appropriate Marito's writing instrument—his typewriter (24)—the diametrical reversal of authorial fortunes with which *La tía Julia y el escribidor* ends acquires a particular significance. After Camacho's mental breakdown Varguitas literally takes over his place at the radio station, charged now with the responsibility of assembling the serials that will be broadcast to replace Camacho's creations. Talking about his new responsibilities at the station and the numerous part-time jobs he contracts in order to support himself and his new wife, Varguitas says that "Con estos trabajos, (que me hacían sentir, un poco, émulo de Pedro Camacho) logré triplicar mis ingresos" (422). [Thanks to all these jobs (which made me feel something like a rival of Pedro Camacho), I contrived to triple my income (351).] Significantly enough, the first thing he does with this income is to redeem his typewriter, which he had pawned earlier (422). But this substitution is accompanied by another supplanting that is structural in nature: the young writer in the end also appropriates for his autobiographical narrative the twentieth and last chapter of the novel, one whose subject matter should have been Camacho's oeuvre, on the basis of the rigorous alternation that has dominated the text until that very juncture. This leaves little reason to doubt that in the contest between textual registers that is implicitly set up by the novel's design, the surviving voice is that of the adolescent now transformed into an established writer. Moreover, in this concluding chapter the first-person narrator manages to deliver the final blow to the scriptwriter by explaining away Camacho's power, his erstwhile envied prodigious capacity for production, as grounded on the inadequate repression of an altogether sordid set of personal circumstances.

Perhaps the clearest indication yet of the connection between the constitution of the autobiographical narrator as a writer and the process through which Camacho becomes undone as a creator can be gleaned from a direct consideration of the even-numbered chapters in the novel. Most commentators have tended to attribute these to Camacho and have subsequently endeavored to compose an artistic and psychological profile of the scriptwriter on the basis of the textual consistencies that they exhibit. But although the subject matter is unequivocally Camacho's radio serials, it is also clear that these are not the actual scripts over which the Bolivian is seen laboring so feverishly in the novel, since they are not written in the dialogic format characteristic of the serial genre. They are, rather, condensed prose renditions of the material broadcast over the radio by Camacho and his group of devoted collaborators. The resulting question regarding the provenance of these chapters can be resolved textually only by proposing that the even-numbered chapters of *La tía Julia y el escribidor*, the "Camacho" installments of the novel, are authored by the aspiring writer Marito, who has produced them as exercises for mastering the craft of storytelling. This interpretation had been originally advanced by Vargas Llosa himself: "Pedro Camacho is a natural storyteller without any kind of sophistication, a genius at that level, with a tremendous capacity to transform reality and fiction into his own form. The other, Varguitas, wants to be a writer but is self-critical. This rigor, in this case, is a kind of impotence. He wants to write a story, while Pedro is pouring out all kinds of dramas and catastrophes. Pedro's dramas are not presented in scripts but are described by Varguitas, who transforms them. That is the apprenticeship he passes through" (Ruas 1982: 15).[12] Vargas Llosa's account of the *purpose* of Marito's transcriptions does not stand to reason, since it would have the young writer apprenticing from a creator who is being characterized at the same time as progressively losing control of his métier. Yet it observes a strangely perfect consonance with the argument that I am developing here. For when viewed from that perspective the even-numbered chapters of the novel become a metaphor for the relationship that links the narrator's attainment of his final status as author to the scriptwriter's decline: Varguitas's final mastery of his craft is achieved through the telling of the story of Camacho's demise as a creator. In this manner, authorship and writing as an activity are linked in an essential fashion to the symbolic murder of a rival, a forerunner whose place and voice the aspiring writer must appropriate for himself as a necessary stratagem for the constitution of his authorial persona.[13] In this agonistic view of the universe of discourse, becoming a writer is equated not just with the claiming of a space of one's own but also with the vanquishing of one's precursors. Such an explicitly oedipal conception of the literary act will be shown to find its just complement in the autobiographical narrative that unfolds in the odd-numbered chapters of the novel.

Aunt Julia

I do not think it difficult to argue that there is a relationship between Varguitas's ascendence to the status of writer and the development of his liaison with Aunt Julia. Marito's apprenticeship of literature is depicted in the novel as shadowing closely his apprenticeship of sexuality and romantic love. Nonetheless, what is being proposed in these chapters is not simply the existence of a correspondence between sexuality and creation, between carnal knowledge and textual wisdom—although Camacho's uncompromising forsaking of sex would appear to lend some credence to that view! At the risk of stating the obvious, it must be underscored that Marito's love object is not just any woman, but his aunt Julia, somebody who is related to him through ties of kinship. The significance of this peculiar selection is amply confirmed toward the end of the text by the narrator's choice of a second wife, this time a first cousin by the name of Patricia. Just as important, though, there is throughout the novel a marked emphasis on the relations of kinship that bind the narrator to his immediate and extended family, ties that spread seemingly in all directions within the city. The narrator lives with his maternal grandparents at the time of the events depicted and meets with other members of his family on a regular and almost ritualistic basis: "Escribía en casa de mis abuelos, a mediodía y en las noches. Esa semana no almorcé donde ninguno de mis tíos, ni hice las visitas acostumbradas a las primas" (59). [I wrote at my grandparents' house, during my lunch hours and at night. During that week I didn't drop in at any of my uncles' houses for the midday meal, and skipped my usual visits to my girl cousins (44).] In all, seventeen aunts, uncles, and cousins either appear directly or are mentioned in the text.[14] Furthermore, it almost seems as if every person outside the immediate family that is remarked on in the novel turns out to be a relative of sorts. For instance: "Hubo una conspiración perfecta para obligarme a casar por la Iglesia, en la que estuvo involucrado hasta el arzobispo de Lima (era, por supuesto, pariente nuestro)" (430). [There was a perfect planned conspiracy to force me to marry in the church, in which even the Archbishop of Lima was involved (he was, it goes without saying, a relative of ours)" (358).] Other examples are Guillermo Osores, "un médico vagamente relacionado con la familia" (118) [a physician who was some sort of distant family relation (155)]; and Senator Adolfo Salcedo, "emparentado de algún modo con la tribu familiar" (60) [distantly related to the familial tribe (45)]. It is not surprising, then, that the protagonist should borrow from the lexicon of ethnological investigation to refer to his family. In at least two occasions he describes his parentage as a *tribu* (60), another time as a *clan* (241), and later as his *selvática parentela* (431). The reader will also remember that the father-son duo that owns the two radio stations, Radio Panamericana and Radio Central, are referred throughout the novel as Genaro-papá and Genaro-hijo. The result of this insistence on familial relations is that the narrator is depicted as moving within a social and affective universe where kinship is both the organizing paradigm and the *doxa*, the indisputable ideological belief-system under which everything else is subsumed.

It is precisely against that background that Marito's affair with Aunt Julia must be examined and against which it acquires its ultimate significance. In the choice of his aunt as an object of sexual desire, Varguitas transgresses the boundaries established by the laws of kinship in a cosmos where, as we have seen, kinship reigns supreme. But this breach is patently considered to be more dangerous by reason of what it connotes than because of the individual who is actually chosen by the transgressor; for what is clearly the burning issue in the family's preoccupation with the affair is not consanguinity—after all, Julia is only a relative by marriage and a foreigner to boot—but rather the couple's difference in age. Hence, the scandal, the disturbance created within the family by the liaison, is primarily attributable to another violation to which the romance alludes in a barely disguised fashion: the possibility of an incestuous relationship between mother and son. Indeed, in what could be regarded as an instance of reverse apophasis (mentioning by denying that one will mention), the text attempts to make light of this interpretation precisely by bringing it up: "La verdad es que estás hablando como si fueras mi mamá—le dije yo. Es que podría ser tu mamá—dijo la tía Julia" (194). ['The truth of the matter is that you're talking to me as though you were my mama.' I said to her. 'The fact is, I *could* be your mama,' Aunt Julia said (161).] And later: "Los munícipes, luego de revisar los documentos, solían hacerme bromas que eran patadas en el estómago: ¿pero cómo, quieres casarte con tu mamá?' " (331) [After looking over my papers, the functionaries would inevitably crack jokes at my expense that were like so many kicks in the belly: 'So you want to marry your mama, do you?' (274).] Understood in this vein, then, the even-numbered sections of the novel would delineate the successful seduction of a symbolic mother-figure by the aspiring writer and the linking of that accomplishment to the attainment of a position of authorial mastery.

One can now begin to discern the metaphoric connection that exists between this conclusion and the one reached earlier concerning the "Camacho" installments of the text. Before, we showed how those chapters told the story of a writer's rise as founded on a rival's silence, on his competitor's symbolic annihilation within what could be described as a zero-sum universe of discursive power. Now, this same process of empowerment is construed as implicating the transgressing of incest restrictions through a sexual liaison with an evident mother surrogate. Both of these symbolic acts of violence and infringement—murder and incest—are represented as making possible the birth of the writer. Authorship is thereby depicted as predicated fundamentally on transgression: the writer is envisaged as a breaker of rules and taboos, as an iconoclastic individual engaged in a struggle with both his literary precursors and the social conventions of his contemporaries. Such a conception of the writer is one that Vargas Llosa has advanced and expounded on in a number of his critical essays, as well as in his monographic studies on authors such as Flaubert and García Márquez.[15] Yet if one were to translate what happens in *La tía Julia y el escribidor* in terms of the oedipal scenario on the basis of which its allegorical tale of a writer's formation is formulated, it would appear that Oedipus *can* murder Laius *and* marry Jocasta without having to atone for his deeds through demotion and punitive self-injury. In the aftermath of this realization, however, an interesting question insinuates itself: is *La tía Julia y el escribidor* a statement on *poiesis* in the guise of an oedipal struggle, or could it be interpreted instead as the reverse—as an oedipal fantasy masquerading as the story of the formation of a writer? In order to explore this question, we will have to inquire into the particulars of another story, one that is carefully yet only partially cloaked in the body of Vargas Llosa's text.

The Father's Signature

After Marito's affair with his aunt becomes public (read familial) knowledge, his parents, who then reside in the United States, make a hasty return home to handle the situation. The mother is relatively swiftly mollified, but the father remains beside himself and beyond such easy assuagement. He composes a letter to his son where he informs him explicitly of his draconian intentions with respect to the entire matter:

> "En cuanto a ti, quiero que sepas que ando armado y que no permitiré que te burles de mí. Si no obedeces al pie de la letra y esa mujer no sale del país en el plazo indicado, te mataré de cinco balazos como a un perro, en plena calle."
>
> *Había firmado con sus dos apellidos y rúbrica y añadido una postdata*: "Puedes ir a pedir protección policial, si quieres. Y para que quede bien claro, aquí firmo otra vez mi decisión de matarte donde te encuentre como a un perro."

Y en efecto, había firmado por segunda vez, con trazo más enérgico que la primera.
(414, my emphasis)

"As for you, I should like to inform you that I am armed and will not allow you to make a fool of me. If you do not obey to the letter and this woman does not leave the country within the time limit that I have indicated above, I shall put five bullets through you and kill you like a dog, right in the middle of the street."

He had signed it with his two family names and added a postscript: "You can go ask for police protection if you wish. And to remove all possible doubts as to my intentions, I herewith affix my signature once again to my decision to kill you, wherever I find you, like a dog." *And he had indeed signed his name a second time, in an even bolder hand than the first time.* (345)

The threat associated with the father is identified here with the re-doubled affixing of the father's name, a repetition that is meant to vouch for the concreteness of the intentions that the signature subscribes. But just as clearly, the threat is signaled by what is described as the *full* rendering of that name, one that encompasses both of the father's family surnames—what in Spanish is commonly referred to as *el nombre con sus dos apellidos*. In this passage, the father's homicidal warning is considered somehow more imminent and real because of the use of his full name to underwrite the sincerity of his menace. This identification of the father's authority with his complete signature—the signature that includes both family names—becomes altogether significant if we take into consideration the important role played by kinship in the novel's universe. I would also like to suggest that this association can assist us in approaching another imperfectly concealed story, the one with which *La tía Julia y el escribidor* concludes: that of the narrator's subsequent wedding to a first cousin by the name of Patricia.

Marito's divorce from Aunt Julia and his second marriage to his cousin Patricia are significant events paradoxically dispensed with in the novel in but a few sentences: "Cuando la tía Julia y yo nos divorciamos hubo en mi dilatada familia copiosas lágrimas, porque todo el mundo (empezando por mi madre y mi padre, claro está) la adoraba. Y cuando, un año después, volví a casarme con una prima (hija de la tía Olga y el tío Lucho, qué casualidad) el escándalo fue menos ruidoso que la primera vez" (429). [When Aunt Julia and I were divorced, copious tears were shed in my vast family, because everyone (beginning naturally with my mother and father) adored her. And when, a year later, I married again, a cousin of mine this time (the daughter of Aunt Olga and Uncle Lucho, what a coincidence), it created less of an uproar within the family than the first time (358).] The expression "what a coincidence" would appear merely to refer to the fact that the same aunt-and-uncle couple has gone from being the narrator's former sister-and brother-in-law to being his new mother-and father-in-law. But, of course, it can also be read as remarking on the seemingly fortuitous circumstance that his second wife should turn out to be a *cousin*, when his first wife happened to be an *aunt*. Such an expression of surprise cannot conceal, however, the consistency in outcomes that it claims to dismiss as mere coincidence, since it serves to underscore the fact that both of the protagonist's choices of love object occur within the closed confines of a world securely bounded by relationships of kin. But how can this internal, endogamous displacement from aunt to cousin be interpreted in terms of the oedipal paradigm that was recognized earlier? The possibility of an answer begins to unfold when we examine the new genealogical arrangement produced by this latest marriage under the light of the previously gained insight: that in *La tía Julia y el escribidor*, the Father's authority is associated with his full name—with that version of his signature that comprises both of his family names.[16] An abbreviated diagram of the essential kinship relations instituted by the narrator's second matrimony would resemble Figure 1.

If we are attentive to the figurative link between the Father's signature and his authority that the novel establishes, one can argue that the narrator's marriage to his cousin provides the final turn in the oedipal fantasy that has been surveyed to this point. For through these nuptials Mario *Vargas Llosa* joins Patricia *Llosa* in a union that may produce a son who can only aspire to be, in name at least, a mere repetition of the father: *Vargas Llosa*. The result of this gambit is that the threat of the son ever overtaking his progenitor is thereby anticipated and canceled metaphorically. The novel becomes, then, a fantasy of triumphant oedipal desire from both sides of the oedipal paradigm: on the one hand, it depicts the emblematic vanquishing of the surrogate father by the son—Marito's supplanting of Pedro Camacho and his seduction of the surrogate mother figure—but also the symbolic annulment of the future oedipal threat represented by a grown man's son. In other words, the fanciful Oedipus portrayed in *La tía Julia y el escribidor* marries his mother and murders his father, and when he becomes an adult he also manages to preempt and neutralize the possibility of sharing Laius's fate at the hands of his own son. By means of this endogamous genealogical stroke the grown narrator's progeny is figuratively foreclosed from mounting any sort of effective

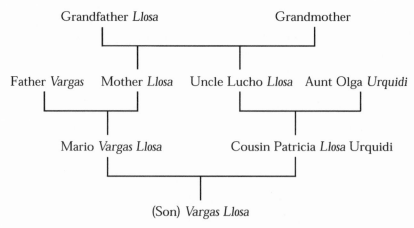

FIGURE 1. Kinship relations after Marito's second marriage

oedipal challenge, since he is always already condemned to merely repeat the Father's name—the very sign of the Father's authority.[17]

In Vargas Llosa's autobiographical accounts of how he became a writer, his father's figure has always loomed large. He has explained on a number of occasions that his father's injunction against writing (out of concern for his developing masculinity) turned literature into a forbidden and therefore secret endeavor: "[Writing] was one of the reasons why there were always disagreements between my father and myself. I used to write in Piura, I remember, and my grandparents, my uncles, applauded me for it. They thought it was cute. When my father discovered that inclination in me he was frightened. He thought something was seriously wrong. . . . So my vocation grew and solidified a bit secretly."[18] Hence, everything Vargas Llosa has ever written could be regarded in some respect as an act of defiance against his father. But I think we would be mistaken in taking this conflict to be the primordial subtext to which the oedipal struggle in *La tía Julia y el escribidor* alludes. For Vargas Llosa's account of his relationship with his father is simply yet another story of how the writer comes into being, a story that is identical in status to the one narrated by the novelistic text, regardless of its autobiographical and therefore avowedly privileged status. On the other hand, the oedipal story is a convenient cultural paradigm for the mise-en-scène that is—as we shall see—at the foundation of Vargas Llosa's conception of writing. Vargas Llosa has asserted that *La tía Julia y el escribidor* ultimately explores "something that has always fascinated me, something to which I devote most of my life but which I have never understood: Why do I write and what does writing mean?"[19] The statement allows us to conjecture that perhaps the novel can be read as providing some sort of answer to Vargas Llosa's perplexed rhetorical questions on writing.

As I have shown, *La tía Julia y el escribidor* enacts a triumphant fantasy of oedipal desire: the successful usurpation of the Father's place, and the self-constitution of the subject into an autonomous and invulnerable agent, one also made symbolically immune to the precise challenge he masterfully carried out. This last maneuver is projected into the text as the proleptic annulment of the son's difference from the Father; the son is compelled to assume the Father's last name, the sign of his authority. Yet this fantasy is conveyed as the story of a writer's acquisition of a persona, of a distinctive literary identity signified by the author's signature: *Vargas Llosa*.[20] The resulting juxtaposition provides an insight into the ideology of writing that underlies Vargas Llosa's textual production, one that could be described in the following terms: literary creation offers the ever renewed opportunity for the phantasmatic affirmation of a self-sufficient and sovereign subjectivity in the face of a persistent threat to the subject's autonomy and self-consistency. In the oedipal narrative of *La tía Julia y el escribidor*, and in Vargas Llosa's autobiographical statements, this threat is identified symbolically with the Father; but it would be more appropriate to construe it in discursive terms as the threat attached to the conception of the decentered subject advanced by the postmodernist aesthetics invoked by Vargas Llosa's text. As a means of warding off this peril, a praxis of writing is instituted that results in the composition of texts that are both warrantors of and monuments to the subjectivity that is responsible for their production. But it is important to understand how this subjectivity is inscribed in Vargas Llosa's texts, since that encoding is not accomplished through the conspicuous author surrogates of the narrator or the implied author. Instead, in Vargas Llosa the presence and authority of the writing subject is hypostatized into the discrete mechanism of textual generation that rules every one of his novels. This is the reason why, at the core of Vargas Llosa's works, there always lies ensconced an implacable and consistent textual machine whose "turns" generate the novel and whose specificity can be abstracted from each one of the texts that it has produced. One has only to think of the careful and almost mathematically parsed orchestration of fragments in *La Casa Verde* and *Conversación en La Catedral*, where specific characters or installments of stories succeed one another following a strict combinatory;[21] or the rigorous alternation of narrative material that creates the text of *La tía Julia y el escribidor*, as well as the more recent *El hablador* and *Elogio de la madrastra*. This is the origin of the "paired" titles shown by many of Vargas Llosa's works, both literary and critical: *La ciudad y los perros*, *Pantaleón y las visitadoras*, *La tía Julia y el escribidor*, *Katie y el hipopótamo*, *Contra viento y marea*, *La orgía perpetua: Flaubert y Madame Bovary*, *José María Arguedas: Entre sapos y halcones*. The complementarity that is announced already in the titles has its counterpart in most of these works in the alternation between two voices or registers that follow one another in a rigorous fashion until the end of the text. The result is that while Vargas Llosa's novels expressly underscore the limited, imperfect, and contingent nature of personal knowledge, the relentless and unwavering generative principle at work in those same texts bespeaks instead a subjectivity in full possession of its rhetorical prerogatives. Every one of Vargas Llosa's works engages in the re-creation of this subjectivity and in the affirmation of its concomitant authority. The reappearance of this mechanism in *La tía Julia y el escribidor* bespeaks the desire to reaffirm those prerogatives above and beyond the programmatic requirements of a postmodern aesthetics. This move—which constitutes Vargas Llosa's *clinamen* in his presumed adoption of a postmodern literary modality—accounts in turn for the difficulties that have invariably accompanied the attempts to subsume Vargas Llosa's recent production under the category of the postmodern, since in spite of the obvious superficial affinities his authoritative and centered discursive posture cannot be easily reconciled with the fundamental postmodern challenge to that very notion of the subject.[22]

Moreover, this interpretation of Vargas Llosa's conception of writing may also help us to understand the controversial political theses that he has propounded for a number of years now and that have brought him both to the forefront of ideological debate in Latin America and to Peru's 1990 presidential compaign. As is well-known, Vargas Llosa is one of a group of Latin American writers and intellectuals who have forsworn the Marxist agenda after a period of initial identification with the achievements and goals of the Cuban Revolution. Citing the moral, political, and economic bankruptcy of what he calls the "utopian" Left and the militaristic Right in Latin America, Vargas Llosa has argued repeatedly for the encouragement of private enterprise and, above all, for the establishment and protection of a free market of both commodities and ideas; an arena where individuals can transact economically and intellectually with a minimum of institutional intervention or obstacles, whether from the state bureaucrat or the revolutionary commissar.[23] In agreement with Fernand Braudel, Vargas Llosa envisions the historical beginnings of this market as "un espacio independiente y soberano donde la acción humana pudo volcarse sin acondicionamientos, en cierto modo desbocarse, de acuerdo sólo al interés y voluntad del individuo que ocurría a él para comprar o vender, para producir o consumir" (*Contra viento* 2:433) [an independent and sovereign space where human activity was allowed to take place, in a sense to boil over without impediment, guided only by the interest and will of the individual who arrived at it to buy or to sell, to produce or to consume]. And later Vargas Llosa adds: "El hombre ... adquiere una cara individual y un espacio propio sólo en los tiempos modernos, cuando la multiplicación de actividades y funciones económicas, sociales y artísticas no controladas ... estimularon la evolución del pensamiento filosófico y político hasta instituir esa noción que rompe con toda la tradición histórica de la humanidad: la de soberanía individual" (*Contra viento* 2:434). [Man ... acquires an individual face and a private space only in modern times, when the multiplicity of non-controlled economic, social and artistic activities and functions ... stimulated the evolution of philosophical and political thought until it arrived at that idea which breaks with the entire historical tradition of Mankind: the notion of individual sovereignty.]

Vargas Llosa's position is admirable in its consistency and courageous in its open espousal of ideas and projects opposite to those that have been traditionally judged politically suitable for a Latin American intellectual to promote. But could one not see in his conception of the market as a domain where free, autonomous subjects also freely assemble to transact in an unconstrained fashion another fantasy essentially similar to the one identified in *La tía Julia y el escribidor?* In other words, could it not be argued that the economic, political, and intellectual subject on which Vargas Llosa's political views are predicated is a repostulation of the self-fashioning and sovereign agent whose phantasmatic creation is portrayed in the text of *La tía Julia y el escribidor*, only that this time the fantasy is played out in the social realm and assumes the form of a convergence of similarly conceived and constituted subjects? The open market, rendered in this vision as a contest between two autonomous agents (a buyer and a seller), a contest ruled by the immutable and unwavering law of supply and demand, becomes, in fact, a text—a perfect analogue for a Vargas Llosa novel: a work where two or more characters, stories, or narrative levels vie for textual space in a contest orchestrated by the principle of textual generation—the textual machine—that controls every one of his works.

But if Vargas Llosa's economic and political views can be seen as analogues of his fictions, that very fact paradoxically relegates him to silence in the political arena, if we examine his own assertions on the nature and purpose of fictive creation. This injunction arises from his persistent characterization of fiction as a compensatory or consoling fantasy and of the dangers inherent in its indiscriminate use outside the realm of artistic creation. In spite of the profound transformations that have occurred in Vargas Llosa's political convictions, he has consistently proposed that the mainspring of fiction is an ineradicable discrepancy between reality and human desire. Most recently, in the prologue to *Kathie y el hipopótamo*, for instance, he has expressed this belief in the following manner:

> El abismo inevitable entre la realidad concreta de una existencia humana y los deseos que la soliviantan y que jamás podrá aplacar, no es sólo el origen de la infelicidad, la insatisfacción y la rebeldía del hombre. Es también la razón de ser de la ficción, mentira gracias a la cual podemos tramposamente completar las insuficiencias de la vida, ensanchar las fronteras asfixiantes de nuestra condición y acceder a mundos más ricos o más sórdidos o más intensos, en todo caso distintos del que nos ha deparado la suerte.[24]

> The inevitable abyss that exists between the concrete reality of human existence and the desires that inflame it and that it will never be able to quiet down is not only the origin of human unhappiness, dissatisfaction, and rebelliousness: it is also fiction's raison d'être, a lie thanks to which we can cheatingly complement the insufficiencies of life, broaden the asphyxiating limits of our condition, and have access to worlds that are richer, or more sordid, or more intense, but in any event different from the one that fortune has bestowed on us.

This discrepancy, he argues, is intrinsic to the human condition, and so is the desire to bridge the resulting chasm through the creation of fictional constructs. But Vargas Llosa has also cautioned against the attempts to impose fictions on reality, which in his view results in ideological dogma and utopian authoritarianism. To this pernicious form of compensatory fantasy he opposes the benign and harmless fabrication of literary or artistic (imaginative) creation. Fiction allows human beings to give free rein to their imaginings born of dissatisfaction with the real, but without the disastrous consequences that ensue when these same impulses are used to make demands on reality in the shape of ideological formulations. Vargas Llosa has warned,

Esta magia—abolir lo real y recrearlo con la fantasía—me parece muy respetable, y la practico con ardor, pues es lo que hacen los novelistas—todos los artistas—pero no es una práctica recomendable para quien quiere saber lo que está ocurriendo a su alrededor en el campo político y social y contribuir de manera efectiva-inmediata-a combatir, allí donde aparezca, alguno de los tentáculos de la hidra de la iniquidad. (*Contra viento* 2:100)

This magic act—abolishing the real and recreating it in the imagination—seems to me quite respectable, and I practice it passionately, since it is what novelists—all artists—do; but it is not an advisable practice for anyone who wants to be aware of what goes on around him in the political and social sphere and who wants to contribute in an effective, direct way to combat the hydra-head of iniquity, wherever its tentacles may show up.

And he avers that although the use of linguistic polysemy is admissible in literature, the same practice leads to chaos and social disintegration when employed outside the confines of the fictional:

[La] prestidigitación verbal es también respetable; ella es el fundamento de la literatura. Pero cuando se emplea esa técnica de la permutación fuera de la novela, el drama o la poesía, en el texto y el contexto político por ejemplo, algo gravísimo acontece: la moral humana se resquebraja y la solidaridad social se diluye. El resultado es la muerte del diálogo, el reino de la desconfianza, la pulverización de la sociedad en seres aislados y recelosos cuando no hostiles unos a otros." (*Contra viento* 2:101)[25]

Verbal prestidigitation is equally worthy; it is the foundation of literature. But when this technique of permutations is employed outside the novel, the play or the poem—in the political text or context, for instance—something very grave occurs: human morality breaks down and social solidarity dissolves. The result is the death of dialogue, the rule of mistrust, the crumbling of society into isolated and suspicious beings, if not openly hostile to one another.

Fiction's salutary value is therefore available only as long as it renounces the world. When the same compensatory impulse that is responsible for its existence is allowed to have an impact on the realm of the real the results are, as the last remarks make clear, apocalyptic. But if, as I have argued, there is a figural similarity between Vargas Llosa's fictional constructs and his ideological pronouncements, the latter become thoroughly compromised by his adamant requirement regarding the mutual exclusivity of the two. In the end the author's stricture that political advocacy be divorced from the stuff of literature returns to haunt him in the guise of the continuity that exists between his own political figurations and the rhetoric of his fictions.[26]

The self-inflicted crisis to which this last realization condemns Vargas Llosa's political discourse is indicative of the existence of a larger rhetorical disjunction underlying his writing, the one I have endeavored to trace throughout this book. Perennially faced with the imminent disallowance of his authority, the discursive predicament of the Spanish American subject makes exceedingly troubling Vargo Llosa's embracing of the postmodern ludic exploration of the subject's disappearance from language and the text. In other words, the casting off of the stable subject and its prerogatives is itself a prerogative of a stable subject, a description that does not reflect accurately the Spanish American discursive situation. Hence, the postmodern agenda presents the Spanish American writer with a multilayered and playful questioning of the subject's authority that he can only feel to be a parodic repetition of his own essential rhetorical condition. This is why, regardless of their overt posturing toward a postmodern aesthetics, Vargas Llosa's works from the 1970s onward engage time and again in a ritualistic reaffirmation of the subject's authority and centrality. Vargas Llosa's attempts to inscribe his novelistic production in the context of a postmodern praxis of literature account for the explicit transformation that took place in his writing, of which *La tía Julia y el escribidor* has been assumed to be an exemplary text. Yet our analysis has shown that this gesturing toward a postmodern aesthetics is made problematic by the existence of a dimension of the novel that expresses an ideology of the subject that is antithetical to postmodern expectations. The fable of authorship and authority that is told by Vargas Llosa's novel finds its correlative expression in its rigid, mechanical formalism, a structural trait that is also an invariant feature of his works. In Vargas Llosa's postboom, "postmodern" literary production the subject is, in the final analysis, not undermined or put in check; it is instead hypostatized into the textual "machine" that generates almost every one of his works. The humor of *La tía Julia y el escribidor* conceals finally a deadly serious struggle. The search for a "modern" writing leads the Spanish American subject to an appropriation of a postmodern literary aesthetics, a mirror in which he is finally confronted with the disturbing reflection of his discursive disempowerment.

If the essential rhetorical crisis of Spanish American cultural discourse is founded on a problematic relationship with modernity, the present questioning and undermining of the ideology of modernity must carry with it profound connotations for the Spanish American cultural enterprise. This is, in fact, the exploration undertaken in the next chapter, in which the outline of what could be a true Spanish American postmodernity will begin to emerge from our reading of two recent novelistic texts.

CHAPTER SEVEN

The Closing of the Circle
The End of Modernity in Spanish America

To be modern is to know clearly what cannot be started over again.
— Roland Barthes, "From Work to Text"

THE PRESENT POSTMODERN MOMENT, with its heady promises of deliverance from the ideological and political programs of modernity, has been both benevolent and unkind to the so-called developing nations. The new dominant cultural configuration has reassured intellectuals of marginalized states that the goals their societies were striving for were illusory and that they should release themselves from the self-imposed pressures and concomitant frustrations under which they labored for countless years. Nonetheless, there is a lingering suspicion in peripheral intellectual circles about the concept of the postmodern, a suspicion that is articulated in a number of fashions but that invariably revolves around the issue of historical timing: why is it that at the precise moment in which developing cultures and oppressed groups seem to be poised to stake a claim for participation in history, history is declared to have ended and the individual subject is discarded as a philosophical phantasm? Neil Larsen gives voice to these concerns when he says poignantly that "I, at least, have often found myself wondering in private whether we ought even to bother with the question at all, whether just consenting to raise the 'issue' of 'Latin America and postmodernism' is already to fall into a clever sort of neocolonizing trap."[1] Yet the many variegated possibilities delineated by the rhetoric of the postmodern still beckon, with their suspicion of rigid ideological commitment, their affirmation of local circumstance, and their depiction of a heterogeneous sphere for political agency.[2]

In Spanish America critical reflection on postmodernity and postmodernism already comprises, regardless of its relative novelty, an enormous and intricate bibliography that is impossible to summarize. The titles and dates of some of these works provide a sense of the debate's breadth: Eduardo Azcuy's *Posmodernidad, cultura y política* (1989), Antonio Benítez Rojo's *La isla que se repite: el Caribe y la perspectiva posmoderna* (1989), Consuelo Corredor's *Modernismo sin modernidad* (1990), Aníbal Quijano's *Modernidad, identidad y utopía en América* (1990), Marta López Gil's *Filosofía, modernidad, posmodernidad* (1990), Edgardo Lander's *Modernidad y universalismo* (1991), and José J. Sebrel's *El asedio a la modernidad: crítica del relativismo cultural* (1991).[3] But even the most superficial examination of that critical oeuvre forces us to realize that the diagnostic spectrum of opinion that it evinces on the phenomenon is articulated between two opposite and antithetical poles: from an absolute denial of the pertinence of the postmodern to the Spanish American situation to the other extreme, in which postmodernity is enthusiastically assumed and its proponents allege that, due to its particular historical characteristics and experiences, one could make the case that Spanish America could be considered postmodern par excellence or, it has even been proposed, *avant la lettre*. Nelly Richard has summarized this last position thus: "The very heterogeneity of the experiences which have created a Latin American space out of its multiple and hybrid past creates, at least on the surface, the very qualities of fragmentation and dispersion associated with the semantic erosion characteristic of the crisis of modernity and modernism as its cultural dominant."[4] Nonetheless, these two antithetical postures arise, regardless of their apparently irreconcilable character, from an identical interpretation of Spanish American modernity, even if the conclusions they derive from that similar interpretation should later take them their separate ways. It would seem logical that in order to understand what postmodernity is for Spanish America one should reach back to that which the latter purports to neutralize or overcome; that we should let ourselves be overtaken by that "post-," that grammatical particle which, in contrast with its function as prefix, openly proclaims its canceling of its own origin. Nevertheless, the similarities that become evident when we go back to the ideas on *modernity* in which the most opposite opinions on *postmodernity* are based could serve as a point of departure for the consideration of the critical literature that addresses that disputed category.

In my view, these two antithetical perspectives on *postmodernity* in Spanish America are predicated on a shared interpretation of Spanish American *modernity* that regards it as weak, incomplete, unfinished, or uneven. The scheme that provides the foundation for this interpretation is derived, in essence, from Weber's ideas on the specificity of the modern, rational society—a paradigm that I mentioned in another context in chapter 1. For Weber, modernity consisted of the substitution of traditional and mutually imbricated forms of traditional knowledge by relatively autonomous discursive spheres, each of which purported to found a knowledge based in the epistemological rigor of a discipline. One of these—perhaps the one that concerns us the most—is the sphere of cultural discourse. According to this view, the peripheral, neocolonial circumstance of Spanish America necessarily translated itself in the incapacity to articulate in a uniform and conclusive fashion the transition proposed by Weber's scheme. That is why, when we examine cultural production in Spanish America, until very recently one spies the clear symptoms of the impossibility of delimiting, of clearing an autonomous space for cultural discourse in Spanish American societies. This accounts for why one finds literature—especially in the nineteenth century—attempting to justify itself through the espousal of projects that are outside itself, instead of centering its self-justification precisely in its distance, its divorce from the material world.

It is easy to see how the two opposed views on postmodernism in Spanish America that were discussed earlier should originate in that interpretation: first, the idea that postmodern experience is consonant with Spanish American experience, either because it ironizes or inverts hierarchies or because it vindicates a historical development that until recently had been marked by the sign of failure. The critique of modernity's program has made possible the reinterpretation of the historical experience of these zones that lived it in an oblique or imperfect fashion, so that the traditional elements that were not displaced by modern disciplines of knowledge are now seen as characteristics of a more complete sensibility, as qualities of a mode of being that did not mutilate itself in order to pursue the rationalism propounded by modernity at the expense of other forms of understanding. The Spanish American capacity to live seemingly in the midst of the most obvious disjunctions between the modern and the traditional is identified, then, with the postmodern rejection of hierarchy and the concomitant desire to level and shuffle around the absolute and mutually exclusive categories of Western knowledge. Our intellectual thinking is and has always been weak—but that adjective is no longer a sign of inferiority or insufficiency.[5] If at the banquet of modernity we were always a second-class invitee, history finally rewarded us when sveltness became the apparent universal fashion. This interpretation has the attractiveness of turning into a virtue what was previously a defect, a fact that explains the enthusiasm with which it is advanced and with which it has been received in some quarters.

The second essential attitude toward postmodernity bases its denial of the viability of the postmodern as an alternative for Spanish America also in the weakness of modernity in the Spanish American circumstance. It has been summarized succinctly in a recent book by William Rowe and Vivian Schelling: "A degree of consensus has arisen around the proposition that the distinctiveness of Latin American modernism is that it occurred without modernity, and that given that a partial and distorted modernization has generally occurred only in recent decades, it is inappropriate to speak of a postmodern condition in Latin America."[6] If one cannot speak unequivocally about a Spanish American *modernity*, how can one even begin to argue for the existence of a specifically Spanish American postmodernity to oppose and surmount it? The present fascination with the postmodern in ever larger circles of Spanish American intellectuals would be only the most recent confirmation of the atavistic subjection of that intelligentsia to metropolitan currents and movements. According to this view, the postmodern moment would be simply a luxury item available only to those who have gone through the amusement ride of modernity and have come out the other end with a dizzying skepticism about the ride; for being released by the hegemonic world powers from the craving for modernity is as illusory, it is argued, as being *given* your freedom, as being *declared* free. Postmodernism would be just another commodity that is dangled before what is now a well-developed market of cultural ideas, only that this one is claimed to satisfy the ultimate consumer desire: the desire to be free from consumption. But in spite of those promises of liberation, the hierarchy that organizes the channels of distribution of that market would have remained unaltered in their most basic structure.

I believe that the fundamental framework of the interpretation of modernity that serves as foundation for these two views on postmodernity in Spanish America is open to a critique from at least two perspectives. The first one is related to the necessarily relative quality of its argumentation. With the adjective "relative" I refer to the fact that the general definition of modernity articulated in it *requires* that modernity in Spanish America be a manqué or lame version of metropolitan modernity. If Spanish America had not seen the evolution of social and discursive structures that the model posits, then modernity in the Spanish American context will have to be, a fortiori, a degraded exemplar of the archetype. In other words, the invocation of the paradigm determines by necessity the mobilization and deployment of a rhetoric of insufficiency, of lack and compensation. Yet it is important to notice that that insufficiency and that lack are only a discursive effect produced by the critical narrative with which the phenomenon of modernity in Spanish America is examined.

From this perspective Spanish American modernity consisted of the appropriation of European and American technologies, discourses, and expectations that had not arisen organically from the context in which they were nevertheless grafted. But why not see in this appropriation a kind of organicity proper to Spanish American circumstance? Why not argue instead that Spanish America experienced the modernity that was organic to it, without having the latter carry forever the mark of a weakness and an incompleteness that only arise from the comparison with its metropolitan counterpart?

The second objection that could be raised against this interpretation of Spanish American modernity is linked to the two rhetorical questions that closed the previous paragraph. It has to do precisely with the concept of organicity that serves as foundation to that interpretation. The category of "organicity" has here the sense of adequation or propriety that is supposed to exist between a specific economic and historical conjuncture and the discursive manifestations that are produced in and from it. The interpretation of Spanish American modernity as incomplete or weak describes it as characterized by the appropriation of discourses and ideologies that were not its own, that arose in and from other socioeconomic circumstances. But the ease in the displacement of discourses that such an accusation postulates—that is, the apparent ability of discourses to disconnect themselves *tout court* from their original context in order to be transferred to a circumstance that is alien to them—militates necessarily against the organicity in which the accusation is founded. Furthermore, and perhaps more important, the argument evinces here its resistance to endowing Spanish America with that same organicity that it assumes as a given in the metropolitan context and that guarantees there the relationship of propriety that is presumed to exist between discourse and infrastructure. Because even if we accept that Spanish American modernity was characterized by the adoption of metropolitan discourses identified as modern, one would still have to recognize that the particular choice of which discourses would be adopted will reflect a degree of adequation between them and the specific historical circumstances of each Spanish American intellectual.

In the ultimate analysis, what I aim to propose is that the distinction between modernity as the accession to a historical, economic, and technological phase and modernity as a collection of discourses is, if not unsustainable, of questionable usefulness. This realization would allow us first to study Spanish American modernity as such, without regarding it consistently as under the sign of insufficiency, as the result of a deviation that always already sees it as distanced from a model of modernity—a model that, as I have argued, is provided by criticism itself. But it will also allow us to understand that modernity as what, in effect, it was: that is, as the deployment in the Spanish American context of a repertoire of discourses identified with modernity. This does not imply that the adoption of these discourses has not been uneventful or wrenching, a notion I hope I dispelled in chapter 1. On the contrary, the evidence of those disjunctions can be readily found in the fissures and internal disarticulations of the Spanish American text. But I think that in the end, the significant project is to define the nature of that internal difference and to determine in which level of the text that difference resides. In my view, these dislocations are the traces of the difficult rhetorical situation that arises when the Spanish American writer wields a discourse for which his or her circumstances are always in danger of becoming the negative object, that is, the counterexample to a norm established by that very discourse and not, as they are interpreted by the schemes under examination, the signs of the inoperability in Spanish America of a certain paradigm of modernity. The contradictions and the internal crevices of the Spanish American work arise when the latter deploys a strategy for the affirmation of its own authority by turning away from a modernity that threatens Spanish American writers through the very discourse chosen by the text as a model, not from the poverty of Spanish American modernity. In the first case contradiction represents a maneuver of discursive authorization, while in the second the internal disjunction is a signal of discursive insufficiency and inadequacy. Is this difference the symptom of Spanish America's historical incapacity to sustain modernity, or is it, as I argue in this book, the trace of a habilitating strategy that searches for a way out of the dead end represented by the adoption of modernity by peripheral societies? The usefulness of this last proposal is that it allows us to think that the complex textual situation I have described may perhaps *be* Spanish

America's modernity, in contrast to the first option, which always reads in the text the imprint of the impossibility of upholding a given metropolitan conception of modernity.

I proposed earlier that the most antithetical opinions with respect to postmodernism in Spanish America have a common backdrop, a shared origin in a similar interpretation of what Spanish American modernity was. From all of the above one can deduce that perhaps the real discussion about the character of postmodernity in Spanish America is still yet to take place. Yet the debate precipitated by the discussion of these issues in Latin America has resulted in the publication of a truly staggering number of related studies in the last fifteen years, which implies that, irrespective of the surreptitious consonance highlighted by the previous analysis, the discussion is touching on something fundamental, something unquestionably important. This is not to say that postmodernity and postmodernism have not been the topic of intellectual and scholarly discussions in Europe and the United States as well; but the force and unanimity with which the topic has monopolized recent cultural deliberations in Latin America is truly a remarkable circumstance. It is also true that in hegemonic circles, the discussion has centered on the specificity of the postmodern, whereas in Latin America the debate has centered on the desirability of *embracing* the postmodern, a discussion that takes for granted a fairly homogeneous definition of the phenomenon. This assumed homogeneity in the understanding of the nature of postmodernity is, I would argue, both consequential and quite revealing. Furthermore, one quality shared by most of these works is a sense of urgency born from the assumption that the outcome of the debate will have profound consequences for Latin America's future, a sense that something truly significant is at stake in the discussion. This is in marked contrast to the dispassionate tenor of the debate in American and European academic circles regarding the postmodern, in which one senses a certain cool exhaustion—a certain jadedness that arises from the incongruity between the frantic speed of the debate and the thoroughly institutional and closed context in which it is taking place.

I would like to argue that the intensity of the polemics on the meaning of postmodernity for Spanish America is indicative of the fact that, at a very fundamental level, cultural discourse in Spanish America is and has always been inextricably tied to the concept and the experience of modernity. And it has been only recently, since the concept of modernity has been scrutinized critically as a historically and ideologically bounded category, that the relationship between modernity and Spanish American cultural discourse has become fully apprehensible to that discourse. Regardless of the outcome of the present debate, the perception—however illusory it might be—that the program of modernity has been superseded (or in any event devalued) has simultaneously created the necessary distance for this realization to obtain. Hence, the polemics is not just a discussion regarding the desirability of embracing the potentialities of the postmodern: in what is perhaps its most significant dimension, it is also an inquiry about the condition and the future of cultural discourse in Spanish America.

Some recent literary texts have become the stage in which this relationship between the end of modernity and Latin American cultural discourse is being explored in its most wrenching and rewarding implications. The two works that are most representative of this phenomenon are Gabriel García Márquez's *El general en su laberinto* and Carlos Fuentes's latest novel, *La campaña*. Both texts are suffused with a liminal intentionality—that is, they enact an explicit desire to revisit the putative beginnings of Spanish America in the early decades of the nineteenth century. This quality makes evident the revisionary intention that informs their writing, inasmuch as their reenactment of that beginning is meant to represent the closing of a circle, a return to the mythical point of departure for Spanish American cultural life and historical existence in order to address the difficulties—rhetorical and otherwise—that accompanied that beginning. The result is a profound meditation that in both cases revolves around the contradictory relationship between Spanish America and modernity. Hence, in my view these texts are not caught in the dialectics of desire and opposition to the modern that I have tried to describe in this book. They offer—perhaps even unbeknownst to them—a diagnosis and a critique of that rhetorical predicament, in a move that points perhaps to its final dissolution as the generating mechanism of Spanish American cultural discourse.

From the beginning of the acknowledgments offered as a postscript to *El general en su laberinto*, Gabriel García Márquez avers that the period of Bolívar's biography that serves as the temporal framework to the novel is the one most bereft of details in a life that could be said to have been recreated to the day by the hagiography surrounding the hero: "Los fundamentos históricos me preocupaban poco, pues el último viaje por el río es el tiempo menos documentado de la vida de Bolívar. Sólo escribió entonces tres o cuatro cartas—un hombre que debió dictar más de diez mil—y ninguno de sus acompañantes dejó memoria escrita de aquellos catorce días desventurados."[7] [I was not particularly troubled by the question of historical accuracy, since the last voyage along the river is the least documented period in Bolivar's life. During this time he only wrote three or four letters—a man who must have dictated over ten thousand—and none of his companions left a written memoir of those fourteen calamitous days.] But García Márquez's explanation begs a significant question, for one could ask, in any event, why this is indeed the least detailed period of Bolívar's biography. It could be argued that the very nature of the Libertador's fluvial journey during his last months must have hindered the collection of facts, anecdotes, conversations, and so on, that have otherwise been skillfully woven together by his biographers to make possible the minute re-creation of his existence up to that moment. It seems to me, nonetheless, that the answer is given to us by the very events narrated by García Márquez in his novel: by that point in his life, Bolívar had already begun to die to Spanish American history. History does not pay the same sedulous attention to the last months of Bolívar's life because by then he had ceased to be the protagonist of historical events and had instead become a figure marginal to them, as is confirmed by the general's frequent and moving fits of rage, engendered as they are by the knowledge of his fitful impotence. Bolívar's own writings attest to many such moments of clarity concerning the caducity of his secular works and days:

> En todo tiempo las obras de los hombres han sido frágiles, más en el día son como los embriones nonatos que perecen antes de desenvolver sus facultades. Por todas partes me asaltan los espantosos ruidos de las caídas, mi época es de catástrofes: todo nace y muere a mi vista como si fuese relámpago, todo no hace más que pasar, ¡y necio de mí si me lisonjease quedar de pie firme en medio de tales convulsiones, en medio de tantas ruinas, en medio del trastorno moral del universo![8]

> In all epochs, the achievements of man have been fragile, but today they are like stillborn embryos that perish without developing their potential. I am accosted from all sides by the thundering clamor of failure; my time is one of catastrophe: everything is born and dies as if it were a lightning flash; everything is fleeting, and I would be a fool if I endeavored to be constant in the middle of such convulsion, in the midst of so much ruin, in the middle of the moral upheaval of the universe!

What we are treated to in the text of *El general en su laberinto* is a Bolívar who has begun his physical denouement, but perhaps more important, his historical agony as well. This is why the first sentences of the novel depict the general floating in a bathtub in such a profound state of trance that he is described as "alguien que ya no era de este mundo" (11) [a man no longer of this world (3)].

But if it is indeed true that García Márquez's novel depicts Bolívar's historical twilight, paradoxically the text is attempting to portray simultaneously the very beginning of Spanish American history. For what is the historical juncture narrated by *El general en su laberinto*, if not the starting point, the zero-degree of Spanish American historical existence? I am alluding, first of all, to the postrevolutionary moment in which the territorial claims and the assertions of personal authority that would shape the future Spanish American nationalities began to manifest themselves. But I am also referring, of course, to the instant in which Bolívar's ideal of continental unity had to acknowledge the impossibility of its being translated into practice, not exclusively because circumstances were unfavorable but because they were not taken into consideration in its formulation. The general's myth of unification was, after all, simply a myth, a cultural and political fiction based on the Enlightenment readings of Bolívar and the other intellectual authors of the independence movement: a chimera that did not take into account the vast geographical expanses involved or the narrow ambitions of the various local protobourgeoisies.[9] But it was a fantasy that has also had a powerful diachronic dimension, since Bolívar's wistful dream has been repeatedly invoked and proposed as an enterprise to be pursued by numerous Spanish American thinkers and politicians throughout the continent's history; one has only to remember the millenarian rhetoric that characterized the celebration of the *Centenario* of independence in Spanish America during the second decade of the twentieth century. I would like to explore in more detail the conjunction established by García Márquez's text between, on the one hand, the last days of Bolívar, and on the other, the beginning of Spanish America's historical and cultural existence. Why should *El general en su laberinto* have it that when we hark back to the origins of the continent's history we should encounter the dying and diminished figure of the Gran Libertador Simón Bolívar in his mournful and sorrowful river journey to the grave? What is the meaning of this text, which freely acknowledges the lack of originality of its subject matter (it had been taken up previously by Alvaro Mutis) and which concludes with the desolate death of its protagonist?[10] Why is it that the very title of *El General en su laberinto* refers explicitly to the instant depicted in the novel in which Bolívar acquires the knowledge of his pitiless and irrevocable personal extinction?

These questions begin to find their answers in the last sentence of the postface to the novel, where García Márquez refers almost in passing but explicitly to "el horror de este libro (272) [the horror of this book (274)]." The phrase's off-handedness cannot diminish its profound impact. The writing of *El general en su laberinto* would seem to respond, then, to a desire to confront the reader with something that is deemed horrific, unbearable. I do not wish to suggest that *El general en su laberinto* purports to be a Gothic tale or anything remotely like it; but if we take into consideration that the events narrated by the novel encompass almost exclusively the excruciatingly slow death of Bolívar, one could conclude that the novel's ultimate intention is to force us to look this death in the eye— that is, to impose on us the direct knowledge of the horror it entails, forcing us to be witnesses to its unfolding. This intent is one whose— shall I call them therapeutic?—implications would have to be recognized as such. It is a matter, it seems, of entering into a new relation with Bolívar's death, arriving at a new pact with it founded on the performance of its painful restaging in front of the reader's gaze.

Given all of the above, I would like to invoke in this discussion of *El General en su laberinto* the Freudian distinction between mourning and melancholia as contrasting and opposing strategies of dealing with the brutal fact of the death of a loved being or the loss of a cherished object.[11] According to Freud, these two activities represent two essential mechanisms for confronting such a loss. Faced with the disappearance of the lost object the libido constructs an image of it as a defense against its absence; hence, the love for the lost object or being becomes love for an introspected image of the disappeared object. In the first of these strategies, that of mourning, the ties to that image become progressively looser until with the passing of time the libido is liberated. But in the case of melancholy, the links to the image remain steadfast; the libido holds onto the internalized image of the lost object, to the point of forming an identification between the ego and that image. By means of this identification, the lost object is kept alive, but as a disappeared object—an object that the superego then admonishes for its desertion. Hence, in melancholia the disappeared object is at once both desired and repudiated. The result of this identification of the ego with the image of the lost object is the self-destructive and paralyzing behavior that characterizes the melancholy being.

The intention that underlies the writing of *El general en su laberinto* is the desire to make the reader pass from a melancholy relationship vis-à-vis the figure of Bolívar to a relationship that has the therapeutic qualities of mourning instead. Yet I immediately hasten to add that in this last sentence "Bolívar" is a metaphor that alludes synecdochically to a more sweeping and general phenomenon in the history of cultural life in Spanish America. For in Bolívar's Enlightenment project of a great confederation of autonomous states and its subsequent crushing failure I propose to read the essential components of Spanish America's problematic relationship with modernity.

I do not think it cavalier to suggest that the rhetorical circumstance that I have consistently addressed in this book coincides, mutatis mutandis, with the dynamics of loss and mourning described earlier.[12] Spanish American intellectuals always experienced modernity as a sort of somber and imperfect mourning—in other words, as the absence of a desired object that was lost after the initial postulation of an unambiguous connection between the new independent continent and the future, that is, modernity. The melancholy introjection and identification with modernity as a desired yet lost object has manifested itself as an internal crisis that has condemned Spanish American culture to experience despondently its cultural and historical life. In *El general en su laberinto* García Márquez goes back to the beginnings of the continent's history in order to expose the enactment, the imprinting of that mechanism of imperfect mourning in the cultural unconscious of Spanish America. The conjunction established by the novel of the beginning of history and of Bolívar's death harks back to this primordial circumstance that articulates itself around the sense of loss. Spanish American history begins with the loss, the negation, of Bolívar's dream of continental unity; and it is under the sign of that original absence that Spanish America's cultural existence has developed to the present day. García Márquez's novel depicts for us a Bolívar trapped in the somber labyrinth of his personal and historical melancholy, so that our own cultural melancholy will recognize itself in that written mirror and will transform itself into beneficent mourning, so that the phantom of the lost object of modernity may cease to rule the libidinal economy of Spanish American cultural discourse and historical life. This is indeed a bleak and funereal book, but one in which the somberness is meant to be at the service of the forces of life.

The possibility, indeed, the need for such a transformation becomes visible only the moment one has achieved an eccentric perspective with respect to modernity—that is, when the latter becomes suspect as a desideratum, when modernity loses its aura as an imperative and universal project. I am alluding, of course, to that multiple and complex circumstance that has come to be referred to with the imprecise label of "postmodernity." It is precisely from this position, already released from the ballast of a modernity experienced as an absence, that the gripping text of *El general en su laberinto* is produced. The recent delegitimation of modernity's program has relieved Spanish American writers from their historical and cultural melancholia, allowing them access to the decentered, transnational, and multidimensional happening of contemporary cultural life. This release explains why *El general en su laberinto* incorporates what could be conceptualized as a postmodern version of Bolívar's myth of continental consolidation—as an affirmation that irrespective of its failure as originally formulated, the unity envisioned by Bolívar has nonetheless been achieved in the illusory yet powerfully real universe of cultural myths. This refashioning is depicted in García Márquez's acknowledgments, in which the author's scriptural praxis is inserted in an impressive and laboriously detailed communications network configured by contemporary devices for the generation, transmission, and duplication of information: telephones, fax machines, telex stations, photocopying machines. I quote from García Márquez's acknowledgments in the text:

Pero mis gratitudes van de manera muy especial para un grupo de amigos, viejos y nuevos, que tomaron como suyo propio y de gran importancia no sólo mis dudas más graves—como el pensamiento político real de Bolívar en medio de sus contradicciones flagrantes—sino también las más triviales—como el número que calzaba. Facio Poyo tuvo la virtud de calmar mis angustias con documentos analgésicos que me leía por teléfono desde París, o que me mandaba con carácter urgente por télex o telefax, como si fueran medicinas de vida o muerte. El historiador colombiano Gustavo Vargas, profesor de la UNAM, se mantuvo al alcance de mi teléfono para aclararme dudas mayores y menores, sobre todo las que tenían que ver con las ideas políticas de la época. . . . Jorge Eduardo Ratter, embajador de Panamá en Colombia y luego canciller en su país, hizo varios vuelos urgentes sólo para traerme algunos libros inencontrables. El expresidente Belisario Betancur me aclaró dudas dispersas durante todo un año de consultas telefónicas. Con Francisco Pividal sostuve en La Habana las lentas conversaciones preliminares que me permitieron formarme una idea clara del libro que debía escribir. . . . Mi viejo amigo Aníbal Noguera Mendoza—desde su embajada de Colombia en Puerto Príncipe—me envió copias de papeles personales suyos, con su permiso generoso para servirme de ellos con toda libertad. (271–72)

<hr>

But my thanks go in a very special way to a group of friends, old and new, who took as their own affair, and one of the utmost importance, not only my most serious questions, such as the real nature of Bolívar's political thought amid all his flagrant contradictions, but also the most trivial, such as the size of his shoes. Fabio Puyo had the ability to soothe my distress with analgesic documents, which he read to me on the telephone from Paris or sent to me with all urgency by telex or telefax, as if they were life-or-death medicines. The Colombian historian Gustavo Vargas, a professor at the Universidad Nacional Autónoma de México, stayed within reach of my telephone to clarify major and minor doubts, above all those related to the political ideas of the period. . . . Jorge Eduardo Ritter, ambassador of Panama to Colombia and then foreign minister of his country, made several urgent plane trips just to bring me books of his that could not be found elsewhere. Ex-President Belisario Betancourt clarified doubts throughout an entire year of telephone consultations. . . . With Francisco Pividal in Havana I held the long preliminary conversations that permitted me to form a clear idea of the book I should write. . . . From his Colombian embassy in Port-au-Prince my old friend Aníbal Noguera Mendoza sent me copies of his personal papers and his generous permission to use them with absolute liberty. (272–73)

Bolívar's dream, García Márquez seems to imply, would have been feasible only in our present era, in which the ideological pressures of nineteenth-century nationalism that checked Bolívar's unifying project have been delegitimized and in which the means of communication and transportation could indeed allow one to imagine the creation of a collectivity of continental proportions. By implicitly underscoring the discrepancy between Bolívar's Enlightenment rhetoric and the material and economic circumstances of his moment, García Márquez brings to light the unavoidable dead end, the inevitable melancholy relationship with modernity that marked Spanish American discourse from its very beginnings in the nineteenth century.

Furthermore, there seems to me to be another reason why Bolívar's projects of continental unity is presented in this fashion—one could say, modulated in another key—in *El general en su laberinto*: no longer as a rhetorical formula but as a transnational communications network. Under this new sign, in this novel version, Bolívar's idea has ceased to be the expression of a personal will to power as it was originally, in order to become simply the *potential* for a communicative operation. For the most one can aspire to do in the contemporary moment is to place oneself strategically at the intersection of various independent acts of communication. The praxis of writing that emerges from García Márquez's description must necessarily produce, as well, a transformation in the figure of the author and his product. Hence, we see, for instance, that García Márquez describes *El general en su laberinto* as the repetition and continuation of a text written and partially published earlier by Alvaro Mutis, and in his postface he asks the reader to conceptualize the novel as a collage of multiple transmissions of information. The simulacrum of the author that is described by *El general en su laberinto* is a metaphor for the radical transformation undergone by the figure of the Spanish American author during the last twenty years. The former conjurer of totalizing fictions that purported to encompass and incorporate in his works the essence of Spanish America disperses himself, disseminates himself in those recent Spanish American texts that appeal to the dialogic multiplicity of the fragment, to eroticism, humor, local circumstance, and personal idiosyncracy. García Márquez has offered us in his novel yet another image to enrich this new repertoire of authorial simulacra: that of a writer who waits for the telephone to ring, or for the fax machine to go on line, to begin his work.

Carlos Fuentes's recent novel, *La campaña*, represents a different perspective on the problematics I outlined earlier. The events depicted in the text are chronologically previous to those narrated in *El general en su laberinto*; one could even say that *La campaña* almost ends where García Márquez's account of Bolívar's last days begins. Yet in the context of the tale of mourning I have identified in *El general en su laberinto*, *La campaña* is emblematic of the successful passing from melancholy to mourning and beyond, that is, to the final awareness that loss must somehow be turned into memory if life is to abide and prevail.

The campaign referred to by the novel's title is, of course, the military campaign of the wars for Spanish American independence during the second and third decades of the nineteenth century. Fuentes narrates the story of a group of young *criollo* friends who are steeped in the Enlightenment's ideas and delight in invoking its rhetoric at the slightest provocation. Eager to achieve the much-sought-after coincidence between thought and action, the most ideologically committed of them, Baltasar Bustos, steals the first-born son of the Spanish Presidente de la Audiencia del Virreinato del Río de la Plata and substitutes in his place the son of a black prostitute as a defiant act against peninsular hegemony and authority. In his retreat from the infant's chambers Baltasar knocks down a candle, causing a fire that kills the black infant he had just replaced in the white baby's crib; this fire is explained in the novel as the arson with which the revolution begins. Baltasar gives the white child to black servants, ordering them with the lapidary sentence of a committed revolutionary: "—Aquí está el otro niño. Denle su destino."[13] [Here is the other baby. Let him live his own fate.]

That this act is meant to be understood as the spark of the insurrection against Spain is underscored by the fact that it is depicted as happening late on the night of May 24, 1810, the eve of the historic uprising that marked the launching of the struggle against Spanish supremacy in what is present-day Argentina. But Baltasar's attempt to achieve political consistency is tainted, contaminated from the outset as it were by a feeling that owes absolutely nothing to Enlightenment reason or ideological rectitude: for some time he had been surreptitiously spying on the president's wife, the Creole beauty Ofelia Salamanca, and had fallen madly in love with her. Racked with guilt upon believing he had condemned his beloved's child to a life of misery, Baltasar engages in a ten-year crusade to find Ofelia in order to beg forgiveness for his deed and to declare his love for her. This is, in fact, the *real* campaign that Fuentes's novel narrates. The text, then, is built around this moment in which there occurs a conjunction between ideology and passion, and the ambiguity of the title, which refers both to the passionate enterprise in which Baltasar engages and the military campaign for independence, is the direct result of this juxtaposition. In the end, Baltasar finally meets with Ofelia in Mexico, but the encounter is short-lived and anticlimactic; Ofelia is deathly ill and in a daze, and Baltasar adopts her son as his own. Having thus achieved the end of his quest by assuming responsibility for the results of his deed, Baltasar is now free to love again—this time a real, tangible woman, not a figment of his mind's creation. The novel ends hopefully with the reappearance in Baltasar's life of Gabriela Cóo, a Chilean actress whom the protagonist had met during his wanderings and whom he had earlier forsworn because of his love for Ofelia Salamanca. But the novel's conclusion is not the closed ending it would seem to be: in the last pages it is revealed that Ofelia's son had been fathered by the novel's narrator, Baltasar's best friend Manuel Varela, who had had an affair with her and would keep this secret from him forever. In this fashion, the novel concludes by inscribing Baltasar's idyll in an even larger, imperfect circle of passion and betrayal.

The result of the conflation achieved in the novel between the military campaign for independence and Baltasar's lovelorn quest is that the familiar historical events depicted in the text—the *montoneras* in Argentina, the Andean battles of San Martín, the Mexican guerrilla priest and his revolutionary crusade—are all there merely as a backdrop to the story of guilt, love, and incomplete redemption enacted in the novel. Hence, the momentous events of the history of the period are relegated to a secondary status, a circumstance that projects Baltasar's passionate search as the prime mover of historical and novelistic deployment. In fact, it could be argued that in this novel Fuentes has endeavored to present passion as *the* prime mover of history, or at least of Spanish American history. To this end, time and again, the reader is treated to a series of disquisitions by several characters regarding the difficulties encountered and the contradictions incurred in when the rhetoric of reason and modernity is invoked in a world ruled instead by affect and impulse. Perhaps the most significant and beautiful of these is the meditation offered by the revolutionary priest Anselmo Quintana in a tempestuous and lucid confession to the protagonist Baltasar Bustos in Mexico:

> Vienes de muy lejos y este continente es muy grande. Pero tenemos dos cosas en común. Nos entendemos hablando español. Y nos guste o no nos guste, llevamos tres siglos de cultura católica cristiana, marcada por los símbolos, los valores, las necedades, los crímenes y los sueños de la cristiandad en América. Conozco a los muchachos como tú: . . . todos ustedes quisieran acabar con ese pasado que les parece injusto y absurdo, olvidarlo. Sí, qué bueno hubiera sido ser fundados por Montescú en vez de Torquemada. Pues no más no. ¿Queremos ahora ser europeos, modernos, ricos, regidos por el espíritu de las leyes y de los derechos universales del hombre? Pues yo te digo que nomás no se va a poder si no cargamos con el muerto de nuestro pasado. Lo que te estoy pidiendo es que no sacrifiquemos nada; ni la magia de los indios, ni la teología de los cristianos, ni la razón de los europeos nuestros contemporáneos. No te dejes separar y encandilar por una sola idea, Baltasar. Pon en un platillo de la balanza todas tus ideas, y cuanto las niega en el otro, y entonces andarás más cerca de la verdad. Obra en contra de tu fe secular, pon al lado de ella mi fe divina, pero como lastre, gravedad, contraste y parte de tu laicismo. No quiero saber dentro de diez años, que eres un enfermo más de utopías frustradas, de ideales traicionados. (243)

> ---

> You've come from far, far away, and this continent is very large. But we have two things in common. We understand each other because we speak Spanish. And, like it or not, we've had three centuries of Catholic, Christian culture, marked by the symbols, values, follies, crimes, and dreams of Christianity in the New World. I know fellows like you: . . . All of you would like to put an end to that past which seems unjust and absurd to you, to

forget it. Yes, how good it would have been to be founded by Montesquieu instead of Torquemada. But it didn't happen that way. Do we want now to be Europeans, modern, rich, governed by the spirit of the laws and the universal rights of man? Well, let me tell you that nothing like that will ever happen unless we carry the corpse of our past with us. What I'm asking you is that we not sacrifice anything: not the magic of the Indians, not the theology of the Christians, not the reason of our European contemporaries. Don't let yourself be divided and dazzled by a single idea, Baltasar. Put all your ideas on one side of the balance, then put everything that negates them on the other, and then you'll be closer to the truth. Work counter to your secular faith. Put next to it my divine faith, but as ballast, weight, contrast, and a part of your secularism. I don't want to find out ten year from now that you became just one more man made sick by frustrated utopias, by betrayed ideals. (230–31)

Quintana's address is not an apology for religion per se but rather an argument for the need to counter the exclusive hegemony of Enlightened reason in Baltasar's mind—and, by extension, in the ideology of the emancipation movement. The priest's admonitions had been preceded by a vision that Baltasar had experienced in the Andes while delirious with a high fever. In it, the protagonist had walked into a cavern, and there he had had a sudden and violent epiphany:

Baltasar sintió algo peor, más insidioso: una náusea parecida a la pérdida de la inocencia, una afirmación sutil como un veneno, de algo totalmente ir-racional, mágico, que desmoronaba con unas cuantas imágenes seductoras e inasibles toda la paciente construcción racional del hombre civilizado. Estaba convencido de que había llegado al pasado más remoto, al origen de todas las cosas, y que este origen mágico de brujería y engaño no era el de una perfecta asimilación del hombre con la naturaleza sino, nuevamente, un divorcio intolerable, una separación que lo hería en lo más seguro de sus convicciones ilustradas. Quería creer en el mito de los orígenes, pero no como mito, sino como realidad de mundo e individuo conciliados. ¿Qué había visto aquí, qué superchería, o qué advertencia: "La unidad con la naturaleza no es necesariamente la receta de la felicidad; no regreses al origen, no busques una imposible armonía, valoriza todas las diferencias que encuentres en tu camino. No creas que al principio fuimos felices. Tampoco se te ocurra que al final lo seremos. (97–98)

Baltasar felt something worse, more insidious: a nausea like that of the loss of innocence, an affirmation as subtle as poison, something totally irrational, magic, which with a few seductive, ethereal images destroyed all the patient, rational structures of civilized man. He was convinced that he had reached the remotest past, the origin of all things, and that this magic origin of sorcery and illusion was not that of a perfect assimilation of man with nature but, again, an intolerable divorce, a separation that wounded him in the most certain of his enlightened convictions. He wanted to believe in the myth of origins, not as a myth but as a reality of the world reconciled with the individual. What had he seen here, what trick or what warning? Unity with nature is not necessarily the formula for happiness; do not go back to the origins, do not seek an impossible harmony, cherish all the differences you find on the road. . . . Do not think that at the beginning we were happy. By the same token, don't think we'll be happy at the end. (87–88)

The two fragments just read are not so much a comment on the historical moment depicted in the novel, of course, or an attempt to represent the debates that went on during that period as a look back from our post-modern present to the entire cultural production of Spanish America that ensued from that moment. Like García Márquez in *El general en su laberinto*, in *La campaña* Fuentes harks back to the historical beginnings of Spanish America in order to identify the existence of a jarring contradiction at the root of Spanish American intellectual and historical life. The unbridled adoption of the rhetoric of modernity by Spanish American intellectuals throughout most of its history determined from the outset the utopian, wrenching, and paradoxical nature of their discourse, a predicament that has become visible, as it were, now that the project of modernity has been put into question, now that we have acquired the necessary critical distance from it. But neither Fuentes nor García Márquez is intent on pointing to opportunities that were missed, to roads not taken, or to what might have been; in that regard they are decidedly not the latest installment of that long-standing gesture that has sought to diagnose the ills of Spanish America in order to argue for impossible or draconian solutions. The return to the beginning effected by both of these novels is not a strategy to gain rhetorical or interpretive authority but rather the mark of a desire to signal the closing of an entire epoch of Spanish American cultural existence. For if, as Barthes has said, "to be modern is to know clearly what cannot be started over again," then these novels are frightfully modern. In their differing ways, *El general en su laberinto* and *La campaña* are positioned similarly vis-à-vis the contemporary moment, and this coincidence is signaled by their common displacement to the perceived point of departure of Spanish American historical development.

Yet I hasten to place some boundaries on what would appear to be a ringing endorsement of the postmodern moment. There is little doubt that postmodernism is the latest product of Western cultural circles, just as there should be no illusion that the economic relationship between developed and developing countries is no longer defined in hegemonic terms.[14] It might even be argued that Spanish America's relationship to postmodernity is analogous to the one that it entertained with modernity and that the former should therefore be forsworn for that very reason. Nonetheless, as Alberto Moreiras has remarked in a recent article, "La emancipación no puede ir contracorriente del movimiento histórico del capital, del que la posmodernidad depende."[15] [Freedom cannot go against the grain of the historical movement of capital, on which postmodernity is dependent.] Through its questioning of the values of modernity, "postmodernism" has acquired a very concrete and particular meaning for Spanish America, one that has led to the reconceptualization of previous Spanish American cultural discourse as unreflectively beholden to hegemonic values and concerns. The creation of spaces for future contestatory practices will depend on such radically situated and ad hoc reappropriations of dominant cultural modalities. For one cannot simultaneously denounce one's economic and cultural subjection on the one hand and claim complete ideological autonomy on the other, since subjection requires one's incorporation into hegemonic arrangements and their respective ideologies. Contestation then must be understood not as a pure negation or reversal but as a complex conversation engaged in by a cynical and suspicious interlocutor; as someone who, like Benjamin's Angel of History—and as I propose is the case with García Márquez and Fuentes here—looks toward the past while forced by the winds of history to recede ineluctably toward the future.

They Have Never Been Modern (Either)

No one has ever been modern. Modernity has never begun. There has never been a modern world.

—Bruno Latour, *We Have Never Been Modern*

IT IS AN AXIOMATIC BELIEF of social and cultural criticism in Spanish America that the economic and intellectual elites of Spanish America mortgaged the future of the continent in their relentless pursuit of the modern at the expense of the real needs of the region or of their individual countries.[1] Indeed, it is difficult not to agree with E. Bradford Burns's indictment of the social elites of Latin America, which reads in part as follows:

> The ideology apparent in the writings of most intellectuals from Sarmiento to da Cunha, and almost all the governments of nineteenth-century Latin America, bore a variety of names: progress, civilization, development, and, retrospectively, modernization. Whatever the name applied, the idea was as constant as it was simple: to copy those aspects of Northern European— and, later, United States—culture which most struck the fancy of the elites, thus creating an imperfect and selective process of remolding their nations after foreign models. Although technology appealed the most to the elites, they also aped certain life-styles and professed the values accompanying them. The intent of the elites was to graft onto Latin America the accoutrements of progress rather that to accommodate new ideas and modes by reforming basic national institutions.[2]

Burns goes on to depict the history of Latin America as a massive conflict between two antagonic positions with respect to the modern:

> On the one hand, the elites, increasingly enamored with the modernization first of an industrializing Europe and then of the United States, insisted on importing those foreign patterns and imposing them on their own fledgling nations. On the other hand, the vast majority of Latin Americans, including

some elites but most particularly the popular classes, recognized the threat inherent in the wholesale importation of modernization and the capitalism accompanying it. They resisted modernization, preferring their long-established living patterns to the more recent foreign novelties and fearing the impact of capitalism in their lives.[3]

Burns is, of course, entirely right. But it is my hope that after finishing this book the reader will understand that this view represents only one aspect of the problem, and not necessarily the most interesting or rewarding. The excoriation of the Spanish American elites evident in these fragments arises from the conviction that the ideologies and discourses of modernization and modernity were *options* that could have been exercised or not, at will, in the process of providing a political and cultural foundation to the republics that arose after independence. As I tried to show in chapter 1, the identification with modernity that is the principal characteristic of cultural discourse in Spanish America was the direct consequence of the counterhegemonic narrative of futurity that the Creole dominant group used against its metropolitan Spanish adversaries. After undergoing subtle transformations, this narrative fulfilled several of the pressing ideological needs of the cultural and economic elites of the emerging nations. This much is consistent with Burns's critique of those groups but dispenses with the moral and ethical component of his inculpation.

The identification with the modern that Burns and others have so amply demonstrated may have created the radical division in Spanish American life proposed by the former's comments. But I have argued in this work that the fundamental chasm that Burns locates between the ruling groups and the masses occurred *within* the very discourse of cultural and economic modernization produced by the elite. The commitment to modernity created a crisis of authority for the Spanish American writer that was addressed through the disavowal of modernity at another level of his text. My aim has been to identify this dynamic in the works that have been analyzed in the preceding chapters.

We saw how in Sarmiento this crisis results in a performative conception of writing in which the latter is linked radically to the moment of its emergence, a strategy that removes Sarmiento's discourse from the rhetorical requirements of the several discursive models whose authority is invoked by his writing. The result is a prose that eschews self-consistence, order, and form and is ruled by a pulsional component that is perhaps the best guarantor of its specificity and éclat.

In the case of antislavery discourse I argued that there is a disjunction between slavery as a subject of study as conceptualized by abolitionist treatises and slavery as it is portrayed by the fictional works that are commonly regarded as merely the literary components or adjuncts of those treatises. The latter texts depict slavery as an object refractory to the analytical procedures and categories employed by the antislavery treatises, which were exemplified by the rhetorical formula of the *memorial* or *memoria*. This opacity and obduracy foils the epistemological transparency taken for granted by that discourse and may further help us understand the persistent presence of slavery and black themes in Cuban literature above and beyond the disappearance of that institution from Cuban soil.

Lucio Mansilla's *Una excursión a los indios Ranqueles* provided yet another rendition of this textual problematics. Mansilla carefully constructed for himself the worldly persona of the dandy, the quintessential modern sensibility as it was defined by Baudelaire. Both his life and his writings affect the levity and superficiality of the flâneur in his passing contact with the stimulus provided by the urban landscape. Yet in *Una excursión* Mansilla articulated a counternarrative to that emplotment of the self as the consummate deracinated modern individual by anchoring his subjectivity on the conservative terrain of the familial. In this and subsequent works, Mansilla constructed a family romance involving the figures of his uncle Juan Manuel de Rosas and Domingo F. Sarmiento as antagonistic father figures through which he managed to establish a claim of immediacy in his relationship to Argentina and its history.

Horacio Quiroga's poetics of the short story were surveyed next. One can detect in Quiroga a conception of fictional writing as a *technè* ruled by an internal economy whose main elements derived from metropolitan literary masters regarded as modern and from contemporaneous discourses on technological invention and experimentation. This is why he describes himself time and again as unabashedly epigonal vis-à-vis those authors in whom he claimed to have discovered the technical requirements of the short story: Poe, Maupassant, Chekhov. Yet we saw how this teleological economy of writing was continually violated by Quiroga's writerly praxis—one in which the end of the story was proleptically unveiled from the very beginning of the narrative.

The study of Mario Vargas Llosa's *La tía Julia y el escribidor* allowed us to see an instance in which the modern is identified with the literary modality of postmodernism. The supposed "postmodern turn" of Vargas Llosa's novelistic production after the publication of *Pantaleón y las visi-*

tadoras is a well-established critical interpretation. I tried to show how the decentering of the subject and the questioning of its prerogatives that is characteristic of that discursive mode is resisted in Vargas Llosa's novel through the projection onto the novel of an oedipal fantasy through which the novelistic subject constitutes itself as an autonomous and authoritative voice instead.

The last chapter began with a consideration of what a relevant and serviceable interpretation of postmodernity for Spanish America might be. I proposed that in its questioning of the essence and universal applicability of the tenets of modernity, postmodernity has had the effect of making visible, as it were, the rhetorical mechanism that has produced Spanish American cultural discourse. I argued that one can see the salutary effect of this revelation in two recent literary texts: Gabriel García Márquez's *El General en su laberinto* and Carlos Fuentes's *La campaña*. Both of these works revisit the liminal moment of Spanish American historical existence in order to rewrite, each in its own way, the inscription of modernity as a negativity that until very recently has ruled Spanish America's cultural and political life.

This awareness of the rhetorical crisis that has generated Spanish American cultural discourse—which I argue is our particular version of postmodernity—can be seen in the recent displacement of the question of identity from the center of cultural enterprise in Spanish America. As I have proposed elsewhere, the surreptitious turning away from modernity that is effected by cultural discourse in Spanish America became reified into the endless cultural project of searching for an identity whose definitive formulation was the presumed responsibility of every Spanish American intellectual and writer.[4] Predictably, this project has come under scrutiny as the crisis that gave birth to it has ceased to be experienced as such. A critical praxis that has surfaced recently as a result of this change in perspective is the one in which a disjunction is revealed between the metaphors and topoi of national identity discourses and the contemporary realities and needs of the country in question. A perfect example of this tendency is Roger Bartra's *La jaula de la melancolía*, in which the author seeks to evince the present unproductive state of Mexican cultural and political discourses—the staleness and rigidity of its founding tropes.[5] Cultural products that indict previous texts belonging to that same tradition are not necessarily a novelty in themselves, since one of the dominant traits of Spanish American cultural discourse has been its internecine critical polemicizing. What is truly remarkable in this new examination of cultural language is that the exercise has no diagnostic or corrective intention. That is, there is no demand for the reformulation of old myths or the creation of new metaphors for cultural life, only the intention of showing the inapplicability and present lack of fit of the old paradigms. Bartra's critical stance, which places itself this side of nostalgia and pre-scription, is presented as a necessary step on the way to finally breaking the hold that the stale discourses of identity still have on the cultural imagination of Spanish America.

On the other hand, there has been a great deal of polemicizing in the last fifteen years about the desirability of a sweeping condemnation of identity discourses; opponents have argued that the usefulness of identity *récits* should be analyzed in the concrete circumstances in which they are invoked and in terms of the strategic opportunities that they make pos-sible.[6] My contention is that the "question of identity" provided until very recently the possibility and the space for Spanish American cultural discourse and that this generative and productive dimension has to be acknowledged fully. But by the same token, since the relationship between Spanish America and the metropolis is no longer mediated by the ideo-logical narrative of modernity—a situation dictated by the metropolis it-self, of course, but true nonetheless—the discourse of identity does not retain any longer the generative and contestatory capabilities it once pos-sessed.

The best way to achieve clarity concerning any future options for Spanish American discourse lies in a thorough understanding of that gen-erative mechanism and the crisis to which it was a response. A sustained exploration of cultural discourse in Spanish America from that perspective would make possible a critical rereading of European modernity itself through the identification and study of the ways in which Spanish Amer-ican authors sought to define a space for disallowing its implications. In other words, identifying the difficulties that Spanish American intellec-tuals faced in creating a modern tradition would allow us to uncover and exploit the constructedness of cultural narratives of modernity in metro-politan circles as well.[7] I believe this is the sort of enterprise that Nelly Richard had in mind when she proposed that "postmodernism offers us the chance to reconsider all that was 'left unsaid' and to inject [modern-ity's] areas of opacity and resistance with the potential for new, as yet undiscovered meanings."[8] One could conceptualize this critical explora-tion as an analogue to the radical deterritorialization of Western mo-dernity carried out by Bruno Latour in his book *We Have Never Been*

Modern. Eschewing as incomplete the critical leverage seemingly offered by the contemporary disavowal of modernity, Latour concentrates instead on identifying the hybrid quasi-objects that modernity simultaneously created and suppressed as part of its coming into being: objects that contravened the avowed dichotomy between the natural and the social on which the modern constitution was founded. Latour's maneuver exposes an entire dimension of the modern disposition that while inconsistent with its tenets, is also constitutive of it, thereby identifying a nonmodernity at the very core of the modern. I propose that we must learn to develop similar habits of reading, but without mystifying the peripheral as a privileged site of contestation. For as Latour says in the course of his argument, "the defence of marginality presupposes the existence of a totalitarian centre. But if the centre and its totality are illusions, acclaim for the margins is somewhat ridiculous."[9] Given that the relationship between Europe, the United States and Spanish America is still customarily defined in hegemonic terms, the lessons of all sorts mastered from the readings of Spanish American texts from the perspective articulated in this book can only redound in the end to our collective benefit.

Notes

All translations are my own unless otherwise specified.

Preface

1. Carlos J. Alonso, *The Spanish American Regional Novel: Modernity and Autochthony* (Cambridge: Cambridge UP, 1990).

2. Simón Bolívar, "Carta al general Santander," in *Doctrina del Libertador* (Caracas: Ayacucho, 1985), 158.

3. Gregory Jusdanis, *Belated Modernity and Aesthetic Culture* (Minneapolis: U of Minnesota P, 1991), xii. See also Anthony Cascardi's ranging consideration of modern subjectivity in *The Subject of Modernity* (Cambridge: Cambridge UP, 1992). Timothy J. Reiss has traced modernity's discursive foundations back to the sixteenth century in his impressive *Discourse of Modernism* (Ithaca: Cornell UP, 1982).

Chapter One

1. Derrida showed in an early article on Benveniste's work that the copula is in any event a very unstable grammatical category. See his "The Supplement of Copula: Philosophy before Linguistics," in *Margins of Philosophy*, trans. Alan Bass (Chicago: U of Chicago P, 1982), 175–205.

2. Barbara Johnson, "Taking Fidelity Philosophically," in *Difference in Translation*, ed. Joseph F. Graham (Ithaca: Cornell UP, 1985), 146.

3. Djelal Kadir has argued in his *Columbus and the Ends of the Earth* (Berkeley: U of California P, 1992), 62–80, that the newness of the New World was produced discursively even before the actual discovery of the continent. See also José Rabasa, *Inventing America: Spanish Historiography and the Formation of Eurocentrism* (Norman: U of Oklahoma P, 1993). In this study of historiographic discourses produced during the first years after the discovery of the Americas, Rabasa examines, among other things, "how an inherited stock of knowledge constitutes a thesaurus for the invention and description of a desirable *new world*" (59). The book which inaugurated this line of inquiry and to which all subsequent efforts are clearly indebted is Edmundo O'Gorman's *La invención de América: el universalismo en la cultura de Occidente* (Mexico City: Fondo de Cultura Económica, 1958).

4. Stephen Greenblatt, *Marvelous Possessions: The Wonder of the New World* (Chicago: U of Chicago P, 1991).

5. Irving Leonard has studied the various implications of the Spanish search for the Amazons in chapters 4 and 5 of his *Books of the Brave* (Berkeley: U of California P, 1992), 36–64. See also Horacio Jorge Becco's compilation of related material in *Historia real y fantástica del Nuevo Mundo* (Caracas: Ayacucho, 1992), as well as Stephen Clissold's *The Seven Cities of Cíbola* (New York: C. N. Potter, 1992) and Constantino Bayle's *El Dorado fantasma* (Madrid: Razón y Fe, 1930).

6. Mario Góngora, *Studies in the Colonial History of Spanish America* (Cambridge: Cambridge UP, 1975), 236–37.

7. Johannes Fabian, *Time and the Other: How Anthropology Makes Its Object* (New York: Columbia UP, 1983).

8. Antonello Gerbi, *La disputa del Nuevo Mundo: historia de una polémica.* (Mexico City: Fondo de Cultura, 1960). Concerning Buffon, Gerbi avers:

> Pero si miramos aún más a fondo, descubriremos también en la teoría buffoniana el reflejo de un problema lógico que todavía sigue sin resolver. Buffon no se lo formula con toda claridad, pero lucha con él a ciegas, con valor desatentado y desafortunado: . . . la existencia y la pensabilidad de especies naturales *semejantes*, pero diferentes, el enigma de conceptos naturalistas vinculados entre sí por indiscutibles analogías y, sin embargo, separados por indiscutibles e irreductibles rasgos individuales. (30)

> But if we look even closer, we shall discover in Buffon's theories the mark of a logical problem that is still unresolved. Buffon does not formulate it clearly, but he struggles with it unknowingly and without success: it is the existence and the possibility of *similar* yet different natural species; the enigma of naturalist concepts linked by undisputable analogies, and nevertheless separated by undisputable and irreducible individual traits.

9. Julio Ortega has argued in *El discurso de la abundancia* (Caracas: Monte Avila, 1990) that there is a discourse of excess and abundance about Spanish America that had its source in the need to represent the novel realities encountered by the conquerors and explorers. The various manifestations of that discourse would later be opposed, Ortega continues, by a *discurso de la carencia* that would signal the discrepancy between the utopian discourse of *abundancia* and the dystopian historical experience of the region. Regardless of my misgivings about the dialectic movement implied by his formulation, I find useful Ortega's notion of a utopian "modelo virtual—que supone una realidad americana discernible en las tensiones del futuro; o sea: en proceso de constituirse y realizarse" (71) [virtual model— which supposes an American reality discernible in the tensions of the future; that is, in the process of constituting and realizing itself].

10. Rafael Gutiérrez Girardot, *Temas y problemas de una historia social de la literatura hispanoamericana* (Bogotá: Cave Canem, 1989), 46.

11. In *Spain and Portugal in the New World, 1492–1700* (Minneapolis: U of Minnesota P, 1984), Lyle N. McAlister argues that the fluidity within the so-called Republic of Spaniards was due to the fact that the Spanish Crown "opposed the presence of a powerful nobility in America" and that "the medieval concept of a republic could not accommodate the millions of non-Europeans who made

up most of the American population" (391). See especially chapter 18, "American Societies and American Identities," 391–422.

12. Richard Morse, "The Heritage of Latin America," in *The Founding of a New Society*, ed. Louis Hartz (New York: Harcourt, 1964), 142. The Crown's first attempt to ban the *encomienda* in New Spain takes place as early as 1523; in 1526 it moved to claim as its prerogative all rights of exploitation of *suelo y subsuelo*.

13. There were, of course, serious challenges to Imperial authority by the *conquistadores* themselves from the very beginning of the Conquest. By the same token, the appointments of some early viceroys by Philip II, such as the Conde de Nieva and especially his successor Francisco de Toledo in Peru (1569–81), were made with the specific intention of curtailing the new prerogatives that the older conquistadores and their immediate descendants had created and continuously sought to arrogate to themselves. See chapter 6 of D. A. Brading's *The First America: The Spanish Monarchy, Creole Patriots and the Liberal State, 1492–1867* (Cambridge: Cambridge UP, 1991), 128–46, for an account of the extended negotiations between the Crown and the *encomenderos*, who alternately demanded and offered to pay for their "right" to their property claims for perpetuity. A more thorough consideration of the topic can be found in Mario Góngora's *El estado en el derecho indiano: época de fundación, 1492–1570* (Santiago: Universidad de Chile, 1951).

14. As Richard Morse has starkly put it, "To state the case more fully, political or social revolution was neither cause nor concomitant of the independence wars." ("Heritage of Latin America," 162).

15. José Luis Romero and Luis Alberto Romero have edited an important two-volume collection of texts and manifestos produced by the separatist cause that leaves no doubt in this regard. See their *Pensamiento político de la emancipación* (Caracas: Ayacucho, 1985). The entire second part of Francisco Bilbao's *El evangelio americano* (Caracas: Ayacucho, 1988) still in 1864 argues for a radical *desespañolización* of all practices and institutions in Spanish America (89–127). See also Joseph Pérez, *Los movimientos precursores de la emancipación en Hispanoamérica* (Madrid: Alhambra, 1982).

16. See, for instance, Simón Bolívar's "Carta de Jamaica" (1815), in which the rubric "Nuevo Mundo" is used alternately with "América" to refer to the Spanish possessions in rebellion. In *Doctrina del Libertador*, 83–99. Ten years earlier, in his "Juramento de Roma," Bolívar had argued that the "enigma" of human freedom would only be finally solved in the unspecified future of the "Nuevo Mundo" (*Doctrina del Libertador*, 4).

17. The sense that the New World offered unlimited opportunities for social advancement did not come to an end with the severance of political ties with Spain after independence, as was demonstrated by the successive waves of Spanish immigrants that landed in both former and remaining Spanish colonies during the nineteenth and early twentieth centuries. James D. Fernández's ongoing work on the figure of the *indiano* in nineteenth-century Spanish letters offers a suggestive consideration of these issues.

18. Jorge Klor de Alva, "Colonialism and Postcolonialism as (Latin) American

Mirages," *Colonial Latin American Review* 1.1–2 (1992): 3–23. A companion essay that appeared three years later takes up again some of the issues first addressed here and allows Klor de Alva to qualify some of his original formulations: "The Postcolonization of the (Latin) American Experience: A Reconsideration of 'Colonialism,' 'Postcolonialism,' and 'Mestizaje,'" in *After Colonialism: Imperial Histories and Postcolonial Displacements*, ed. Gyan Prakash (Princeton: Princeton UP, 1995), 241–75.

19. Klor de Alva avers further that "the close identification of the post-independence national cultures with their European templates makes it evident that the Americas, in contrast to many Asian and African societies, did not experience decolonization in the course of their assumed postcoloniality. From this I conclude that where there was no decolonization there could be no postcolonialism, and where in a post-independence society no postcolonialism can be found, the presence of a preexisting colonialism should be put in question" (4). By way of criticizing Klor's ideas, Fernando Coronil has argued for a functional definition of postcoloniality as subordination that allows him to subsume the neocolonial phase of Spanish American history under the mantle of the postcolonial. See his "Can Postcoloniality Be Decolonized?: Imperial Banality and Postcolonial Power," *Public Culture* 5.1 (1992): 89–108.

20. Kwame Anthony Appiah, *In My Father's House: Africa in the Philosophy of Culture* (New York: Oxford UP, 1992), 149. In his study of the "messianic" component of postcolonial African literature, *Resistance in Postcolonial African Fiction* (New Haven: Yale UP, 1990), Neil Lazarus says as much:

> Now, with the rare exception of a figure like Ousmane Sembene, African writers of the independence era belonged themselves to the African national bourgeoisies. Almost all of them were comparatively highly educated; many, indeed, were "been-to's," people who had traveled abroad—usually to the West—for education or professional training. By virtue of their qualifications and experience, they, along with the rest of their class, stood poised at independence to inherit privileged and responsible positions in the postcolonial society. (11)

21. Anderson discusses the formation of a collective subjectivity among the Spanish American Creoles as based, among other things, on their perceived sense of being thwarted as a group in their bureaucratic advancement during the colonial regime. See Benedict Anderson, *Imagined Communities: Reflections on the Origin and Spread of Nationalism* (London: Verso, 1983), especially chapters 4 and 5, pp. 50–79. See also Camilo Torres's "Memorial de agravios," in *Pensamiento político de la emancipación: 1790–1825*, 2 vols., ed. José L. Romero and Luis A. Romero, (Caracas: Ayacucho, 1985), 1:25–42.

22. Michael Hechter, *Internal Colonialism: The Celtic Fringe in British National Development, 1536–1966* (Berkeley: U of California P, 1975), 37.

23. This might be the right moment to make a brief but important point. I am cognizant of the long line of indigenous revolts in Spanish America that attest to a resistance to the commitment to modernity on the part of the Creole elite: the Túpac Amaru and Túpac Kitari rebellions of the late eighteenth century, and the Chamula revolt in Mexico and the "Guerra de las castas" in Yucatán during

the nineteenth century, for instance; rebellions that were repressed with equal savagery by both the Spanish colonial authorities and the Creole national ruling classes. Nonetheless, in this study I am concerned with the cultural projects articulated by the Spanish American elites after independence—that is, those of the class that was in a position to impose its cultural templates on the rest of the population and to claim for those programs a false collective representativeness and unanimity precisely through its repression of those alternative proposals. Even though my argument does not address the latter explicitly, I would caution the reader to keep in mind that the voices heard here arrogated to themselves their right to speak through that silencing operation.

24. By calling formulations of national identity "artificial" I mean to say that they are constructs, not that they are in any way arbitrary.

25. I am referring to the period 1810–70 in that country, which included the administrations of José Gaspar de Francia, Antonio Carlos López, and Francisco Solano López.

26. Anthony Pagden has studied the profound difficulties attendant to the various attempts made by colonial writers to formulate a Creole identity based on the existence of a connection with the pre-Spanish past. See his essay "Fabricating Identity in Spanish America," *History Today* (1992): 44–49, and the anthology edited by Pagden and Nicholas Canny entitled *Colonial Identity in the Atlantic World, 1500–1800* (Princeton: Princeton UP, 1987). In this regard one could also mention the cultural and governmental programs of Rafael Carrera's administration in Guatemala (1838–65), which endeavored to incorporate the indigenous element into the political body. See E. Bradford Burns's evaluation of Carrera's regime in "Cultures in Conflict: The Implication of Modernization in Nineteenth-Century Latin America," in *Elites, Masses, and Modernization in Latin America, 1850–1930* (Austin: U of Texas P, 1979), 49–56.

27. John Lynch has famously referred to this Spanish bureaucratic initiative as a "second conquest" in *The Spanish American Revolutions, 1808–1826* (New York: Norton, 1973), 7. As Claudio Véliz summarizes, "These measures were not the outcome of a successful agitation by mercantile circles in the colonies, but on the contrary, were based on the economic ideas of Charles III's ministers, principally Campillo and Campomanes and were decreed by the metropolis against the wishes of the local traders." In *The Centralist Tradition of Latin America* (Princeton: Princeton UP, 1980), 126–27. See also Brian R. Hamnett's "Between Bourbon Reforms and Liberal Reforma: The Political Economy of a Mexican Province— Oaxaca, 1750–1850," in *The Political Economy of Spanish America in the Age of Revolution, 1750–1850*, ed. K. Andrien and Lyman Johnson (Albuquerque: U of New Mexico P), 39–62.

28. Simón Bolívar, "Carta al General Santander" (1825), in *Doctrina del Libertador*, 182.

29. I am not arguing that the results were indeed novel in Spanish America but rather that such an expectation greatly influences the narrative outcome.

30. See chapter 1 of Alonso, *The Spanish American Regional Novel*.

31. For instance, Robert T. Conn has intelligently studied the ideological uses of the concept of *americanismo* in the works of Alfonso Reyes. See his " 'Ameri-

canismo andante': Alfonso Reyes and the 1930s," *Latin American Literary Review* 23.46 (1995): 83–98.

32. Victor Bulner-Thomas has referred to this access to the international capital market as a "poisoned chalice" in his *The Economic History of Latin America since Independence* (Cambridge: Cambridge UP, 1994), 28. For an overview of the economic problems entailed by independence for the new republics see David Bushnell and Neill Macaulay's *The Emergence of Latin America in the Nineteenth Century* (New York: Oxford UP, 1994). See also *The Frank G. Dawson's First Latin American Debt Crisis: The City of London and the 1822–25 Loan Bubble*: (New Haven: Yale UP, 1990) and J. Fred Rippy's *British Investments in Latin America, 1822–1949* (Minneapolis: U of Minnesota P, 1959), in which the uneven financial relationship between British trusts and the new Spanish American countries is detailed. Roberto Cortés Conde has studied the implications of these beginnings for the second half of the Spanish American nineteenth century in his *First Stages of Modernization in Spanish America* (New York: Harper and Row, 1974).

33. Enrique Dussel has written extensively about how the myth of modernity allowed Europe to constitute itself as the center through its simultaneous constitution of a periphery. He then uses this essential internalization of the peripheral that is present in the center's definition of itself to explode the myth from within. See his *Invention of the Americas: Eclipse of "the Other" and the Myth of Modernity*, trans. Michael D. Barber (New York: Continuum, 1985), and "Eurocentrism and Modernity (Introduction to the Frankfurt Lectures)," *boundary 2* 20.3 (1993): 65–76. Here he claims that

> Modernity is, for many (for Jürgen Habermas or Charles Taylor, for example), an essentially or exclusively European phenomenon. In these lectures, I will argue that modernity is, in fact, a European phenomenon, but one constituted in a dialectical relation with a non-European alterity that is its ultimate content. Modernity appears when Europe affirms itself as the "center" of a World history that it inaugurates; the periphery" that surrounds this center is consequently part of its self-definition. The occlusion of this periphery (and of the role of Spain and Portugal in the formation of the modern world system from the late fifteenth to the mid-seventeenth centuries), leads the major contemporary thinkers of the "center" into a Eurocentric fallacy in their understanding of modernity. If their understanding of the genealogy of modernity is thus partial and provincial, their attempts at a critique or defense of it are likewise unilateral and, in part, false. (66)

34. Nelly Richard, "Postmodernism and Periphery," in *Postmodernism: A Reader*, ed. Thomas Docherty (Hertfordshire: Harvester Wheatsheaf, 1993), 464. Or, as Bruno Latour has said, "modern temporality is the result of a retraining imposed on entities which would pertain to all sorts of times and possess all sorts of ontological statuses without this harsh disciplining." *We Have Never Been Modern*, trans. Catherine Porter (Hertfordshire: Harvester Wheatsheaf, 1993), 72.

35. The transition implicit in this sentence is the topic of chapter 7 of this study.

36. Vincent Descombes, *L'Inconscient malgré lui* (Paris: Minuit, 1977).

37. Descombes concludes, "The statements of the master have found their

authority on the authority of his name, and the authority of that name is guaranteed by the voice of the public" (119). I have also found useful for this discussion Antoine Compagnon's study of quotation as a textual praxis in his now classic *La Seconde main, ou le travail de la citation* (Paris: Seuil, 1979).

38. *Una modernidad periférica* constitutes the ideological backbone of Sarlo's study of Argentine modernization, an effort that spans two other books as well: *El imperio de los sentimientos* (Buenos Aires: Diálogos, 1986) and *La imaginación técnica: sueños modernos de la cultura argentina* (Buenos Aires: Nueva Visión, 1992).

39. Spain's relationship with modernity shares in some of the qualities that characterize the Spanish American case. Indeed, at the time some European capitalist powers were competing to establish Spanish American markets, Spain was undergoing a similar neocolonial penetration from those very countries and then some: Britain, France, Belgium, and Germany. This common experience of economic and material peripheralness determined that modernity be construed in both geographic enclaves as something that was judged to exist only in metropolitan centers, as a commodity that had to be appropriated, imported, and then protected if it was to have a chance to thrive in an initially inhospitable context. But by the same token, once this belief took hold, the rhetorical dialectics that I describe in this chapter were also set into motion; that is, even in those texts that would seem to argue for the unbridled adoption of the program of modernity, there was simultaneously the expression of a desire to distance oneself from the modern, an affirmation of the incommensurableness of the local by the epistemological and discursive instruments of modernity. This troping away from modernity that takes place in these texts is a movement that ought to be studied in its various manifestations. I am by no means an expert in Spanish letters, but a number of notable instances come immediately to mind in that specific context: Feijóo's apologies of Scholastic doctrine; Blanco White's struggle against orthodoxy, which paradoxically took the form of a series of conversions from one religion to another; Larra's deep and well-known ambivalence with respect to the modern; and Zorrilla's salvific rewriting of Tirso's play, which effectively cancels the quintessential modernity that critics such as Michel Serres and Shoshana Felman have seen in the previous avatars of the Don Juan figure. See Felman's *The Literary Speech Act: Don Juan with J. L. Austin, or Seduction in Two Languages* (Ithaca: Cornell UP, 1983) and Michel Serres's "The Apparition of Hermes: *Dom Juan*," in *Hermes: Literature, Science, Philosophy*, ed. J. Harari and D. Bell (Baltimore: Johns Hopkins UP, 1982), 3–14.

40. Ducrot and Todorov: "Linguistic production may be regarded either as a sequence of sentences identified without reference to any specific circumstances of occurrence (the sentences may be pronounced, transcribed by means of various writing systems, printed) or as an act in the course of which these sentences are actualized, assumed by a particular speaker in specific spatial and temporal circumstances. From this alternative stems the opposition between the *utterance* (énoncé) and the speech situation, sometimes called the *enunciation* (énonciation)." *Encyclopedic Dictionary of the Sciences of Language* (Baltimore: Johns Hopkins UP, 1983), 323.

41. Enrico Mario Santí has argued forcefully against that logic in our larger

disciplinary context. See his "Latinamericanism and Restitution," *Latin American Literary Review* 20 (1992): 88–96. See also Alberto Moreiras's "Restitution and Appropriation in Latinamericanism," *Journal of Interdisciplinary Literary Studies* 7 (1995): 1–43.

42. Richard Terdiman, *Discourse/Counter-Discourse: The Theory and Practice of Symbolic Resistance in Nineteenth-Century France* (Ithaca: Cornell UP, 1985), 77.

43. I am thinking, for instance, of works such as Angel Rama's *Transculturación narrativa en América Latina* (Mexico City: Siglo XXI, 1982), Gustavo Pérez Firmat's *The Cuban Condition: Translation and Identity in Modern Cuban Literature* (Cambridge: Cambridge UP, 1989) and Mary Louise Pratt's *Imperial Eyes: Travel Writing and Transculturation* (New York: Routledge, 1992).

44. Fernando Ortiz, *Contrapunteo cubano del tabaco y el azúcar* (Caracas: Ayacucho, 1978).

45. Pratt, *Imperial Eyes*, 228, note 4.

46. To my mind the best critique of the use of the concept of *transculturación* in the Latin American context is by the Cuban anthropologist Manuel Moreno Fraginals in an essay entitled "Aportes culturales y deculturación," in *Africa en América Latina*, ed. Manuel Mareno Fraginals (Mexico City: Siglo XXI, 1987), 13–33. Speaking about the experience of Africans brought to the Americas as slaves he argues:

> En nuestra opinión no puede llegarse a la raíz de este problema si partimos del esquema antropológico prefijado que considera la transculturación como un fenómeno de choque y síntesis entre un grupo de inmigrantes que son insertados en una sociedad de moldes culturales europeos. La realidad de las que, muy vagamente pudiéramos llamar "zonas negras del Caribe" es otra totalmente distinta. Desde sus inicios se trata de sociedades *nuevas* donde africanos y europeos van llegando simultáneamente: los primeros en condición de pueblos sojuzgados en una guerra de rapiña capitalista y los segundos en condiciones de grupo explotador. No hay pues una sociedad preexistente, a la europea, que se impregna de aportaciones africanas. Por lo tanto, es falso como método la simple búsqueda de africanismos para sopesar cuantitativamente cuántos se insertaron en los moldes establecidos. (31)

> In my view, we cannot arrive at the root of this problem if we take as our point of departure the anthropological paradigm that regards transculturation as a phenomenon of clash and synthesis between a group of immigrants that are inserted into a society of European cultural traits. The reality of what one could imprecisely call the "Black zones of the Caribbean," is completely other. From their beginnings these are new societies to which Africans and Europeans arrived simultaneously: the first as vanquished peoples in a capitalist war of spoils, and the latter as the exploiting group. Hence there is no preexisting, European-based society that is then inflected with African contributions. Therefore, it is a useless methodology to engage in the search of africanisms to determine quantitatively how many of them found their way into the official molds.

See also Antonio Benítez Rojo's *La isla que se repite: el Caribe y la perspectiva posmoderna* (Hanover, N.H.: Ediciones del Norte, 1989) for a superb reconceptualization—and performance—of cultural exchange in the Caribbean.

47. Samir Amin has criticized this sort of contestatory maneuver, referring to

it as "inverted Eurocentrism" in his *Eurocentrism* (New York: Monthly Review P, 1989). Some recent critical works attempt to transcend the limitations of the bipolar model of cultural exchange under hegemonic rule by exploring precisely the dependence of metropolitan discourses on the enterprise of empire. Their effort is to arrive at a dynamic formulation of hegemony that approximates the activity depicted by Moreno Fraginal's earlier quotation. Nancy Armstrong has argued in *Desire and Domestic Fiction: A Political History of the Novel* (New York: Oxford UP, 1987) that histories of hegemonic institutions "tend to ignore the degree to which the forms of resistance themselves determine the strategies of domination" (22). See also Edward Said's *Culture and Imperialism* (New York: Knopf, 1993), and his essay "Secular Interpretation, the Geographical Element, and the Methodology of Imperialism," in *After Colonialism: Imperial Histories and Postcolonial Displacements*, ed. Gyan Prakash (Princeton: Princeton UP, 1995), 21–39.

48. I have found most illuminating Brett Levinson's meditations on this subject in his "The Death of the Critique of Eurocentrism: Latinamericanism as Global Praxis/Poiesis," *Revista de Estudios Hispánicos* 31.2 (1997): 169–201.

49. In this regard I must open an extended parenthesis here to deal with one influential work on this theme, Roberto González Echevarría's splendid book *Myth and Archive: A Theory of Latin American Narrative* (Cambridge: Cambridge UP, 1990). González's argument is that there have been three master rhetorical forms that have informed colonial and postindependence novelistic production from its beginning to the present: the forensic template of the *relación* for the colonial period, the scientific travelogue for the nineteenth century, and anthropological discourse for the twentieth. The scheme is founded on the idea that the principal quality of the novel as a genre is to pretend that it is something other than literature: hence, the novel models its form after nonliterary, referential discourses that are imbued with prestige and authority at a given time in order to partake in their prominent status.

As is evident even from this short account, González's reading of Spanish American cultural production in its relation to a succession of hegemonic discourses is related to my undertaking in this book. There is, however, a crucial difference: his reduction of those discourses to the three mentioned earlier is unnecessarily limiting: it leads him to devalue significant works that do not conform to the scheme and to force others into harmonizing with it (e.g., the outright dismissal of *María* and *Amalia*, as well as the bewildering interpretation of Borges's story "Tlön Uqbar, Orbis Tertius" as a parody of a telluric novel). By contrast, the argument that I am proposing sees each text as choosing from a much larger repertoire of hegemonic discourses that are invoked as models on account of their perceived prestige, which allows for a more nuanced contextualization and understanding of their paradoxical engagement with those models.

50. Matei Calinescu, *Five Faces of Modernity: Modernism, Avant-Garde, Decadence, Kitsch, Postmodernism* (Durham: Duke UP, 1987), 41.

51. Marshall Berman, *All That Is Solid Melts into Air: The Experience of Modernity* (New York: Simon and Schuster, 1982), 87–129.

52. Claudio Véliz, *The New World of the Gothic Fox: Culture and Economy in English and Spanish America* (Berkeley: U of California P, 1994), 197. Véliz goes

on to say: "Without an Industrial Revolution, there could not have been re-
sponses, intelligent and otherwise, to its consequences; in the absence of smoke-
belching satanic mills, it is unlikely to find poets calling for new Jerusalems surrounded by greenery" (197).

53. Berman, *All That Is Solid Melts into Air*, 231–32. Simon Gikandi has described the phenomenon succinctly in its Caribbean manifestation: "Once they
have been displaced from what I call their Eurocentric zones of origin, modernism,
modernity, and modernization proffer contradictory meanings that are, nevertheless, the conditions that make Caribbean literature possible." In *Writing in Limbo:
Modernism and Caribbean Literature* (Ithaca: Cornell UP, 1992), 254. For another
magnificent study of the ambivalent modernism of peripheral areas see Leopoldo
Zea's *Discurso desde la marginación y la barbarie* (Barcelona: Anthropos, 1988).

54. Mary Louise Pratt, "Reinventing America/Reinventing Europe: Creole
Self-fashioning," in *Imperial Eyes*, 172–97; William Katra, "Rereading *Viajes*: Race,
Identity, and National Destiny," in *Sarmiento: Author of a Nation*, ed. Tulio Hal-
perín Donghi, et al. (Berkeley: U of California P, 1994), 73–100. See also Cris-
tóbal Pera's "Una excursión en la modernidad: Sarmiento en París," in *Actas XXIX
Congreso del IILI* (Barcelona: PPU, 1994), 319–37.

55. Jusdanis describes this phenomenon as follows: "Belated modernization,
especially in non-western societies, necessarily remains 'incomplete' not because
it deviates from the supposedly correct path but because it cannot culminate in a
faithful duplication of western prototypes. The imported models do not function
like their European counterparts. Often they are resisted. The project of becoming modern thus differs from place to place. This is why it is possible to speak of
many modernities. Peripheral societies, however, internalize the incongruity between western originals and local realities as a structural deficiency. The lack of
modernity is seen as a flaw. Hence, 'incomplete' attempts to catch up with the
West are followed by calls for a new phase of modernization" (*Belated Modernity
and Aesthetic Culture*, xiii). One also has to mention here Roberto Schwarz's striking concept of "misplaced ideas," which he develops to address Brazilian appro-
priations of modern ideology. See his *Misplaced Ideas: Essays on Brazilian Culture*,
ed. and trans. John Gledson (London: Verso, 1992).

56. In a recent article, Bhabha put it succinctly thus: "It has been my growing
conviction that the encounters and negotiations of differential meanings and values within the governmental discourses and cultural practices that make up 'colonial' textuality have enacted, *avant la lettre*, many of the problematics of signification and judgment that have become current in contemporary theory: aporia,
ambivalence, indeterminacy, the question of discursive closure, the threat to
agency, the status of intentionality, the challenge to 'totalizing' concepts, to name
but a few." From "Freedom's Basis in the Indeterminate," in *The Identity in Question*, ed. John Rajchman (New York: Routledge, 1995), 49.

Bhabha goes on to make a claim for the proleptic "postmodernism" of the
colonial situation: "To put it in general terms, there is a 'colonial' countermod-
ernity at work in the eighteenth- and nineteenth-century matrices of Western
modernity that, if acknowledged, would question the historicism that, in a linear
narrative, analogically links late capitalism to the fragmentary, simulacral, pas-

tiche-like symptoms of postmodernity" (49). I disagree with this claim, for reasons that I will address in chapter 7. See also Spivak's *In Other Worlds: Essays in Cultural Politics* (London: Methuen, 1987) and Niranjana's *Siting Translation: History, Post-Structuralism, and the Colonial Context* (Berkeley: U of California P, 1992).

57. Homi Bhabha, "The Commitment to Theory," in *The Location of Culture* (New York: Routledge, 1994), 36. I have also found illuminating Ora Avni's "solution" out of the impasse between semantic and deictic conceptions of language by positing a third semiotic position that is attentive to the heterogeneous interaction between these two functions of language—which I see as the dimension in which discourse can be seen to be inflected by hierarchical difference. See Avni, *The Resistance of Reference: Linguistics, Philosophy, and the Literary Text* (Baltimore: Johns Hopkins UP, 1990), especially 230–64.

58. Partha Chatterjee, *The Nation and Its Fragments: Colonial and Postcolonial Histories* (Princeton: Princeton UP, 1993).

59. Fredric Jameson, "Third-World Literature in the Era of Multinational Capitalism," *Social Text* 15 (1986): 65–88. Aijaz Ahmad's critique of Jameson's thesis, "Jameson's Rhetoric of Otherness and the National Allegory" (*Social Text* 17 [1986]: 3–25), appears in a subsequent issue of the same journal and was reprinted in his book *In Theory: Classes, Nations, Literatures* (London: Verso, 1992). It reads in part as follows: "If this 'Third World' is *constituted* by the singular 'experience of colonialism and imperialism,' and if the only possible response is a nationalistic one, then what else is there that is more urgent to narrate than this 'experience'? In fact, there is *nothing else* to narrate. For if societies here are defined not by relations of production but by relations of intra-national domination; . . . if the motivating force for history here is neither class formation and class struggle nor the multiplicities of intersecting conflicts based upon class, gender, nation, race, region, and so on, but the unitary 'experience' of national oppression (if one is merely the *object* of history, the Hegelian slave), then what else *can* one narrate but that national oppression? Politically, we are Calibans all. Formally, we are fated to be in the poststructuralist world of Repetition with Difference; the same allegory, the nationalist one, over and over again, until the end of time" (102). There is a powerful rejoinder to Ahmad's critique of Jameson by Madhava Prasad: "On the Question of Theory of (Third World) Literature," *Social Text* 31–32 (1992): 57–83.

In a passage that echoes Ahmad's critique, Chatterjee has said: "If nationalisms in the rest of the world have to choose their imagined community from certain 'modular' forms already made available to them by Europe and the Americas, what do they have left to imagine? History, it would seem, has decreed that we in the postcolonial world shall only be perpetual consumers of modernity. Europe and the Americas, the only true subjects of history, have thought out on our behalf not only the script of colonial enlightenment and exploitation, but also that of our anticolonial resistance and postcolonial misery. Even our imaginations must remain forever colonized" (5).

60. Paul de Man's classic study "The Rhetoric of Temporality" offers an overview of romantic critiques of allegory. In *Interpretation: Theory and Practice* (Baltimore: Johns Hopkins UP, 1969), 173–209.

61. "When the atoms are being carried, each by its own weight, straight downward through the void, at utterly unfixed times and places they swerve a little from their course, just enough so that you can say that the direction is altered. If the atoms did not have this swerve, they would all fall straight down through the deep void like drops of rain, and no collisions would occur nor would the atoms sustain any blows. Thus, Nature would never have created anything." From Lucretius *On Nature*, trans. Russell M. Geer (New York: Bobbs-Merrill, 1965), 47. I have borrowed the critical use of this term from Harold Bloom's invocation of it to name one of the "revisionary ratios" that can obtain between a poet and his precursor. In *The Anxiety of Influence: A Theory of Poetry* (New York: Oxford UP, 1973).

62. Rama's concept of the *ciudad letrada* has also been proposed as a model for both colonial and contemporary literary studies. See, for instance, the following essays by Adorno and Kubayanda: "La *ciudad letrada* y los discursos coloniales," *Hispamérica* 48 (1987): 3–24, and "Order and Conflict: *Yo el Supremo* in Light of Rama's *ciudad letrada* Theory," in *The Historical Novel in Latin America*, ed. Daniel Balderston (Gaithersburg, Md.: Hispamérica, 1986), 129–37. Upon Rama's death there were a number of special issues of reviews and entire sections of journals devoted exclusively to his work: *Prismal-Cabral* 12–13 (1984); *Hispamérica* 39 (1984); and *Sin Nombre* 14.3 (1984). An important appraisal of Rama's works can be found in José Eduardo González, "¿El final de la modernización literaria?: técnica y technología en la crítica de Angel Rama," *MLN* 113.2 (1998): 380–406. See also the essays collected in *Angel Rama y los estudios latinoamericanos*, ed. Mabel Moraña (Pittsburgh: IILI, 1997).

63. Angel Rama, *La ciudad letrada* (Hanover, N.H.: Ediciones del Norte, 1984), 55–57.

64. For more on Hostos see, for instance, Juan Manuel Rivera's "*La peregrinación de Bayoán*: fragmentos de una lectura disidente," *Cuadernos Americanos* 35 (1992): 158–79, and Richard Rosa's "Literatura y construcción de naciones en el Caribe: una lectura de los textos de Eugenio María de Hostos" (Ph.D. diss., Harvard University, 1996). See also three special issues of *Cuadernos Americanos*: two devoted to Martí (51 and 52 [1995]) and one to Mariátegui (48[1994]).

65. Weber's influence on the study of nineteenth-century Spanish American studies is related to his discussion of the formation of autonomous spheres of rationalized discourses in the modern state, a theory whose full implications for literary discourse are subsequently developed by Habermas and Bürger.

66. I am thinking here of monographs such as Beatriz González Stephan's *La historiografía literaria del liberalismo hispanoamericano del siglo XIX* (Havana: Casa de las Américas, 1987), Julio Ramos's *Desencuentros de la modernidad en América Latina: literatura y política en el siglo XIX* (Mexico City: Fondo de Cultura Económica, 1989), and Susana Rotker's *La invención de la crónica* (Buenos Aires: Ediciones Letra Buena, 1992). There are two notable exceptions in this collection of critical works that study the state function of literature. The first is Josefina Ludmer's *El género gauchesco: un tratado sobre la patria* (Buenos Aires: Sudamericana, 1988), and the other is Doris Sommer's *Foundational Fictions: The National Romances of Latin America* (Berkeley: U of California P, 1991). In both of these works literature's role *as*

literature in the formation of the modern Latin American states from the outset is amply documented. See also Ricardo Piglia's masterful discussion of what he calls the "self-autonomization" of Argentine literature from its very beginnings in the nineteenth century in "Sarmiento the Writer," in *Sarmiento: Author of a Nation*, ed. Halperín Donghi et al. (Berkeley: U of California P, 1994), 127–44.

67. Ramos, *Desencuentros*, 172–73.

68. The topic of Spanish America's "incomplete" modernity will be retaken in chapter 7 in the context of an examination of the debates concerning post-modernity in the Spanish American milieu.

69. Iris M. Zavala has studied in detail the implications of this fin-de-siècle perceived imminence of modernity in the Hispanic context in her *Colonialism and Culture: Hispanic Modernisms and the Social Imaginary* (Bloomington: Indiana UP, 1992).

70. See Alvin Kernan's "The Idea of Literature," *New Literary History* 1.1 (1973): 31–40, and Tzvetan Todorov's "The Notion of Literature," *New Literary History* 1.1 (1973): 5–16. The first two chapters of Luiz Costa Lima's *Control of the Imaginary: Reason and Imagination in Modern Times*, trans. Ronald W. Souza (Minneapolis: U of Minnesota P, 1988) are also relevant to this discussion.

71. For an extended consideration of literature's internalization of modernity—which in his view has characterized literature since its appearance—see Octavio Paz's justly famous *Los hijos del limo: del romanticismo a la vanguardia* (Barcelona: Seix Barral, 1984).

Chapter Two

1. Domingo Sarmiento, "Carta a José Posse," in his *Memorias*, in *Obras completas*, 51 vols., ed. A. Belín Sarmiento (Buenos Aires: Imprenta y Litografía Mariano Moreno, 1899), 49:267. All quotations will be taken from this source, which will be referred to henceforth as *Obras*.

2. I offer here a shortened reproduction of a list compiled by Barreiro, who asserts, "Cuando enfrentó la polémica, [Sarmiento] perdió todo dominio y fue deslenguado, safio, procaz, implacable. . . . Ingenieros afirmará que 'Sarmiento contestó con golpes de hacha a las finísimas estocadas de su adversario.' " [When he polemicized (with Alberdi), (Sarmiento) lost all self-control and became foul-mouthed, disrespectful, impudent, and implacable. . . . Ingenieros said that "Sarmiento answered with the strokes of an ax the subtle sword thrusts of his adversary."] In *Cartas y discursos políticos: itinerario de una pasión republicana*, vol. 3 of *Edición especial de seis tomos de la obra de D. F. Sarmiento* (Buenos Aires: Ediciones Culturales Argentinas, 1965), 75.

3. Sarmiento, *Obras*, 15: 370.

4. Ibid., 3:26.

5. Sarmiento, letter to Echeverría, in Alberto Palcos, *Historia de Echeverría* (Buenos Aires: Emecé, 1960), 254–55.

6. See, for instance, Diana Sorensen Goodrich's account of the history of *Facundo*'s reception, *Facundo and the Construction of Argentine Culture* (Austin: U of Texas P, 1996).

7. Tulio Halperín Donghi, "El antiguo orden y su crisis como tema de *Recuerdos de provincia*," *Boletín del Instituto de Historia Argentina y Americana "Dr. E. Ravignani"* 1 (3d. series) (1989): 22. Another clear example is given by Ana María Barrenechea's reading of Sarmiento's compositional modus operandi. Speaking about Sarmiento's relationship with his reader, she tries to ascribe two irreducibly antithetical rhetorical strategies to Sarmiento's will:

> Por una parte excita su interés con un diálogo constante que no le deja desviar la atención, con preguntas, respuestas, exclamaciones, recursos que subrayan las opiniones, sacudimientos y virajes súbitos, respiros y sorpresas, pausas y nuevas arremetidas. Por otra parte, temiendo que se extravíe entre tantas digresiones y no mantenga el hilo de su razonamiento, le recuerda a cada paso el plan que lo guía para que al final quede claro el camino recorrido y pueda acabar con la fórmula tradicional *quod erat demostrandum*.

> ────────────

> On the one hand he engages the reader with a constant dialogue that does not allow him to lose attention: questions, answers, exclamations, the underscoring of opinions, jolts and sudden turns, stops and surprises, pauses and new thrusts. On the other hand, afraid that the reader will get lost in so many digressions and lose the thread of his reasoning, he reminds him continuously about the plan that he is unfolding so that in the end the road traveled will be clear, and he may be able to invoke the traditional formula *quod erat demostrandum*.

"La configuración del *Facundo*," in *Textos hispanoamericanos: de Sarmiento a Sarduy* (Caracas: Monte Avila, 1978), 40.

8. Adolfo Prieto, *La literatura autobiográfica argentina* (Buenos Aires: Facultad de Filosofía y Letras, 1966), 51.

9. Quoted in Ezequiel Martínez Estrada, *Sarmiento* (Buenos Aires: Argos, 1947), 164.

10. Enrique Anderson Imbert, Prologue to *Recuerdos de provincia* (Buenos Aires: Editorial de Belgrano, 1981), 59.

11. By the same token, Manuel Gálvez refers to an incident in Sarmiento's youth that reveals, according to him, "la impremeditación que tendrá toda su vida" [the lack of premeditation of his entire existence]. In *Vida de Sarmiento: el hombre de autoridad* (Buenos Aires: Editorial Tor, 1952), 51. Later he argues that "Sarmiento procedía por impulsos espontáneos e incontenibles que se renovaban sin cesar, sobre todo cuando algo los obstaculizaba." (444).[Sarmiento advanced through spontaneous and unbounded impulses that renewed themselves continually, and especially when something impeded them.]

12. Carlos Altamirano and Beatriz Sarlo, "Una vida ejemplar: la estrategia de *Recuerdos de provincia*," *Escritura* 9 (January–June 1980): 8.

13. Carlos Alberto Erro, Prologue to *Páginas escogidas de Sarmiento*, vol. 4 of *Edición especial de la obra de Domingo Faustino Sarmiento* (Buenos Aires: Ediciones Literarias Argentinas, 1963), x.

14. Immanuel Kant, *Critique of Judgment*, trans. J. H. Bernard (New York: Hafner Press, 1951), 83.

15. Witness, for instance, the following poignant characterization of Sarmiento's oeuvre by William Katra: "La contradictoria presencia de Sarmiento,

entonces y hoy, seguirá desafiando toda clasificación. . . . Sus escritos han sido continuo objeto de polémicas, si no de disputas. Pero después de bajar los puños y calmarse las voces, los lectores de Sarmiento siempre terminan por afirmar la extraña belleza y la inexplicable atracción de esta obra apasionante." [Then as now, Sarmiento's contradictory being continues to defy all classification. . . . His writings have been the subject of polemics, if not outright fights. Yet after fists have been unclenched and voices have been lowered, Sarmiento's readers always end up acknowledging the strange beauty and the inexplicable attraction of this impassioned oeuvre.] In "Sarmiento frente a la generación de 1837," *Revista Iberoamericana* 143 (April–June 1988): 549.

16. See J. L. Austin's *How to Do Things with Words*, ed. J. O. Urmson and Marina Sbisà (Cambridge: Harvard UP, 1975).

17. My argument here reflects recent trends and polemics in anthropological thought. See, for instance, Johannes Fabian's *Language and Colonial Power: The Appropriation of Swahili in the Former Belgian Congo, 1880–1938* (Cambridge: Cambridge UP, 1986); Clifford Geertz's *The Interpretation of Cultures* (New York: Basic Books, 1973) and *Local Knowledge: Further Essays in Interpretive Anthropology* (New York: Basic Books, 1983); Marshall Sahlins's *Historical Metaphors and Mythical Realities* (Ann Arbor: Michigan UP, 1981); James Clifford's *The Predicament of Culture; Twentieth-Century Ethrography, Literature, and Art* (Cambridge: Harvard UP, 1988); and Elizabeth Traube's *Cosmology and Social Life: Ritual Exchange among the Mambai of East Timor* (Chicago: U of Chicago P, 1986).

18. Françoise Pérus, "Modernity, Postmodernity, and Novelistic Form in Latin America," in *Latin American Identity and Constructions of Difference*, ed. Amaryll Chanady (Minneapolis: U of Minnesota P, 1994), 51.

19. Emile Benveniste, "The Nature of Pronouns," in *Problems in General Linguistics*, trans. Mary Elizabeth Meek (Coral Gables, Fla.: University of Miami P, 1971), 45.

20. Martínez Estrada, *Sarmiento*, 136.

21. Ibid.

22. Walter Benjamin, "The Task of the Translator," in *Illuminations*, trans. Harry Zohn, ed. and intr. Hannah Arendt (New York: Schocken, 1976), 80.

23. Jacques Derrida, "Force and Signification," in *Writing and Difference*, trans. and intr. Alan Bass (Chicago: U of Chicago P, 1978), 4.

Chapter Three

1. An early example of this revisionist view is Raúl Cepero Bonilla's *Azúcar y abolición* (Havana: Editorial de Ciencias Sociales, 1971).

2. José Antonio Saco, *Historia de la esclavitud desde los tiempos más remotos hasta nuestros días* (Paris: Tipografía Lahure, 1875–77).

3. Salvador Bueno, *El negro en la literatura hispanoamericana* (Havana: Editorial Letras Cubanas, 1986), 61.

4. Domingo del Monte, *Centón Epistolario de Domingo del Monte* (Havana: Imprenta Siglo XX, 1923–38), 1:201.

5. Ibid., 1:201–2.

6. In his article " 'I Was Born': Slave Narratives, Their Status as Autobiography and as Literature," James Olney argues precisely this point, in terms that are perhaps too absolute. According to him, "just as the triangular relationship embracing sponsor, audience, and ex-slave made of the later something other than an entirely free creator in the telling of his life story, so also it made of the narrative produced (always keeping the exceptional case in mind) something other than autobiography in any full sense and something other than literature in any reasonable understanding of that term as an act of creative imagination." In *The Slave's Narrative*, ed. Charles T. Davis and Henry Louis Gates Jr. (New York: Oxford UP, 1985), 168.

7. David T. Haberly, "Abolitionism in Brazil: Anti-Slavery and Anti-Slave," *Luso Brazilian Review* 9.2 (1972): 30–46.

8. As reported by Herbert Klein in his *African Slavery in Latin America and the Caribbean* (New York: Oxford UP, 1986), 244.

9. For a fascinating account of the political maneuverings that were part of the transaction, see David R. Murray's *Odious Commerce: Britain, Spain, and the Abolition of the Cuban Slave Trade* (Cambridge: Cambridge UP, 1980).

10. Del Monte, *Escritos de Domingo del Monte* (Havana: Cultural, 1929), 48.

11. Saco, *Memoria sobre la vagancia en la Isla de Cuba* (Santiago de Cuba: Instituto Cubano del Libro, 1974), and *Memoria sobre caminos* (New York: G. F. Bunce, 1830). See also "Mi primera pregunta: ¿La abolición del comercio de esclavos africanos arruinará o atrasará la agricultura cubana?" (Madrid: M. Calero, 1837) and "Paralelo entre la isla de Cuba y algunas colonias inglesas" (Madrid: Tomás Jordán, 1837).

12. Félix Varela, *Escritos políticos* (Havana: Editorial de Ciencias Sociales, 1977), 260–76, and Francisco Arango y Parreño, *Obras*, 2 vols. (Havana: Ministerio de Educación, 1952).

13. Francisco Arango y Parreño, *Obras*, 2:367. One finds in *Cecilia Valdés* the summary of one such genealogical chain as detailed by the black slave María de Regla: "Es querer decir que Magdalena, negra como yo, tuvo con un blanco a señá Chepilla, parda; que señá Chepilla, tuvo con otro blanco, a señá Charito Alarcón, parda clara, y que señá Charito tuvo con otro blanco a Cecilia Valdés, blanca" (2:147). [It means that Magdalena, black like me, had Chepilla, a dark mulatta, with a white man; that Chepilla had Charito Alarcón, a light mulatta, with another white man, and that Charito had Cecilia Valdes—a white woman— with another white man.] For a detailed study of racial ideology during this period see Verena Martínez-Alier, *Marriage, Class, and Colour in Nineteenth-Century Cuba* (Ann Arbor: U of Michigan P, 1989).

14. See part 2 of Michel Foucault, *The Order of Things* (New York: Vintage, 1973), 217–387.

15. Lorna Williams's recent book on antislavery narrative, *The Representation of Slavery in Cuban Fiction* (Columbia: U of Missouri P, 1994), hints in several moments at this dimension of the works. She speaks, for instance, about the "sadism" of Ricardo in Suárez y Romero's *Francisco* and argues that "the novel postulates that controlling the slaves' sexuality constitutes the planter's dominant concern" (68). See also her discussion of Avellaneda's *Sab* (84–118).

16. Gertrudis Gómez de Avellaneda, *Sab* (Salamanca: Anaya, 1970), 41–42. The most significant study of the "monstrosity" ascribed to mulattos in these works—and especially to female characters—is Vera Kutzinski, *Sugar's Secrets: Race and the Erotics of Cuban Nationalism* (Charlottesville: UP of Virginia, 1993).

17. See, for instance, Ivan Schulman's introduction to his edition of Manzano's autobiography (Madrid: Ediciones Guadarrama, 1975) as well as Susan Willis's "Crushed Geraniums: Juan Francisco Manzano and the Language of Slavery," in Davis and Gates, *The Slave's Narrative*, 199–224.

18. Sylvia Molloy, "From Serf to Self: The Autobiography of Juan Francisco Manzano," in *At Face Value: Autobiographical Writing in Spanish America* (Cambridge: Cambridge UP, 1991), 54. See also Antonio Vera León's excellent article "Juan Francisco Manzano: El estilo bárbaro de la nación," *Hispamérica* 60 (1991): 3–22, and Thomas Bremer's "The Slave Who Wrote Poetry: Comments on the Literary Works and the Autobiography of Juan Francisco Manzano," in *Slavery in the Americas*, ed. Wolfgang Binder (Würzburg: Königshausen und Neumann, 1993), 487–501. In addition, Julio Ramos has an enlightening reading of Manzano's work in his "La ley es otra: literatura y constitución de la persona jurídica," *Revista de Crítica Literaria Latinoamericana* 20.40 (1994): 305–35, esp. pp. 310–21.

19. In his *Suite para Juan Francisco Manzano* (Havana: Editorial Arte y Literatura, 1977), Roberto Friol raises explicitly the erotic component of the relationship between Manzano and the Marquesa (51–52).

20. Mercedes Rivas, *Literatura y esclavitud en la novela cubana del siglo XIX* (Seville: Escuela de Estudios Hispano-Americanos de Sevilla, 1990), 196.

21. Carolyn L. Karcher, "Lydia Maria Child's *A Romance of the Republic*," in *Slavery and the Literary Imagination*, ed. Deborah E. McDowell and Arnold Rampersad (Baltimore: Johns Hopkins UP, 1989), 81. See also Hortense Spillers's powerful essay "Changing the Letter: The Yokes, the Jokes of Discourse, or, Mrs. Stowe, Mr. Reed," in the same collection, 25–61, as well as the essays included in *The Discourse of Slavery: Aphra Behn to Toni Morrison*, ed. Carl Plasa and Betty J. Ring (London: Routledge, 1994).

22. William Hill Brown, *The Power of Sympathy*, ed. Herbert Brown (Boston: New Frontiers P, 1961).

23. Reinaldo Arenas, *La Loma del Angel* (Barcelona: Dador, 1989), 9.

24. William Luis's study of the theme of slavery in nineteenth- and twentieth-century Cuban literature amply substantiates this conclusion through his analysis of works written throughout almost 150 years of Cuban literary history: *Literary Bondage: Slavery in Cuban Literature* (Austin: U of Texas P, 1990). See also Lourdes Martínez Echazábal's *Para una semiótica de la mulatez* (Madrid: Porrúa Turanzas, 1990) for a study of antislavery works in the broader Spanish American context.

25. Benítez Rojo, *La isla que se repite*, 127.

Chapter Four

1. The fact that, as I argue throughout this book, Spanish American writing is continually dealing with issues of rhetorical authority accounts principally

for the received notion that Spanish American literature has a persistently romantic strain. As we know, romanticism was intensely preoccupied with the problem of discursive legitimacy—that is, how to provide a foundation for new modalities of writing without the benefit of the authority provided by the canonical genres.

The bibliography on romanticism is so vast as to preclude even a short reference to key works. Nevertheless, I would like to make special mention of Esteban Tollinchi's monumental two-volume work *Romanticismo y modernidad: Ideas fundamentales de la cultura del siglo XIX*, 2 vols. (Río Piedras: U de Puerto Rico, 1989).

2. Derek Flitter, *Spanish Romantic Literary Theory and Criticism* (Cambridge: Cambridge UP, 1992). See also Jenaro Talens's study of Espronceda's work, in which he proposes a critical revision of Spanish romanticism: *Romanticism and the Writing of Modernity: Espronceda and the Collapse of Literature as Institutionalized Discourse* (Valencia: Fundación Instituto Shakespeare, 1889).

3. Véliz, *The New World of the Gothic Fox*, 201. In *The Dark Side of Reason* (Stanford: Stanford UP, 1992) Luiz Costa Lima has described the phenomenon in the following fashion:

> If in the European literatures that were the contemporaries of our colonial period, nature served the ideological purpose of valuing rural life against the appeal of urban centers, when transplanted to America it served as a backdrop for an exaltation—though a cautious one—of Natural man . . . .
>
> Thus, at least apparently, South American writers seem to have done no more than follow the lesson of *normalized* romanticism. And so it is that they are usually interpreted. But this overlooks a decisive difference. In early romanticism, particularly in Germany but also in Britain, the contemplation of nature gave rise to a specific dialectic, which involved observation and introspection. This was the source of both the early thematization of the imaginary—so evident in Coleridge, for instance and the intense interchange between the poetic and the philosophical (one need only mention Novalis and Hölderlin, or Coleridge and Wordsworth). In Latin America, on the contrary, the articulation of romanticism with philosophy and introspection gave way to sentimentality, often rhetorical or merely lachrymose. The themes of *want* and social incongruency are privatized into nostalgia, exile, and idealization of women. The topos of nature, in fact, led not to a dialectical tension but to a laudatory description of its hugeness or variety, to emphasis on the description of the human types that appeared in it. (168)

4. Andrés Bello's position in this regard was also significant and atypical. His lifelong insistence on the need to acknowledge the classical and Spanish tradition exposed him to and continues to make him a target of charges of literary and political conservatism. But to my mind his views arise from what I believe to be a profound understanding on his part of the difficulties to which the unquestioning identification of Spanish America with modernity would lead. In all his writings, Bello endeavored to place Spanish America in the larger context of Western culture and history, thereby undermining the claims of unconditional originality and modernity that was the founding intellectual conceit—as well as the rhetorical dead end—of the new republics. This assertion is backed by Antonio Cussen's

revisionary reading of Bello in his *Bello and Bolívar: Poetry and Politics in the Spanish American Revolution* (Cambridge: Cambridge UP, 1992). See also Servando Echeandía's "La fundación de la tradición poética hispanoamericana" (Ph.D. diss., Harvard University, 1996).

5. Martínez Estrada, "Ningún libro se ha leído peor que *Facundo, Amalia, Una excursión a los indios Ranqueles*," in *Sarmiento*, 121. Of late Mansilla's writings have been accorded a more sustained critical attention. See especially the following excellent essays: David W. Foster, "Knowledge in Mansilla's *Una excursión a los indios Ranqueles*," *Revista Hispánica Moderna*, new series 41.1 (1988); 19–29; Sylvia Molloy, "Recuerdo y sujeto en *Mis memorias* de Mansilla," *Nueva Revista de Filología Hispánica* 36.2 (1988): 1207–20, and "Imagen de Mansilla," in *La Argentina del Ochenta al Centenario*, ed. Gustavo Ferrari and Ezequiel Gallo (Buenos Aires: Sudamericana, 1980), 745–59; Julio Ramos, "Entre otros: *Una excursión a los indios Ranqueles* de Lucio Mansilla," *Filología* 21.1 (1986): 143–71; Nicolas Shumway, *The Invention of Argentina* (Berkeley: U of California P, 1991), 250–61, and Mirta Stern, "*Una excursión a los indios Ranqueles*: espacio textual y ficción topográfica," *Filología* 20.2 (1985): 115–38.

6. For this and other aspects of the literary representation of urban space (particularly Buenos Aires) see Rosalba Campra, ed., *La selva en el damero: espacio literario y espacio urbano en América Latina* (Pisa: Giardini Editori, 1989).

7. For a discussion of how the concept of "el desierto" has helped shaped Argentine cultural forms, see Beatriz Sarlo's "En el origen de la cultura argentina: Europa y el desierto. Búsqueda del fundamento," in *10. Seminario Latinoamericano de Literatura Comparada (Porto Alegre, September 8–10, 1986)*, (Porto Alegre, Brazil: Universidade Federal do Rio Grande do Sul, 1987).

8. Peter Earle, for instance, affirms, "Mansilla . . . tuvo un propósito concretamente político al lanzarse a su expedición: establecer bajo su propio criterio (independiente de las exigencias anti-indigenistas de Sarmiento) un nuevo tratado humanitario con los Ranqueles." [Mansilla . . . had a specific political motivation when he set out in his expedition: to establish of his own accord (and against Sarmiento's anti-Indian demands) a new more humanitarian treaty with the Ranqueles.] "La excursión de Mansilla," in *Essays on Lucio Victorio Mansilla*, ed. Hugo Rodríguez Alcalá and Alberto Blasi, Latin American Studies Program Commemorative Series, no. 5 (Riverside, Calif.: Latin American Studies Program of the University of California, Riverside, 1981), 39. See also Julio Caillet-Bois, Introduction to Mansilla's *Una excursión a los indios Ranqueles* (Mexico City: Fondo de Cultura, 1947), xxii.

9. Mansilla, *Una excursión a los indios Ranqueles* (Caracas: Ayacucho, 1984), 302. All subsequent references are to this edition and will be included parenthetically in the text. Earlier, Mansilla had made the following remark: "Después de algunas palabras encomiando su conducta [the Ranqueles chieftain's] entré a explicar que el tratado de paz debiendo ser sometido a la aprobación del Congreso, no podía ser puesto en ejercicio inmediatamente" (210). [After praising his conduct I began to explain that since the peace treaty had to be submitted to Congress for approval, its provisions could not be placed into effect immediately.]

10. I have benefited greatly from the archival investigations undertaken by

Silvia M. Fernández, which have allowed her to establish authoritatively the precise chronology of these events. See her "Mansilla y los Ranqueles: ¿Por qué Lucio V. Mansilla escribió *Una excursión a los indios Ranqueles*?" in *Congreso Nacional de Historia sobre la Conquista del Desierto*, 4 vols. (Buenos Aires: Academia Nacional de la Historia, 1980), 4:361–75. Fernández finally does not offer any reasons that would satisfactorily explain the discrepancies that she has so carefully documented.

11. See Carlos Mayol Laferrére, "El coronel Lucio V. Mansilla y la ocupación del Río Quinto en 1869," in *Congreso Nacional de Historia sobre la Conquista del Desierto* (Buenos Aires: Academia Nacional de la Historia, 1980), 2:93.

12. Other such moments appear on pages 11, 48, 74, 109, 166, 190, 244, 314, 323, 330, and 365 of *Una excursión a los indios Ranqueles*.

13. Throughout this chapter I use the phrase "family romance" as defined by Freud principally in his famous essay of the same name: as a story whereby the child fantasizes that he or she is actually the offspring of another set of parents or parent.

14. See, for instance, Mansilla's *causeries* entitled "Los siete platos de arroz con leche" (87–101) and "¿Por qué . . . ?" (47–82). In *Entre-nos: causeries del jueves* (Buenos Aires: Hachette, 1963).

15. Mansilla, *Entre-nos*, 510–11, and *Mis memorias* (Buenos Aires: Hachette, 1955), 126.

16. Mansilla's description of his mother's sewing room as "famous" would have been understood by any Argentine reader of the time. He is alluding to a scene in José Mármol's novel *Amalia* whose setting was that very room. As a youth, Mansilla had insulted Mármol publicly on account of this passage and even challenged him to a duel that never took place.

17. Sarmiento himself alluded in two occasions to this incident in passing and without details. See his *Obras*, 14:294 and 49:271.

18. Domingo Fidel Sarmiento (Dominguito) was born on April 25, 1845. His mother, Benita Pastoriza, who had become a young widow of twenty-three soon after his birth, married Domingo Faustino Sarmiento a few years later, in 1848. Sarmiento officially adopted Dominguito and gave him his family name at the age of three. Eighteen years later, at twenty-one, Dominguito died during the Guerra del Paraguay, in a unit led by Mansilla. Seized by the desire to memorialize his only male child, he began the redaction of a composition on the biography of Dominguito. These first jottings were subsequently misplaced and presumed lost. Twenty years later, when Sarmiento was seventy-five (and two years away from his death), he decided to undertake again the story of Dominguito's life, spurred, he claimed, by an editor's request for some facts about Dominguito for a memorial notice on the twentieth anniversary of his death. *Vida de Dominguito* appeared in serial form beginning in June 1886 and was published in book form later in the same year. These facts are important because Mansilla's remarks about Dominguito are mediated by his previous reading of Sarmiento's biography of his son and because the revisionist intention displayed by them is meant also as a challenge to Sarmiento's book.

19. Quoted in Enrique Popolizio, *Vida de Lucio V. Mansilla* (Buenos Aires: Peuser, 1954), 116.

20. Later on, Mansilla argues that his dream of conversion has become real:

Me quité las botas y las medias, saqué el puñal que llevaba a la cintura y me puse a cortar las uñas de los pies, ni más ni menos que si hubiera estado solo en mi cuarto, haciendo la policía matutina. Mi compadre y los convidados estaban encantados. Aquel Coronel cristiano parecía un indio. ¿Qué más podían ellos desear? Yo iba a ellos. Me les asimilaba. Era la conquista de la barbarie sobre la civilización. El *Lucio Victorius, Imperator*, del sueño que tuve en Leubucó la noche en que Mariano Rosas me hizo beber un cuerno de aguardiente, estaba allí transfigurado. (243–44).

I took off by boots and my socks, reached for the knife I wore at my waist and began to clip my toenails, just as if I were alone in my room doing my morning ablutions. My partner and the invited guests were delighted. The white Colonel behaved like an Indian. ¿What else could they wish? I was going toward them, I was becoming them. It was the victory of barbarism over civilization. The *Lucio Victorius, Imperator*, of the dream I had had in Leubucó the night Mariano Rosas had me drink a horn full of liquor was there in the flesh.

21. See Roberto González Echevarría's gripping discussion of this scene in *Myth and Archive*; 110–25.

22. Mayol Laferrére, "El coronel Lucio V. Mansilla y la ocupación del Río Quinto en 1869," 2:94.

23. Rafael Pineda Yánez, *Cómo fue la vida amorosa de Rosas* (Buenos Aires: Plus Ultra, 1972), 45–60.

24. See, for instance, Mansilla's bizarre, paradoxical *semblanza* of Sarmiento in his *Retratos y recuerdos* (Buenos Aires: El Ateneo, 1927), 21–28. Mansilla's enigmatic relationship with Sarmiento has elicited the following comment from one of his biographers, who devotes an entire chapter to the relationship between the two: "El vínculo entrecortado de altibajos entre ambos hombres, sus encontronazos, recriminaciones recíprocas, desinteligencias y malentendidos constituye uno de los capítulos más curiosos de la biografía de Mansilla." [The on-again, off-again bond between the two men, their clashes, reciprocal recriminations, awkwardness, and misunderstandings is one of the most intriguing chapters of Mansilla's biography.] In Homero M. Guglielmini, *Mansilla* (Buenos Aires: Ediciones Culturales Argentinas, 1961), 89.

25. Mansilla, *Rozas: ensayo histórico-psicológico* (Paris: Garnier, 1898).

26. Ibid., 1. In one of his *causeries*, "Cómo se formaban los caudillos," Mansilla repeated this etymological argument (265). He insisted once more on the "correct" spelling in another *causerie* entitled "Historia argentina" (521).

27. Or, in Nicolas Shumway's words, "Mansilla . . . provides a sad portrait of the intellectual who looked at everything, but never quite found a cause deserving of his energy. His literary persona as a result is the one he carefully sculpted: that of the dandy, the raconteur, the witty observer, the sprightly conversationalist, paralyzed by too much sophistication and too aware of the world to ever commit to it" (*The Invention of Argentina*, 261).

28. For my reading of Mansilla I have found extremely useful Lynn Hunt's analysis of the familial rhetoric surrounding the French Revolution. See her *Family Romance of the French Revolution* (Berkeley: U of California P, 1992).

29. Luiz Costa Lima, *The Dark Side of Reason*, 151.

30. Adolfo Prieto dedicates a chapter (pp. 125–54) to Mansilla in his book *La literatura autobiográfica argentina*, in which he argues that Mansilla was preoccupied with his genealogy in order to make a personal claim to history in the face of the onslaught of new immigrants at the end of the nineteenth century. He bases this diagnosis on the fact that Mansilla's autobiographical work *Mis memorias* appeared in 1904, at the height of the immigration pressure on the old order. But as my argument makes clear, the articulation of Mansilla's genealogical romance precedes by many years the anxieties about immigration in late-nineteenth-century Argentina.

Chapter Five

1. Jaime Alazraki, "Relectura de Horacio Quiroga," in *El cuento hispanoamericano ante la crítica*, ed. Enrique Pupo-Walker (Madrid: Castalia, 1973), 65.

2. Noé Jitrik, *Horacio Quiroga: una obra de experiencia y riesgo* (Buenos Aires: Ediciones Culturales Argentinas, 1959), 113. In Jitrik's excellent book, which continues to be obligatory reading in any attempt to approach Quiroga's work, the entire chapter entitled "Muerte figurada, muerte real" (111–29) treats the theme of death in the life and works of the Uruguayan writer.

3. H. A. Murena, *El pecado original de América* (Buenos Aires: Editorial Sudamericana, 1965), 79.

4. In addition to the article by Alazraki already cited, see the following as well: Nicolás Bratosevich, *El estilo de Horacio Quiroga en sus cuentos* (Madrid: Gredos, 1973); Angel Flores, ed., *Aproximaciones a Horacio Quiroga* (Caracas: Monte Avila, 1976); Roy Howard Shoemaker, "El tema de la muerte en los cuentos de Horacio Quiroga," *Cuadernos Americanos* 220 (1978): 248–64.

5. All of these texts have been published in a volume entitled *Sobre literatura*, vol. 7 of the *Obras inéditas y desconocidas de Horacio Quiroga*, ed. Angel Rama (Montevideo: Ediciones Arca, 1969). All references to Quiroga's writings concerning literature in general or the poetics of the short story in particular refer to this volume.

6. Edgar Allan Poe, *Literary Criticism of Edgar Allan Poe*, ed. Robert L. Hough (Lincoln: U of Nebraska P, 1965), 136.

7. For a more sustained discussion of Poe's influence on Quiroga, see Margo Glantz, "Poe en Quiroga," in Flores, *Aproximaciones a Horacio Quiroga*, 93–118, and José Luis Martínez Morales, *Horacio Quiroga: teoría y práctica del cuento* (Mexico City: Centro de Investigaciones Lingüístico-literarias, Universidad Veracruzana, 1982). I am not arguing, of course, that Quiroga is a derivative writer but that his poetics of the short story was formulated as an echo of similar reflections by other metropolitan writers.

8. In *El desterrado: vida y obra de Horacio Quiroga* (Buenos Aires: Editorial Losada, 1968), Emir Rodríguez Monegal correctly notes that "De Edgar Poe y sobre todo de Maupassant había aprendido el arte de preparar un final que cerraba el relato con una sorpresa" [From Edgar Poe and especially from Maupassant he had learned the art of concocting an end that closed the story with a surprise] (179).

9. Letter to José María Delgado (June 8, 1917), in *Cartas inéditas de Horacio Quiroga*, vol. 2, intr. Mercedes Ramírez de Rossiello (Montevideo: Instituto Nacional de Investigaciones y Archivos Literarios, 1959), 62.

10. Norman Holland studies Quiroga's appeal to scientific discourse in his " 'Doctoring' in Quiroga," *Confluencia* 9.2 (1994): 64–72.

11. Quiroga, "El almohadón de pluma," in *Cuentos completos*, ed. Alfonso Llambías de Azevedo, 2 vols. (Montevideo: Ediciones de la Plaza, 1979), 1:59. All subsequent quotations from Quiroga's stories refer to this edition and will be noted parenthetically in the text.

12. I underscore the fortuitous character of the situation because many critics have seen nature in Quiroga as intent on destroying man. For instance, Leonor Fleming concludes in an article entitled "Horacio Quiroga: escritor a la intemperie" that in Quiroga's work "la naturaleza sobrepasa al hombre en todas sus dimensiones: lo atrae, pero no para acogerlo, sino para devorarlo" [nature overwhelms man in all its dimensions: it attracts him, not to welcome him but to devour him]. (*Revista de Occidente* 113 [1990]: 111). This seems to me an erroneous reading that attempts to identify Quiroga *tout court* with the *tremendista* dimension of the telluric literature of the first thirty years of this century. Not even in "La miel silvestre," which emphasizes the disjunction between reality and the character's romantic vision of nature, can we speak of the natural environment as a conscious agent bent on man's annihilation.

13. I have compiled a partial list of other stories that in their fundamental structure have a dynamic similar to that of the stories already mentioned: "La meningitis y su sombra," "Anaconda," "En la noche," "El vampiro" (in *Anaconda*), "Miss Dorothy Phillips, mi esposa," "Un peón," "Los tres besos," "El potro salvaje," "El techo de incienso," "Más allá," "El vampiro" (in *Más allá*), and "El conductor del rápido."

14. "Las moscas" appeared in *El Hogar* on July 7, 1933.

15. "El hombre muerto," perhaps Quiroga's best-known story along with "A la deriva," was published in the newspaper *La Nación* on June 27, 1920.

16. A number of Quiroga's reviews and other writings on literature make it clear that he never meant for his work to be read as part of the movement for an autochthonous literature at the beginning of the century. See, for example, "La oligarquía poética" (58–60), "Los trucos del perfecto cuentista" (65–69) and "Sobre *El ombú* de Hudson" (122–26) in *Sobre literatura*. This is why Quiroga's oeuvre has consistently resisted its inclusion into the nativist canon, in spite of the repeated and well-meaning attempts to incorporate it into that literary modality.

17. Paul de Man has described the creation of a biographical persona in order to satisfy the exigencies of a poetic formula—in this particular instance autobiographical discourse—as follows: "We assume that life *produces* the autobiography as an act produces its consequences, but can we not suggest, with equal justice, that the autobiographical project may itself produce and determine the life, and that whatever the writer *does* is in fact governed by the technical demands of self-portraiture and thus determined, in all aspects, by the resources of his medium?" In his "Autobiography as Defacement," in *The Rhetoric of Romanticism* (New York: Columbia UP, 1984), 69.

18. As is well-known, the cinema and film are the subjects of a number of Quiroga's short stories. See Emma S. Speratti-Piñero's "Horacio Quiroga, precursor de la relación cine-literatura en la América Hispánica," *NRFH* 36.2 (1988): 1239–49. Also, Walter Rela's bibliography on Quiroga includes an interview in which Quiroga defends the medium from the accusations leveled at it by its critics (55–58). See also Sarlo's discussion of Quiroga's understanding of film in *La imaginación técnica*, 26–30.

19. Ross Chambers, *Story and Situation: Narrative Seduction and the Power of Fiction* (Minneapolis: U of Minnesota P, 1984), 51.

20. In her most recent work Doris Sommer has explored texts that strategically hold information back from the reader in the context of Spanish American narrative in general. See her "Rigoberta's Secrets," *Latin American Perspectives* 18.3 (1991): 32–50, and "Who Can Tell?: Filling in Blanks for Villaverde," *American Literary History* 6.2 (1994): 213–33. See also Lennard J. Davis's *Resisting Novels: Ideology and Fiction* (New York: Methuen, 1987).

Chapter Six

1. What is perhaps the most thorough articulation of this position can be found in M. Keith Booker's *Vargas Llosa among the Postmodernists* (Gainesville: UP of Florida, 1994), in which Vargas Llosa's entire career is examined from the perspective of the modernism/postmodernism divide—which is deemed to have reflected itself in Vargas Llosa's production with the appearance of *Pantaleón y las visitadoras*.

2. Roberto González Echevarría, *La ruta de Severo Sarduy* (Hanover, N.H.: Ediciones del Norte, 1987), 244.

3. The analogy that sees the Spanish American boom as the counterpart of Anglo-American modernism has been indirectly challenged by Ivan Schulman and Evelyn Picón Garfield's *"Las entrañas del vacío:" ensayos sobre la modernidad hispanoamericana* (Mexico City: Ediciones Cuadernos Americanos, 1984), in which the authors argue for a filiation between Spanish American *modernismo* and the various modernist movements of the early twentieth century.

4. For instance, Raymond L. Williams's recent *The Postmodern Novel in Latin America: Politics, Culture, and the Crisis of Truth* (New York: St. Martin's P, 1995) begins with a chapter entitled "Introduction to the Spanish American Modernist and Postmodern Novel." See also *De García Márquez al post-boom* (Madrid: Orígenes, 1986) and *Roa Bastos, precursor del post-boom* (Mexico: Katún, 1983), by Juan Manuel Marcos; and *Más allá del boom: literatura y mercado*, ed. Angel Rama (Mexico City: Marcha, 1981).

5. Mario Vargas Llosa, *La tía Julia y el escribidor* (Barcelona: Seix Barral, 1987), 112. (*Aunt Julia and the Scriptwriter*, trans. Helen R. Lane [New York: Farrar, Straus, Giroux, 1982], 90). Page references are given parenthetically for both editions. Page references given in the text not accompanying a direct quotation refer to the English version.

6. A number of critics have specifically addressed these and related issues in *La tía Julia y el escribidor*: Luis de Arrigoitia, "Machismo, folklore y creación en

Mario Vargas Llosa," *Sin Nombre* 13.4 (1983): 7–24; Rosario Ferré, "Mario Vargas Llosa o el escribidor," *Sin Nombre* 9.2 (1978): 86–90; J. C. González, "De la sub-literatura a la literatura," *Anales de Literatura Hispánica* 6 [7] (1978): 141–56; Stephen M. Machen, " 'Pornoviolence' and Point of View in Mario Vargas Llosa's *La tía Julia y el escribidor*," *Latin American Literary Review* 9 [17] (Fall–Winter 1980): 9–16; Ellen McCracken, "Vargas Llosa's *La tía Julia y el escribidor*: The New Novel and the Mass Media," *Ideologies and Literature* 3 [13] (June–August 1980): 54–69; Saúl Sosnowski, "Mario Vargas Llosa: entre radioteatros y escribidores," in *Latin American Fiction Today* (Taconic Parkway and Montclair State College: Ediciones Hispamérica, 1980), 75–82; and Domingo Yndurain's "Vargas Llosa y el escribidor," *Cuadernos Hispanoamericanos* 370 (1981): 150–57.

7. The narrator's literary apprenticeship has been remarked on previously by a number of critics. See, for instance, the following works: Alicia Andreu, "Pedro Camacho: prestidigitador del lenguaje," *Modern Language Studies* 16.2 (Spring 1986): 19–25; Rosemary Geisdorfer Feal, *Novel Lives: The Fictional Autobiographies of Guillermo Cabrera Infante and Mario Vargas Llosa*, North Carolina Studies in the Romance Languages and Literatures, no. 226 (Chapel Hill: University of North Carolina Department of Romance Languages, 1986); Julie Jones, "*La tía Julia y el escribidor*: Mario Vargas Llosa's Versions of Self," *Critique* 21.1 (1979): 73–82; José Miguel Oviedo, "*La tía Julia y el escribidor*, or the Coded Self-Portrait," in *Mario Vargas Llosa: A Collection of Critical Essays*, ed. Charles Rossman and Alan W. Friedman (Austin: U of Texas P, 1978), 166–81; René Prieto, "The Two Narrative Voices in Mario Vargas Llosa's *Aunt Julia and the Scriptwriter*," *Latin American Literary Review* 11 [22] (Spring–Summer 1983): 15–25; and J. Soubeyroux, "El narrador y sus dobles: *La tía Julia y el escribidor*," in *Hommage à J. L. Flecmakosca par ses collègues*, 2 vols. (Montpellier: Université Paul Valéry, 1984), 2: 383–402. Of these, I have found Oviedo, Prieto, and Feal (particularly Feal's discussion of Marito's relationship with his father) to be the most suggestive for the interpretive approach developed in this chapter.

8. Or, as William Kennedy phrased it in his review of the English translation of *La tía Julia y el escribidor*, the novel is "a work that celebrates story." "Review of *Aunt Julia and the Scriptwriter*," *New York Times Book Review*, August 1, 1982, 14.

9. Julia Urquidi Illanes, *Lo que Varguitas no dijo* (La Paz: Khana Cruz, 1983).

10. The serious threats of legal action made by Raúl Salmón, the real man on whom Vargas Llosa based the character of Camacho, also attest to the similarities between the two versions. See Marvin A. Lewis, *From Lima to Leticia: The Peruvian Novels of Mario Vargas Llosa* (Lanham, Md.: UP of America, 1983), 144.

11. I am not convinced that a consistent lesson on the proper relationship between literature and reality can be gleaned from the novel's depiction of Pedro Camacho or from Varguitas's ulterior success. For example, John Lipski has argued that the novel advances a proposition regarding literary composition: "[Varguitas's] early attempts are of little value because they lean too heavily on reality and too little on creative imagination; the endlessly churned out stories of Camacho are equally worthless for the opposite reason: unrestrained imagination without the creative shaping tempered by daily reality. It is only by synthesizing

the two extremes that a lasting literature will result." "Reading the Writers: Hidden Meta-structures in the Modern Spanish American Novel," *Perspectives in Contemporary Literature* 6 (1980): 122. While this interpretation may account for Camacho's collapse as a creator, it does not help understand Varguitas's ascendance to a clear position of authorial hegemony in the novel. Moreover, it appears to be a restatement of Vargas Llosa's previously cited comments regarding the composition of *Aunt Julia and the Scriptwriter* concerning his avowed desire to balance a "truthful" story with a "fictive" creation in order to produce an effective novel. I agree, rather, with Sara Castro-Klarén when she proposes that "La novela no diferencia, o no esclarece las diferencias entre Camacho y el nuevo fabulador." [The novel does not distinguish, or does not clarify, the difference between Camacho and the new novelist.] *Mario Vargas Llosa: análisis introductorio* (Lima: Latinoamericana Editores, 1988), 109.

12. Sharon Magnarelli has echoed Vargas Llosa's statement by proposing that the even-numbered chapters should be considered "practice prose pieces rewritten by the would-be writer Marito, since they share several characteristics in common with the stories we know he has written in the odd-numbered chapters." "The Diseases of Love and Discourse: *La tía Julia y el escribidor* and *María*," *Hispanic Review* 54.2 (1986): 204.

13. This formulation is reminiscent of the process of poetic self-constitution that has been proposed by Bloom in a number of his works, but especially in *The Anxiety of Influence* and *A Map of Misreading* (New York: Oxford UP, 1975). Bloom's ideas about poetic misprison are not transferable pell-mell to the writing of prose; but since the subject of *La tía Julia y el escribidor* is precisely the self-constitution of a narrator as the outcome of an Oedipal struggle with a predecessor, his insights are apposite in this case.

14. The immediate family roster reads as follows: parents: Dora and "Father"; grandparents: Carmen and "Grandfather"; aunts: Olga, Laura, Gaby, Hortensia, Jesús, Eliana, Celia, Julia; uncles: Lucho, Juan, Jorge, Alejandro, Pedro, Javier, Pancracio; cousins: Jaime, Nancy, Patricia.

15. See, for instance, Vargas Llosa, "El novelista y sus demonios," in *García Márquez: historia de un deicidio* (Barcelona: Seix Barral, 1971), and *La orgía perpetua: Flaubert y "Madame Bovary"* (Barcelona: Seix Barral, 1975).

16. In Spanish an individual's last name is *always* double, a combination of the father's paternal last name and the mother's paternal last name; the latter is what would be called in American usage the mother's maiden name.

17. In an article entitled "My Son, the Rastafarian," Vargas Llosa described his younger son's rebellious adoption of Rastafarian philosophy as an adolescent and his subsequent abandonment of the movement. In this instance the son's defiance was tamed in two fundamental ways: first, it is used as material for the Father's authorial discourse; and second, the crisis is described as having ended when the son begins to work and write for the Instituto Libertad y Democracia, a Peruvian organization whose political and economic views have received ample support from his father and which played a principal role in Vargas Llosa's unsuccessful bid for the Peruvian presidency. *New York Times Magazine*, February 16, 1986, 20, 22–23.

18. Luis Harss and Barbara Dohmann, *Into the Mainstream* (New York: Harper and Row, 1967), 354. In another place he asserts that his father "found out that I was writing poems, [and] feared for my future (a poet is doomed to die of hunger) and for my 'manhood' (the belief that poets are homosexual is still very widespread)." In "A Passion for Perú," *New York Times Magazine*, November 20, 1983, 99–100).

19. Vargos Llosa, *Kathie y el hipopótamo* (Barcelona: Seix Barral, 1983), 108.

20. Vargas Llosa's first published work, *Los jefes*, an uneven collection of short stories written during his twenties, listed the author's name as Mario *Vargas*. In 1963 he published his first novel, *La ciudad y los perros [The Time of the Hero]*, which received the Seix Barral Prize and catapulted him to the recognition and status he has enjoyed since. The author's signature this time, as it would be from this moment on, was Mario *Vargas Llosa*. (I would like to thank Sylvia Molloy for bringing to my attention this significant detail.)

Later, in a polemic that pitted Vargas Llosa against the late Uruguayan critic Angel Rama, the author complained explicitly about Rama's practice of referring to him using an abridged version of his last name. In an earlier exchange Rama had consistently alluded to Vargas Llosa simply as *Vargas*, and Vargas Llosa accuses him of being disrespectful: "Rama enfrenta a mis opiniones un pronóstico de Darcy Ribeiro. Dice: "En las antípodas de la concepción que maneja Vargas (¿qué es esa malacrianza de acortarme el apellido?) Darcy Ribeiro piensa que . . .' " [Rama rebukes my opinions with an assertion by Darcy Ribeiro. He says: 'Opposite to Vargas's position [why the insolent shortening of my last name?] Darcy Ribeiro believes that . . .' " In Vargas Llosa and Rama, *García Márquez y la problemática de la novela* (Buenos Aires: Corregidor, 1973), 54. (I thank Efraín Kristal for pointing me to this exchange.) By the same token, it is significant that in *Aunt Julia and the Scriptwriter* all of the protagonist's relatives are referred to by name except for his father and grandfather, whose names are never revealed.

21. For instance, Oviedo has averred that "the structural regularity of *La Casa Verde* is almost maniacal." *Mario Vargas Llosa: la invención de una realidad* (Barcelona: Barral Editores, 1970), 143. Regarding *Conversación en La Catedral*, Dick Gerdes says that "as in Vargas Llosa's previous novels, the plot lines or narrative segments are presented in an orderly fashion that repeats itself based on . . . a sequence." *Mario Vargas Llosa* (Boston: Twayne, 1985), 102.

22. See, for instance, Marina Gálvez Avero's "Vargas Llosa y la Postmodernidad," in *La novela hispanoamericana contemporánea* (Madrid: Taurus, 1987), 135–44. In *The New Novel in Latin America* (Manchester: Manchester UP, 1995), Philip Swanson studies the problems that arise from the grafting of popular forms onto the formal novelistic ethos of the boom. In *Reclaiming the Author: Figures and Fictions from Spanish America* (Durham: Duke UP, 1992) Lucille Kerr ably documents how Spanish American authors have invoked the formula of the "death of the author" yet have not produced works consonant with that philosophical and aesthetic stance. Nonetheless, she pulls back from advancing a comprehensive explanation for that contradictory praxis.

23. A two-volume compilation of Vargas Llosa's essays entitled *Contra viento y marea* (Barcelona: Seix Barral, 1986), chronicles his ideological evolution from

the early 1960s to the present. All quotations refer to this edition. Also an important text in this regard is his prologue to Hernando de Soto's explosive book *El otro sendero* (Lima: Instituto Libertad y Democracia, 1987), where de Soto argues that the illegal and allegedly parasitical underground economy of Lima is more effective and productive than the official and bureaucratically hampered economic structure. Here Vargas Llosa says the following: "Lo fundamental es que este Estado recuerde siempre que, antes de distribuir la riqueza, hay que producirla. Y que, para conseguirlo, es indispensable que la acción estatal sea lo menos obstructora de la acción de los ciudadanos, ya que éstos saben mejor que nadie lo que quieren y lo que les conviene" (xxviii). [It is crucial for the State to remember always that before one can distribute wealth one has first to produce it. And that, to accomplish this it is imperative that acts by the State exert the least amount of control on its citizens' actions, since they know better than anybody what they want and what is to their advantage.] Regarding intellectual life he has argued elsewhere that "El estado debe garantizar la libertad de expresión y el libre tránsito de las ideas, fomentar la investigación y las artes, garantizar el acceso a la educación y a la información de todos, pero no imponer ni privilegiar doctrinas, teorías o ideologías, sino permitir que éstas florezcan y compitan libremente" (*Contra viento* 2:319). [The State must guarantee free speech and the unchecked flow of ideas, encourage research and arts, guarantee all its citizens access to education and information, without imposing or privileging any doctrine, theory or ideology, letting these flourish and compete with one another freely.]

24. P. 10. And also: "Los hombres no están contentos con su suerte y casi todos . . . quisieran una vida distinta de la que llevan. Para aplacar—tramposamente—ese apetito nacieron las ficciones. Ellas se escriben y se leen para que los seres humanos tengan las vidas que no se resignan a no tener. En el embrión de toda novela hay una inconformidad y un deseo inalcanzado" (*Contra viento* 2:419). [Men are not happy with their lot and most of them . . . would like to have a life different from the one they lead. To deceitfully appease this appetite, fictions were born. They are written and read to provide human beings with the lives they are unresigned to not having. At the core of every novel there is inconformity and unfulfilled desire.] From "El arte de mentir," *Contra viento*, 2:418–24. This entire essay is meaningful to the present discussion.

25. With pragmatic assurance Vargas Llosa has therefore concluded that "En política no hay más remedio que ser realista. En literatura no y por eso es una actividad más libre y duradera que la política" (Contra viento 2:180). [In politics there is no choice but to be a realist. That is not the case in literature, and that is why it is a more independent and lasting endeavor.].

26. For a sustained ideological critique of Vargas Llosa's economic liberalism see William Rowe's "Liberalism and Authority: The Case of Mario Vargas Llosa," in *On Edge: The Crisis of Contemporary Latin American Culture*, ed. George Yúdice, J. Franco, and Juan Flores (Minneapolis: U of Minnesota P, 1992), 45–64, and Gerald Martin's "Mario Vargas Llosa: Errant Knight of the Liberal Imagination," in *Modern Latin American Fiction*, ed. John King (London: Faber and Faber, 1987), 205–33. In a recent essay, Eduardo González has made the following perceptive remark: "I am far from being among those who would fault [Vargas Llosa] for

his cultural and political affiliation with the West. Instead, I find fault in the way in which he exaggerates the splendid and problematic European achievement of a differentiated and autonomous sphere for literary fictions, placed beside but beyond political and religious dogmas." "A Condo of One's Own," *MLN* 112.5 (1997): 955.

Chapter Seven

1. Neil Larsen, "The Cultural Studies Movement in Latin America," in *Reading North by South: On Latin American Literature, Culture, and Politics* (Minneapolis: U of Minnesota P, 1995), 189.

2. See John Gray, *Enlightenment's Wake: Politics and Culture at the Close of the Modern Age* (New York: Routledge, 1995), for a representative enthusiastic endorsement of postmodern possibilities.

3. Other significant works on the question of postmodernism in Spanish America as well as in the context of American academia are the following: Larsen, *Reading North by South*, especially pp. 155–204; Néstor García Canclini, "El debate posmoderno en Iberoamérica," *Cuadernos Hispanoamericanos* 463 (1989): 79–82; George Yúdice, "¿Puede hablarse de postmodernidad en América Latina?" *Revista de Crítica Literaria Latinoamericana* 15.29 (1989): 105–28; John Beverley, "Postmodernism in Latin America," *Siglo XX/20th Century* 9.1–2 (1991–92): 9–29; Santiago Colás, *Postmodernity: The Argentine Paradigm* (Durham: Duke UP, 1994); José Joaquín Brunner, *Un espejo trizado: ensayos sobre cultura y políticas culturales* (Santiago: FLACSO, 1988); the special issues of *South Atlantic Quarterly* 92.3 (1993) and *boundary* 2 20.3 (1993), and the double issue of *Nuevo Texto Crítico* 3.6–7 (1990), all of which are devoted to the topic.

4. Richard, "Postmodernism and Periphery," 467.

5. I am alluding here to Gianni Vattimo's concept of *pensiero debole*, as defined in his article "Dialettica, differenza, pensiero debole," in *Il pensiero debole*, ed. Vattimo and P. Rovatti (Milan: Feltrinelli, 1983), 12–28.

6. William Rowe and Vivian Schelling, *Memory and Modernity: Popular Culture in Latin America* (London: Verso, 1993), 196.

7. Gabriel García Márquez, *El General en su laberinto* (Bogotá: La Oveja Negra, 1989), 269–70. (*The General in His Labyrinth*, tr. Edith Grossman [New York: Knopf, 1990], 271–72). Page references are given parenthetically for both editions.

8. Simón Bolívar, "Carta al general Santander," in *Doctrina del Libertador*, 177.

9. For a study of the influence of Enlightenment philosophy on Spanish American intellectuals, see Gustavo Escobar Valenzuela's *La ilustración en la filosofía latinoamericana* (Mexico City: Editorial Trillas, 1980), María Angeles Eugenio Martínez's *La Ilustración en América (siglo XVIII): pelucas y casacas en los trópicos* (Madrid: Anaya, 1988), and John Tate Lanning's *Academic Culture in the Spanish Colonies* (Oxford: Oxford UP, 1940). José Carlos Chiaramonte has edited a volume of the most significant documents of this period, entitled *Pensamiento de la Ilustración* (Caracas: Ayacucho, 1979). Speaking about Bolívar's commitment to Enlightenment ideas, Eduardo Subirats has made a remark that summarizes to some degree the overarching argument of this book: "El conflicto interior entre una

independencia que se afirmaba como inherente a la realidad americana, y al mismo tiempo se identificaba con una ley exterior, explica la flotante identidad histórica de la doctrina bolivariana." [The internal conflict between an independence that was deemed intrinsic to American reality but which was simultaneously identified with an exterior Law, accounts for the floating historical identity of Bolívar's doctrines.] *El continente vacío: la conquista del nuevo mundo y la conciencia moderna* (Barcelona: Anaya & Mario Muchnik, 1994), 468.

Benedict Anderson has a number of insightful comments on the difficulties faced by the South American patriots with respect to the establishment of a viable political organization when compared to their northern counterparts, in the chapter entitled "Old Empires, New Nations" (51–65) in his *Imagined Communities*:

> The Protestant, English-speaking creoles to the north were much more favourably situated for realizing the idea of 'America' and indeed eventually succeeded in appropriating the everyday title of 'Americans.' The original Thirteen Colonies comprised an area smaller than Venezuela, and one third the size of Argentina. Bunched geographically together, their market centres in Boston, New York, and Philadelphia were readily accessible to one another, and their populations were relatively tightly linked by print as well as commerce. The 'United States' could gradually multiply in numbers over the next 183 years, as old and new populations moved westwards out of the old east coast core. Yet even in the case of the USA there are elements of comparative 'failure' or shrinkage—non-absorption of English-speaking Canada, Texas's decade of independent sovereignty (1835–46). Had a sizeable English-speaking community existed in California in the eighteenth century, is it not likely that an independent state would have arisen there to play Argentina to the Thirteen Colonies' Peru? Even in the USA, the affective bonds of nationalism were elastic enough, combined with the rapid expansion of the western frontier and the contradictions generated between the economies of North and South, to precipitate a war of secession almost a century after the Declaration of Independence; and this war today sharply reminds us of those that tore Venezuela and Ecuador off from Gran Colombia, and Uruguay and Paraguay from the United Provinces of the Río de la Plata. (64)

The differences translated themselves quickly into the distrust with which the United States contemplated the Spanish American revolution from the outset. See Piero Gleijeses, "The Limits of Sympathy: The United States and the Independence of Spanish America," *Journal of Latin American Studies* 24.1 (1992): 481–505.

10. In his acknowledgments to *El General en su laberinto*, García Márquez writes:

> Durante muchos años le escuché a Alvaro Mutis su proyecto de escribir el viaje final de Simón Bolívar por el río Magdalena. Cuando publicó *El Ultimo Rostro*, que era un fragmento anticipado del libro, me pareció un relato tan maduro, y su estilo y su tono tan depurados, que me preparé para leerlo completo en poco tiempo. Sin embargo, dos años más tarde tuve la impresión de que lo había echado al olvido, como nos ocurre a tantos escritores aun con nuestros sueños más amados, y sólo entonces me atreví a pedirle que me permitiera escribirlo. (269)

For many years I listened to Alvaro Mutis discussing his plan to write about Simón Bolívar's final voyage along the Magdalena River. When he published *El Ultimo*

Rostro, a fragment of the projected book, the story seemed so ripe, and its style so polished, that I expected to read it in its complete form very soon afterwards. Nevertheless, two years later I had the impression that he had relegated it to oblivion, as so many writers do even with our best-loved dreams, and only then did I dare ask permission to write it myself. (271)

Similarly, Gerald Martin has said that the novel "begins with a presumption of death," and has wondered why "a novel about the man who achieved the most glorious triumphs in Latin American history should focus upon his darkest hours?" *Journeys through the Labyrinth: Latin American Fiction in the Twentieth Century* (London: Verso, 1988), 292–93.

11. Sigmund Freud, "Mourning and Melancholia," in *The Standard Edition of the Complete Psychological Works of Sigmund Freud*, 24 vols., ed. and trans. James Strachey (London: Hogarth P and the Institute of Psycho-Analysis, 1974), 14: 237–58.

12. The reading I am proposing in this chapter has benefited a great deal from Henry Rousso's study on the repression of French memory of the Vichy period (*Le Syndrome de Vichy, 1944–198 . . .* [Paris: Seuil, 1987]), as well as from Pierre Nora's monumental work *Les Lieux de mémoire*, 7 vols. (Paris: Gallimard, 1984–92).

13. Carlos Fuentes, *La campaña* (Mexico City: Fondo de Cultura Económica, 1990), 23. (*The Campaign* [New York: Farrar, Straus, Giroux, 1991], 16). Page references are to both editions and are given parenthetically in the text.

14. In this regard, Santiago Colás has offered the following perceptive remarks: "There is still a center and occupying it still carries with it power. This discussion of marginality may allow us to say, however, that what has happened today is that center-margin relationships are constantly being renegotiated and reconfigured and dispersed along not always geographically calibrated lines; something very different than saying that there is no center. If we no longer inhabit a world in which power is always distributed along a binary axis—imperialist center and neo-colonial margin, or capitalist and wage laborer—we equally do not inhabit a world in which power and inequality have disappeared, but rather one in which they are allocated (or we now recognize for the first time that they are allocated) via diverse structures, practices and discourses." In "The Third World in Jameson's *Postmodernism, or the Cultural Logic of Late Capitalism*," *Social Text* 31–32 (1992): 267. Enrique Dussel has argued about the *necessity* of the existence of national boundaries for transnational capitalism. See his "Marx's Economic Manuscripts of 1861–63 and the 'Concept' of Dependency," *Latin American Perspectives* 17.2 (1990): 62–101.

Of course, Fredric Jameson has explored the ideological dimension of postmodernism in a number of essays that have been collected in the title mentioned in Colás's article (Durham: Duke UP, 1991). See also his "Third-World Literature in the Era of Multinational Capitalism," 65–88. There is also an important collection of essays that discuss Jameson's ideas on postmodernism: *Postmodernism, Jameson, Critique*, ed. Douglas Kellner (Washington, D.C.: Maisonneuve, 1989).

15. Alberto Moreiras, "Transculturación y pérdida del sentido: el diseño de la

posmodernidad en América Latina," *Nuevo Texto Crítico* 3.6 (1990): 116–17. See also Walter Mignolo, "Occidentalización, imperialismo, globalización: herencias coloniales y teorías postcoloniales," *Revista Iberoamericana* 61.170–71 (1995): 27–40; and Colás, "Of Creole Symptoms, Cuban Fantasies, and Other Latin American Postcolonial Ideologies," *PMLA* 110.3 (1995): 382–96.

Epilogue

1. The title of this chapter is a playful take on Latour's work, which argues through an examination of the scientific discourses of the modern age that modernity never achieved consonance with its stated principles in metropolitan circles.

2. Burns, "Cultures in Conflict: The Implications of Modernization in Nineteenth-Century Latin America," in *Elites, Masses, and Modernization in Latin America, 1850–1930* (Austin: U of Texas P, 1979), 27–28.

3. Ibid., 11. This struggle is dealt with in more detail in Burns's *Poverty of Progress: Latin America in the Nineteenth Century* (Berkeley: U of California P, 1980).

4. Alonso, *The Spanish American Regional Novel*, chapter 1.

5. Roger Bartra, *La jaula de la melancolía: identidad y metamorfosis del mexicano* (Mexico City: Grijalbo, 1987).

6. The bibliography of this debate is enormous; most of it deals with the problem in the context of race and gender. Some recent and significant examples of the debate include Elizabeth Abel, "Black Writing; White Reading: Race and the Politics of Feminist Interpretation," *Critical Inquiry* 19 (1993): 470–98; Linda Alcoff, "Cultural Feminism versus Post-Structuralism: The Identity Crisis in Feminist Theory," *Signs* 13 (1988): 405–36; Paul Smith, *Discerning the Subject* (Minneapolis: U of Minnesota P, 1987); Susan S. Friedman, "Post/Poststructuralist Feminist Criticism: The Politics of Recuperation and Negotiation," *New Literary History* 22 (1991): 465–90; and Jennifer Wicke, "Postmodern Identities and the Politics of the (Legal) Subject," *boundary* 2 (1992): 10–33.

7. In this regard see Eric Hobsbawm's "Mass-Producing Traditions: Europe, 1870–1914," in *The Invention of Tradition*, ed. Eric Hobsbawm and Terence Ranger (Cambridge: Cambridge UP, 1983), 263–307.

8. Richard, "Postmodernism and Periphery," 469.

9. Latour, 124.

Bibliography

Abel, Elizabeth. "Black Writing, White Reading: Race and the Politics of Feminist Interpretation." *Critical Inquiry* 19 (1993): 470–98.

Adorno, Rolena. "La *ciudad letrada* y los discursos coloniales." *Hispamérica* 48 (1987): 3–24.

Ahmad, Aijaz. *In Theory: Classes, Nations, Literatures*. London: Verso, 1992.

———. "Jameson's Rhetoric of Otherness and the National Allegory." *Social Text* 17 (1986): 3–25.

Alazraki, Jaime. "Relectura de Horacio Quiroga." In *El cuento hispanoamericano ante la crítica*, ed. Enrique Pupo-Walker. Madrid: Castalia, 1973, 64–80.

Alcoff, Linda. "Cultural Feminism versus Post-Structuralism: The Identity Crisis in Feminist Theory." *Signs* 13 (1988): 405–36.

Alonso, Carlos J. "Civilización y barbarie." *Hispania* 72 (May 1989): 256–63.

———. "*Facundo* y la sabiduría del poder." *Cuadernos Americanos* 226 (September–October 1979): 116–30.

———. *The Spanish American Regional Novel: Modernity and Autochthony*. Cambridge: Cambridge UP, 1990.

Altamirano, Carlos, and Beatriz Sarlo. "Una vida ejemplar: la estrategia de *Recuerdos de provincia*." *Escritura* 9 (January–June 1980): 3–48.

Amin, Samir. *Eurocentrism*. New York: Monthly Review P, 1989.

Anderson, Benedict. *Imagined Communities: Reflections on the Origin and Spread of Nationalism*. London: Verso, 1983.

Anderson Imbert, Enrique. Prologue to *Recuerdos de provincia*. Buenos Aires: Editorial de Belgrano, 1981.

Andreu, Alicia. "Pedro Camacho: Prestidigitador del lenguaje." *Modern Language Studies* 16.2 (Spring 1986): 19–25.

Appiah, Kwame Anthony. *In My Father's House: Africa in the Philosophy of Culture*. New York: Oxford UP, 1992.

Arango y Parreño, Francisco. *Obras*. Havana: Ministerio de Educación, 1952.

Arenas, Reinaldo. *La Loma del Angel*. Barcelona: Dador, 1989.

Armstrong, Nancy. *Desire and Domestic Fiction: A Political History of the Novel*. New York: Oxford UP, 1987.

Arrigoitia, Luis de. "Machismo, folklore y creación en Mario Vargas Llosa." *Sin Nombre* 13.4 (1983): 7–24.

Austin, J. L. *How to Do Things with Words*. Ed. J. O. Urmson and Marina Sbisà. Cambridge: Harvard UP, 1975.

Auza, Nestor Tomás. *Lucio V. Mansilla: la Confederación*. Buenos Aires: Plus Ultra, 1978.

Avni, Ora. *The Resistance of Reference: Linguistics, Philosophy, and the Literary Text*. Baltimore: Johns Hopkins UP, 1990.

Azcuy, Eduardo. *Posmodernidad, cultura y política*. Buenos Aires: Fundación Nuevo Mundo, 1989.

Bakhtin, Mikhail. "Author and Hero in Aesthetic Activity." In *Art and Answerability*. Austin: U of Texas P, 1990, 4–256.

Barreiro, José P., ed. *Cartas y discursos políticos: itinerario de una pasión republicana*. Vol. 3 of *Edición especial de seis tomos de la obra de D.F. Sarmiento*. Buenos Aires: Ediciones Culturales Argentinas, 1965.

Barrenechea, Ana María. "La configuración del *Facuado*." In *Textos hispanoamericanos: de Sarmiento a Sardvy*. Caracas: Monte Avila, 1978.

Barthes, Roland. "From Work to Text." In *Image Music Text*, ed. and trans. Stephen Heath. New York: Hill and Wang, 1977, 155–64.

———. *The Pleasure of the Text*. Trans. Richard Howard. New York: Hill and Wang, 1975.

Bartra, Roger. *La jaula de la melancolía: identidad y metamorfosis del mexicano*. Mexico: Grijalbo, 1987.

Bayle, Constantino. *El Dorado fantasma*. Madrid: Razón y Fe, 1930.

Beardsell, Peter R. *Quiroga: Cuentos de amor de locura y de muerte*. Critical guides to Spanish Texts, 44. London: Grant and Cutler, 1986.

Becco, Horacio Jorge. *Historia real y fantástica del Nuevo Mundo*. Caracas: Ayacucho, 1992.

Benda, Julien. *La trahison des clercs*. Paris: B. Grasset, 1927.

Benítez Rojo, Antonio. *La isla que se repite: el Caribe y la perspectiva posmoderna*. Hanover, N.H.: Ediciones el Norte, 1989.

Benjamin, Walter. "The Task of the Translator." In *Illuminations*, trans. Harry Zohn, ed. and intr. Hannah Arendt. New York: Schocken, 1976, 69–82.

Benveniste, Emile. "The Nature of Pronouns." In *Problems in General Linguistics*, trans. Mary Elizabeth Meek. Coral Gables, Fla.: U of Miami P, 1971.

Berman, Marshall. *All That Is Solid Melts into Air: The Experience of Modernity*. New York: Simon and Schuster, 1982.

Beverley, John. "Postmodernism in Latin America." *Siglo XX/20th Century* 9.1–2 (1991–92): 9–29.

Bhabha, Homi. "The Commitment to Theory." In *The Location of Culture*. New York: Routledge, 1994, 19–39.

———. "Freedom's Basis in the Indeterminate." In *The Identity in Question*, ed. John Rajchman. New York: Routledge, 1995, 47–61.

Bilbao, Francisco. *El evangelio americano*. Caracas: Ayacucho, 1988.

Bloom, Harold. *The Anxiety of Influence: A Theory of Poetry*. New York: Oxford UP, 1973.

———. *A Map of Misreading*. New York: Oxford UP, 1975.

———. *Poetry and Repression: Revisionism from Blake to Stevens*. New Haven: Yale UP, 1976.

Bolívar, Simón. *Doctrina del Libertador*. Caracas: Ayacucho, 1985.

Booker, N. Keith. *Vargas Llosa among the Postmodernists*. Gainesville: UP of Florida, 1994.

Borges, Jorge Luis. Prologue to *Recuerdos de provincia*. *Prólogos*. Buenos Aires: Torres Agüero Editor, 1975, 129–33.

Brading, D. A. *The First America: The Spanish Monarchy, Creole Patriots and the Liberal State, 1492–1867*. Cambridge: Cambridge UP, 1991.

Bratosevich, Nicolás. *El estilo de Horacio Quiroga en sus cuentos*. Madrid: Gredos, 1973.

Bremer, Thomas. "The Slave Who Wrote Poetry: Comments on the Literary Works and the Autobiography of Juan Francisco Manzano." In *Slavery in the Americas*, ed. Wolfgang Binder. Würzburg: Königshausen und Neumann, 1993, 487–501.

Brown, William Hill. *The Power of Sympathy*. Ed. Herbert Brown. Boston: New Frontiers P, 1961.

Brunner, José Joaquín. *Un espejo trizado: ensayos sobre cultura y políticas culturales*. Santiago: FLACSO, 1988.

Buehrer, David. " 'A Second Chance on Earth': The Postmodern and the Post-apocalyptic in García Márquez's *Love in the Time of Cholera*." *Critique* 32.1 (1990): 15–26.

Bueno, Salvador. *Las ideas literarias de Domingo Delmonte*. Havana: Editorial Hércules F. Fernández y Cía, 1954.

———. *El negro en la literatura hispanoamericana*. Havana: Editorial Letras Cubanas, 1986.

————. *¿Quién fue Domingo del Monte?* Havana: UNEAC, 1986.

Bulner-Thomas, Victor. *The Economic History of Latin America since Independence.* Cambridge: Cambridge UP, 1994.

Burns, E. Bradford. "Cultures in Conflict: The Implications of Modernization in Nineteenth-Century Latin America." In *Elites, Masses, and Modernization in Latin America, 1850–1930.* Austin: U of Texas P, 1979, 11–77.

————. *The Poverty of Progress: Latin America in the Nineteenth Century.* Berkeley: U of California P, 1980.

Bushnell, David, and Neill Macaulay. *The Emergence of Latin America in the Nineteenth Century.* New York: Oxford UP, 1994.

Caillet-Bois, Julio. Introduction to *Una excursión a los indios Ranqueles,* by Lucio V. Mansilla. Mexico City: Fondo de Cultura, 1947, vii–xxxvi.

Calinescu, Matei. *Five Faces of Modernity: Modernism, Avant-Garde, Decadence, Kitsch, Postmodernism.* Durham: Duke UP, 1987.

Campra, Rosalba, ed. *La selva en el damero: espacio literario y espacio urbano en América Latina.* Pisa: Giardini Editori, 1989.

Carilla, Emilio. *Literatura argentina.* Buenos Aires: Ministerio de Educación de la Nación, 1954.

Cascardi, Anthony J. *The Subject of Modernity.* Cambridge: Cambridge UP, 1992.

Castro-Klarén, Sara. *Mario Vargas Llosa: análisis introductorio.* Lima: Latinoamericana Editores, 1988.

Cepero Bonilla, Raúl. *Azúcar y abolición.* Havana: Editorial de Ciencias Sociales, 1971.

Chambers, Ross. *Story and Situation: Narrative Seduction and the Power of Fiction.* Minneapolis: U of Minnesota P, 1984.

Chatterjee, Partha. *The Nation and Its Fragments: Colonial and Postcolonial Histories.* Princeton: Princeton UP, 1993.

Chiaramonte, José Carlos. *Pensamiento de la Ilustración: economía y sociedad iberoamericanas en el siglo XVIII.* Caracas: Ayacucho, 1979.

Clarasó, Mercedes. "Horacio Quiroga y el cine." *Revista Iberoamericana* 45 (1979): 613–22.

Clifford, James. *The Predicament of Culture: Twentieth-Century Ethnography, Literature, and Art.* Cambridge: Harvard UP, 1988.

Clissold, Stephen. *The Seven Cities of Cíbola.* New York: C. N. Potter, 1962.

Colás, Santiago. "Of Creole Symptoms, Cuban Fantasies, and Other Latin American Postcolonial Ideologies." *PMLA* 110.3 (1995): 382–96.

————. *Postmodernity: The Argentine Paradigm.* Durham: Duke UP, 1994.

————. "The Third World in Jameson's *Postmodernism, or the Cultural Logic of Late Capitalism.*" *Social Text* 31–32 (1992): 258–70.

Compagnon, Antoine. *La Seconde main, ou le travail de la citation.* Paris: Seuil, 1979.

Conn, Robert T. " 'Americanismo andante': Alfonso Reyes and the 1930s." *Latin American Literary Review* 23.46 (1995): 83–98.

Coronil, Fernando. "Can Postcoloniality Be Decolonized?: Imperial Banality and Postcolonial Power." *Public Culture* 5.1 (1992): 89–108.

Corredor, Consuelo. *Modernismo sin modernidad.* Bogotá: Centro de Investigación y Educación Popular, 1990.

Cortés Conde, Roberto. *The First Stages of Modernization in Spanish America.* New York: Harper and Row, 1974.

Costa Lima, Luiz. *Control of the Imaginary: Reason and Imagination in Modern Times.* Trans. Ronald W. Sousa. Minneapolis: U of Minnesota P, 1988.

————. *The Dark Side of Reason: Fictionality and Power.* Stanford: Stanford UP, 1992.

Cussen, Antonio. *Bello and Bolívar: Poetry and Politics in the Spanish American Revolution.* Cambridge: Cambridge UP, 1992.

Davis, Lennard J. *Resisting Novels: Ideology and Fiction.* New York: Methuen, 1987.

Dawson, Frank G. *The First Latin American Debt Crisis: The City of London and the 1822–25 Loan Bubble.* New Haven: Yale UP, 1990.

Delgado, José M., and Alberto J. Brignole. *Vida y obra de Horacio Quiroga*. Montevideo: Claudio García, 1939.

Del Monte, Domingo. *Centón Epistolario de Domingo del Monte*. Havana: Imprenta Siglo XX, 1923–38.

———. *Escritos de Domingo del Monte*. Havana: Editorial Cultural, 1929.

De Man, Paul. "Autobiography as Defacement." In *The Rhetoric of Romanticism*. New York: Columbia UP, 1984, 67–81.

———. "The Rhetoric of Temporality." In *Interpretation: Theory and Practice*. Baltimore: Johns Hopkins UP, 1969, 173–209.

Derrida, Jacques. *Dissemination*. Trans. Barbara Johnson. Chicago: U of Chicago P, 1981.

———. "Force and Signification." In *Writing and Difference*, trans. and intr. Alan Bass. Chicago: U of Chicago P, 1978, 3–30.

———. *Margins of Philosophy*. Trans. Alan Bass. Chicago: U of Chicago P, 1982.

———. *Of Grammatology*. Trans. Gayatri Chakravorty Spivak. Baltimore: Johns Hopkins UP, 1976.

Descombes, Vincent. *L'Inconscient malgré lui*. Paris: Minuit, 1977.

Ducrot, Oswald, and Tzvetan Todorov. *Encyclopedic Dictionary of the Sciences of Language*. Baltimore: Johns Hopkins UP, 1983.

Dussel, Enrique. "Eurocentrism and Modernity (Introduction to the Frankfurt Lectures)." *boundary 2* 20.3 (1993): 65–76.

———. *The Invention of the Americas: Eclipse of "the Other" and the Myth of Modernity*. Trans. Michael D. Barber. New York: Continuum, 1985.

———. "Marx's Economic Manuscripts of 1861–63 and the 'Concept' of Dependency." *Latin American Perspectives* 17.2 (1990): 62–101.

Earle, Peter. "La excursión de Mansilla." In Rodríguez Alcalá and Blasi, 35–42.

Echeandía, Servando. "La fundación de la tradición poética hispanoamericana." Ph.D. diss., Harvard University, 1996.

Erro, Carlos Alberto. Prologue to *Páginas escogidas de Sarmiento*. Vol. 4 of *Edición especial de la obra de Domingo Faustino Sarmiento*. Buenos Aires: Ediciones Literarias Argentinas, 1963, i–xv.

Escobar Valenzuela, Gustavo. *La ilustración en la filosofía latinoamericana*. Mexico: Editorial Trillas, 1980.

Eugenio Martínez, María Angeles. *La Ilustración en América (siglo XVIII): pelucas y casacas en los trópicos*. Madrid: Anaya, 1988.

Fabian, Johannes. *Language and Colonial Power: The Appropriation of Swahili in the Former Belgian Congo, 1880–1938*. Cambridge: Cambridge UP, 1986.

———. *Time and the Other: How Anthropology Makes Its Object*. New York: Columbia UP, 1983.

Faulkner, William. *Absalom, Absalom!* New York: Random House, 1972.

Feal, Rosemary Geisdorfer. *Novel Lives: The Fictional Autobiographies of Guillermo Cabrera Infante and Mario Vargas Llosa*. North Carolina Studies in the Romance Languages and Literatures, no. 226. Chapel Hill: University of North Carolina Department of Romance Languages, 1986.

Felman, Shoshana. *The Literary Speech Act: Don Juan with J. L. Austin, or Seduction in Two Languages*. Ithaca: Cornell UP, 1983.

Fernández, Silvia Mirta. "Mansilla y los Ranqueles: ¿Por qué Lucio V. Mansilla escribió *Una excursión a los indios Ranqueles?*" In *Congreso Nacional de Historia sobre la Conquista del Desierto*, 4 vols. Buenos Aires: Academia Nacional de la Historia, 1980, 4: 361–75.

Ferré, Rosario. "Mario Vargas Llosa o el escribidor." *Sin Nombre* 9.2 (1978): 86–90.

Fleming, Leonor. "Horacio Quiroga: escritor a la intemperie." *Revista de Occidente* 113 (1990): 95–111.

Flitter, Derek. *Spanish Romantic Literary Theory and Criticism*. Cambridge: Cambridge UP, 1992.

Flores, Angel, ed. *Aproximaciones a Horacio Quiroga*. Caracas: Monte Avila, 1976.

Foster, David W. "Knowledge in Mansilla's *Una excursión a los indios Ranqueles.*" *Revista Hispánica Moderna*, new series, 41.1 (1988): 19–29.

Foucault, Michel. *The Archeology of Knowledge.* Trans. A. M. Sheridan Smith. New York: Pantheon, 1972.

———. *The Order of Things.* New York: Vintage, 1973.

———. "Preface to Transgression." In *Language, Countermemory, Practice: Selected Essays and Interviews by Michel Foucault*, ed. Donald F. Bouchard. Ithaca: Cornell UP, 1981, 29–52.

Freud, Sigmund. "Family Romances." In *The Standard Edition of the Complete Psychological Works of Sigmund Freud*, 24 vols., ed. and trans. James Strachey. London: Hogarth P and the Institute of Psycho-Analysis, 1974, 9:236–41.

———. "Mourning and Melancholia." In *The Standard Edition of the Complete Psychological Works of Sigmund Freud*, 24 vols., ed. and trans. James Strachey. London: Hogarth P and the Institute of Psycho-Analysis, 1974, 14:237–58.

Friedman, Susan S. "Post/Poststructuralist Feminist Criticism: The Politics of Recuperation and Negotiation." *New Literary History* 22 (1991): 465–90.

Friol, Roberto. *Suite para Juan Francisco Manzano.* Havana: Editorial Arte y Literatura, 1977.

Fuentes, Carlos. *La campaña.* Mexico City: Fondo de Cultura Económica, 1990.

Gálvez, Manuel. *Vida de Sarmiento: el hombre de autoridad.* Buenos Aires: Editorial Tor, 1952.

Gálvez Avero, Marina. *La novela hispanoamericana contemporánea.* Madrid: Taurus, 1987.

Gambarini, Elsa K. "El discurso y su transgresión: 'El almohadón de pluma' de Horacio Quiroga." *Revista Iberoamericana* 46 (1980): 443–57.

García Canclini, Néstor. *Culturas híbridas: estrategias para entrar y salir de la modernidad.* Mexico City: Grijalbo, 1990.

———. "El debate posmoderno en Iberoamérica." *Cuadernos Hispanoamericanos* 463 (1989): 79–82.

García Márquez, Gabriel. *El General en su laberinto.* Bogotá: Oveja Negra, 1989.

Geertz, Clifford. *The Interpretation of Cultures.* New York: Basic Books, 1973.

———. *Local Knowledge: Further Essays in Interpretive Anthropology.* New York: Basic Books, 1983.

Gerbi, Antonello. *La disputa del Nuevo Mundo.* Mexico City: Fondo de Cultura, 1960.

Gerdes, Dick. *Mario Vargas Llosa.* Boston: Twayne, 1985.

Gikandi, Simon. *Writing in Limbo: Modernism and Caribbean Literature.* Ithaca: Cornell UP, 1992.

Glantz, Margo. "Poe en Quiroga." In Flores, 93–118.

Gleijeses, Piero. "The Limits of Sympathy: The United States and the Independence of Spanish America." *Journal of Latin American Studies* 24.1 (1992): 481–505.

Gómez de Avellaneda, Gertrudis. *Sab.* Salamanca: Anaya, 1970.

Góngora, Mario. *El estado en el derecho indiano: época de fundación, 1492–1570.* Santiago: Universidad de Chile, 1951.

———. *Studies in the Colonial History of Spanish America.* Cambridge: Cambridge UP, 1975.

González, Eduardo. "A Condo of One's Own." *MLN* 112.5 (1997): 944–57.

González, J. C. "De la subliteratura a la literatura." *Anales de Literatura Hispánica* 6 [7] (1978): 141–56.

González, José Eduardo. "¿El final de la modernización literaria?: técnica y technología en la crítica de Angel Rama." *MLN* 113.2 (1998): 380–406.

González Echevarría, Roberto. "García Márquez y la voz de Bolívar." *Cuadernos Americanos*, new series, 28 (July–August 1991): 63–76.

———. *Myth and Archive: A Theory of Latin American Narrative.* Cambridge: Cambridge UP, 1990.

———. *La ruta de Severo Sarduy.* Hanover, N.H.: Ediciones del Norte, 1987.

González Stephan, Beatriz. *La historiografía literaria del liberalismo hispanoamericano del siglo XIX.* Havana: Ediciones Casa de las Américas, 1987.

Goodrich, Diana Sorensen. *Facundo and the Construction of Argentine Culture.* Austin: U of Texas P, 1996.

Graham, Joseph F., ed. *Difference in Translation*. Ithaca: Cornell UP, 1985.

Gray, John. *Enlightenment's Wake: Politics and Culture at the Close of the Modern Age*. New York: Routledge, 1995.

Greenblatt, Stephen. *Marvelous Possessions: The Wonder of the New World*. Chicago: U of Chicago P, 1991.

Guglielmini, Homero M. *Mansilla*. Buenos Aires: Ediciones Culturales Argentinas, 1961.

Gutiérrez Girardot, Rafael. *Temas y problemas de una historia social de la literatura hispanoamericana*. Bogotá: Cave Canem, 1989.

Haberly, David T. "Abolitionism in Brazil: Anti-Slavery and Anti-Slave." *Luso Brazilian Review* 9.2 (1972): 30–46.

Haber, Stephen, ed. *How Latin America Fell Behind: Essays on the Economic Histories of Brazil and Mexico, 1800–1914*. Stanford: Stanford UP, 1997.

Halperín Donghi, Tulio. "El antiguo orden y su crisis como tema de *Recuerdos de provincia*." *Boletín del Instituto de Historia Argentina y Americana "Dr. E. Ravignani"* 1, 3d series (1989): 7–22.

Halperín Donghi, Tulio, et al., eds. *Sarmiento: Author of a Nation*. Berkeley: U of California P, 1994.

Hamnett, Brian R. "Between Bourbon Reforms and Liberal Reforma: The Political Economy of a Mexican Province—Oaxaca, 1750–1850." In *The Political Economy of Spanish America in the Age of Revolution, 1750–1850*, ed. K. Andrien and Lyman Johnson. Albuquerque: U of New Mexico P, 39–62.

Harss, Luis, and Dohmann, Barbara. *Into the Mainstream*. New York: Harper and Row, 1967.

Hechter, Michael. *Internal Colonialism: The Celtic Fringe in British National Development, 1536–1966*. Berkeley: U of California P, 1975.

Hobsbawm, Eric. "Mass-Producing Traditions: Europe, 1870–1914." In Hobsbawm and Ranger, 263–307.

Hobsbawm, Eric, and Terence Ranger, ed. *The Invention of Tradition*. Cambridge: Cambridge UP, 1983.

Holland, Norman. " 'Doctoring' in Quiroga." *Confluencia* 9.2 (1994): 64–72.

Hood, Edward W. "The Liberator in the Literary Labyrinth of Gabriel García Márquez." *SECOLAS* 22 (1991): 68–73.

Hunt, Lynn. *The Family Romance of the French Revolution*. Berkeley: U of California P, 1992.

Jameson, Fredric. *Postmodernism or the Cultural Logic of Late Capitalism*. Durham: Duke UP, 1991.

———. "Third-World Literature in the Era of Multinational Capitalism." *Social Text* 15 (1986): 65–88.

Jitrik, Noé. *Horacio Quiroga: una obra de experiencia y riesgo*. Buenos Aires: Ediciones Culturales Argentinas, 1959.

———. *Muerte y resurrección de "Facundo."* Buenos Aires: Centro Editor de América Latina, 1968.

Johnson, Barbara. "Taking Fidelity Philosophically." In Graham, 142–48.

Jones, Charles. "Intereses comerciales e influencia política británica en Latinoamérica durante el siglo diecinueve." In *Iberoamérica en el siglo XIX: nacionalismo y dependencia*. Ed. Juan Bosco Amores et al. Pamplona: Eunate, 1995.

Jones, Julie. "*La tía Julia y el escribidor*: Mario Vargas Llosa's Versions of Self." *Critique* 21.1 (1979): 73–82.

Jusdanis, Gregory. *Belated Modernity and Aesthetic Culture*. Minneapolis: U of Minnesota P, 1991.

Kadir, Djelal. *Columbus and the Ends of the Earth*. Berkeley: U of California P, 1992.

———. *Questing Fictions: Latin America's Family Romance*. Minneapolis: U of Minnesota P, 1986.

Kant, Immanuel. *Critique of Judgment*. Trans. J. H. Bernard. New York: Hafner P, 1951.

Karcher, Carolyn L. "Lydia Maria Child's *A Romance of the Republic*." In *Slavery and the Literary Imagination*, ed. Deborah E. McDowell and Arnold Rampersad. Baltimore: Johns Hopkins UP, 1989, 81–103.

Katra, William. "Rereading *Viajes*: Race, Identity, and National Destiny." In Halperín Donghi et al., 73–100.

———. "Sarmiento frente a la generación de 1837." *Revista Iberoamericana* 143 (April–June 1988): 525–49.

Kellner, Douglas, ed. *Postmodernism, Jameson, Critique*. Washington, D.C.: Maisonneuve P, 1989.

Kennedy, William. "Review of *Aunt Julia and the Scriptwriter*." *New York Times Book Review*, August 1, 1982, 1–20.

Kermode, Frank. *The Sense of an Ending: Studies in the Theory of Fiction*. New York: Oxford UP, 1968.

———. "Sensing Endings." *Nineteenth-Century Fiction* 33 (1978): 144–58.

Kernan, Alvin. "The Idea of Literature." *New Literary History* 1.1 (1973): 31–40.

Kerr, Lucille. *Reclaiming the Author: Figures and Fictions From Spanish America*. Durham: Duke UP, 1992.

Klein, Herbert. *African Slavery in Latin America and the Caribbean*. New York: Oxford UP, 1986.

Klor de Alva, J. Jorge. "Colonialism and Postcolonialism as (Latin) American Mirages." *Colonial Latin American Review* 1.1–2 (1992): 3–23.

———. "The Postcolonization of the (Latin) American Experience: A Reconsideration of 'Colonialism,' 'Postcolonialism,' and 'Mestizaje.' " In *After Colonialism: Imperial Histories and Postcolonial Displacements*, ed. Gyan Prakash. Princeton: Princeton UP, 1995, 241–75.

Kubayanda, Josaphat. "Order and Conflict: *Yo el Supremo* in Light of Rama's *ciudad letrada* Theory." In *The Historical Novel in Latin America*, ed. Daniel Balderston. Gaithersburg, Md.: Hispamérica, 1986, 129–37.

Kutzinski, Vera. *Sugar's Secrets: Race and the Erotics of Cuban Nationalism*. Charlottesville: UP of Virginia, 1993.

Lacan, Jacques. *Ecrits I*. Paris: Seuil, 1971.

Lander, Edgardo. *Modernidad y universalismo*. Caracas: Nueva Sociedad, 1991.

Lanning, John Tate. *Academic Culture in the Spanish Colonies* Oxford: Oxford UP, 1940.

Lanuza, José Luis. *Genio y figura de Lucio V. Mansilla*. Buenos Aires: Editorial Universitaria de Buenos Aires, 1965.

Larsen, Neil. *Reading North by South: On Latin American Literature, Culture, and Politics*. Minneapolis: U of Minnesota P, 1995.

Latour, Bruno. *We Have Never Been Modern*. Trans. Catherine Porter. Hertfordshire: Harvester Wheatsheaf, 1993.

Lazarus, Neil. *Resistance in Postcolonial African Fiction*. New Haven: Yale UP, 1990.

Leonard, Irving. *Books of the Brave*. Berkeley: U of California P, 1992.

Levinson, Brett. "The Death of the Critique of Eurocentrism: Latinamericanism as Global Praxis/Poiesis." *Revista de Estudios Hispánicos* 31.2 (1997): 169–201.

Lewis, Marvin A. *From Lima to Leticia: The Peruvian Novels of Mario Vargas Llosa*. Lanham, Md.: UP of America, 1983.

Lipski, John. "Reading the Writers: Hidden Meta-Structures in the Modern Spanish American Novel." *Perspectives in Contemporary Literature* 6 (1980): 117–24.

López Gil, Marta. *Filosofía, modernidad, posmodernidad*. Buenos Aires: Editorial Biblos, 1990.

Lucretius. *On Nature*. Trans. Russell M. Geer. New York: Bobbs-Merrill, 1965.

Ludmer, Josefina. *El género gauchesco: un tratado sobre la patria*. Buenos Aires: Sudamericana, 1988.

Luis, William. *Literary Bondage: Slavery in Cuban Literature*. Austin: U of Texas P, 1990.

Lukács, Georg. *The Theory of the Novel*. Cambridge: MIT P, 1983.

Lynch, John. *The Spanish American Revolutions, 1808–1826*. New York: Norton, 1973.

Machen, Stephen M. " 'Pornoviolence' and Point of View in Mario Vargas Llosa's *La tía Julia y el escribidor*." *Latin American Literary Review* 9 [17] (Fall–Winter 1980): 9–16.

Magnarelli, Sharon. "The Diseases of Love and Discourse: *La tía Julia y el escribidor* and *María*." *Hispanic Review* 54.2 (1986): 195–205.

Mansilla, Lucio V. *Entre-nos: causeries del jueves*. Buenos Aires: Hachette, 1963.
——. *Una excursión a los indios Ranqueles*. Caracas: Ayacucho, 1984.
——. *Mis memorias*. Buenos Aires: Hachette, 1955.
——. *Retratos y recuerdos*. Buenos Aires: El Ateneo, 1927.
——. *Rozas: ensayo histórico-psicológico*. Paris: Garnier, 1898.
Manzano, Juan Francisco. *Autobiografía*. Ed. and intr. Ivan A. Schulman. Madrid: Ediciones Guadarrama, 1975.
——. *Autobiografía, cartas y versos de Juan Fco. Manzano*. Ed. José L. Franco. Havana: Municipio de La Habana, 1937.
Marcos, Juan Manuel. *De García Márquez al post-boom*. Madrid: Orígenes, 1986.
——. *Roa Bastos, precursor del post-boom*. Mexico: Katún, 1983.
Martin, Gerald. *Journeys through the Labyrinth: Latin American Fiction in the Twentieth Century*. London: Verso, 1989.
——. "Mario Vargas Llosa: Errant Knight of the Liberal Imagination." In *Modern Latin American Fiction*, ed. John King. London: Faber and Faber, 1987, 205–33.
Martínez-Alier, Verena. *Marriage, Class, and Colour in Nineteenth-Century Cuba*. Ann Arbor: U of Michigan P, 1989.
Martínez Echazábal, Lourdes. *Para una semiótica de la mulatez*. Madrid: Porrúa Turanzas, 1990.
Martínez Estrada, Ezequiel. *Sarmiento*. Buenos Aires: Argos, 1947.
Martínez Morales, José Luis. *Horacio Quiroga: teoría y práctica del cuento*. México: Centro de Investigaciones Lingüístico-literarias, Universidad Veracruzana, 1982.
Mathieu-Higginbotham, Corina. "El concepto de Civilización y Barbarie en *Una excursión a los indios Ranqueles*." *Hispanófila* 89 (1987): 80–87.
Mayol Laferrére, Carlos. "El coronel Lucio V. Mansilla y la ocupación del Río Quinto en 1869." In *Congreso Nacional de Historia sobre la Conquista del Desierto*. 4 vols. Buenos Aires: Academia Nacional de la Historia, 1980, 2:83–96.
McAlister, Lyle N. *Spain and Portugal in the New World, 1492–1700*. Minneapolis: U of Minnesota P, 1984.
McCracken, Ellen. "Vargas Llosa's *La tía Julia y el escribidor*: The New Novel and the Mass Media." *Ideologies and Literature* 3 [13] (June–August 1980): 54–69.
Mignolo, Walter. "Occidentalización, imperialismo, globalización: herencias coloniales y teorías postcoloniales." *Revista Iberoamericana* 61.170–71 (1995): 27–40.
Miller, D. A. *Narrative and Its Discontents: Problems of Closure in the Traditional Novel*. Princeton: Princeton UP, 1981.
Miller, J. Hillis. "The Problematic of Ending in Narrative." *Nineteenth-Century Fiction* 33 (June 1978): 3–7.
Molloy, Sylvia. "From Serf to Self: The Autobiography of Juan Francisco Manzano." In *At Face Value: Autobiographical Writing in Spanish America*. Cambridge: Cambridge UP, 1991, 36–54.
——. "Imagen de Mansilla." In *La Argentina del Ochenta al Centenario*, ed. Gustavo Ferrari and Ezequiel Gallo. Buenos Aires: Sudamericana, 1980, 745–59.
——. "Inscripciones del yo en *Recuerdos de provincia*." *Sur* 350–51 (January–December 1982): 131–40.
——. "Recuerdo y sujeto en *Mis memorias* de Mansilla." *Nueva Revista de Filología Hispánica* 36.2 (1988): 1207–20.
——. "Sarmiento, lector de sí mismo en *Recuerdos de provincia*." *Revista Iberoamericana* 143 (April–June 1988): 407–18.
Moraña, Mabel, ed. *Angel Rama y los estudios latinoamericanos*. Pittsburgh: IILI, 1997.
Moreiras, Alberto. "Restitution and Appropriation in Latinamericanism." *Journal of Interdisciplinary Literary Studies* 7 (1995): 1–43.
——. "Transculturación y pérdida del sentido: el diseño de la posmodernidad en América Latina." *Nuevo Texto Crítico* 3.6 (1990): 105–19.
Moreno Fraginals, Manuel. "Aportes culturales y deculturación." In *Africa en América Latina*, ed. Manuel Moreno Fraginals. Mexico City: Siglo XXI, 1987, 13–33.

Morse, Richard. *El espejo de Próspero: un estudio de la dialéctica del Nuevo Mundo.* Mexico City: Siglo XXI, 1982.

———. "The Heritage of Latin America." In *The Founding of a New Society*, ed. Louis Hartz. New York: Harcourt, 1964, 123–76.

———. *New World Soundings: Culture and Ideology in the Americas.* Baltimore: Johns Hopkins UP, 1982.

Murena, H. A. *El pecado original de América.* Buenos Aires: Editorial Sudamericana, 1965.

Murray, David R. *Odious Commerce: Britain, Spain, and the Abolition of the Cuban Slave Trade.* Cambridge: Cambridge UP, 1980.

Nallim, Carlos Orlando. "La visión del indio en Lucio V. Mansilla." *Latino América* 7 (1974): 101–33.

Niranjana, Tejaswini. *Siting Translation: History, Post-Structuralism, and the Colonial Context.* Berkeley: U of California P, 1992.

Nora, Pierre, ed. *Les Lieux de mémoire.* 7 vols. Paris: Gallimard, 1984–92.

O'Gorman, Edmundo. *La invención de América: el universalismo en la cultura de Occidente.* Mexico City: Fondo de Cultura Económica, 1958.

Olney, James. " 'I Was Born': Slave Narratives, Their Status as Autobiography and as Literature." In *The Slave's Narrative*, ed. Charles T. Davis and Henry Louis Gates Jr. New York: Oxford UP, 1985, 148–75.

Ortega, Julio. *El discurso de la abundancia.* Caracas: Monte Avila, 1990.

———. "El lector en su laberinto." *Hispanic Review* 60 (1992): 165–79.

Ortiz, Fernando. *Contrapunteo cubano del tabaco y el azúcar.* Caracas: Ayacucho, 1978.

Oviedo, José Miguel. "A Conversation with Mario Vargas Llosa about *La tía Julia y el escribidor.*" In *Mario Vargas Llosa: A Collection of Critical Essays*, ed. Charles Rossman and Alan W. Friedman. Austin: U of Texas P, 1978, 151–65.

———. *Mario Vargas Llosa: la invención de una realidad.* Barcelona: Barral Editores, 1970.

———. "*La tía Julia y el escribidor*, or the Coded Self-Portrait." In *Mario Vargas Llosa: A Collection of Critical Essays*, ed. Charles Rossman and Alan W. Friedman. Austin: U of Texas P, 1978, 166–81.

Pagden, Anthony. "Fabricating Identity in Spanish America." *History Today* (1992): 44–49.

Pagden, Anthony, and Nicholas Canny, eds. *Colonial Identity in the Atlantic World: 1500–1800.* Princeton: Princeton UP, 1987.

Palcos, Alberto. *Historia de Echeverría.* Buenos Aires: Emecé, 1960.

Pasco, Allan H. "On Defining Short Stories." *New Literary History* 22 (Spring 1991): 407–22.

Paz, Octavio. *Los hijos del limo: del romanticismo a la vanguardia.* Barcelona: Seix Barral, 1984.

Pera, Cristóbal. "Una excursión en la modernidad: Sarmiento en París." In *Actas del XXIX Congreso del IILI.* Barcelona: PPU, 1994, 319–37.

Pérez, Joseph. *Los movimientos precursores de la emancipación en Hispanoamérica.* Madrid: Alhambra, 1982.

Pérez Firmat, Gustavo. *The Cuban Condition: Translation and Identity in Modern Cuban Literature.* Cambridge: Cambridge UP, 1989.

Pérus, Françoise. *Literatura y sociedad en América Latina.* Mexico City: Siglo XXI, 1976.

———. "Modernity, Postmodernity, and Novelistic Form in Latin America." In *Latin American Identity and Constructions of Difference*, ed. Amaryll Chanady. Minneapolis: U of Minnesota P, 1994, 43–66.

Picón Salas, Mariano. "Las formas y las visiones." In *Viejos y nuevos mundos*, ed. Guillermo Sucre. Caracas: Ayacucho, 1983, 397–405.

Piglia, Ricardo. *Respiración artificial.* Buenos Aires: Sudamericana, 1988.

———. "Sarmiento the Writer." In Halperín Donghi et al., 127–44.

Pineda Yánez, Rafael. *Cómo fue la vida amorosa de Rosas.* Buenos Aires: Plus Ultra, 1972.

Plasa, Carl, and Betty J. Ring, eds. *The Discourse of Slavery: Aphra Behn to Toni Morrison.* London: Routledge, 1994.

Poe, Edgar Allan. *Literary Criticism of Edgar Allan Poe.* Ed. Robert L. Hough. Lincoln: U of Nebraska P, 1965.

Pope, Randolph. "Lectura literaria de *El General en su laberinto*." *Revista de Estudios Colombianos* 7 (1989): 36–38.

Popolizio, Enrique. *Vida de Lucio V. Mansilla*. Buenos Aires: Peuser, 1954.

Prasad, Madhava. "On the Question of a Theory of (Third World) Literature." *Social Text* 31–32 (1992): 57–83.

Pratt, Mary Louise. *Imperial Eyes: Travel Writing and Transculturation*. New York: Routledge, 1992.

Prieto, Adolfo. *La literatura autobiográfica argentina*. Buenos Aires: Facultad de Filosofía y Letras, 1966.

Prieto, René. "The Two Narrative Voices in Mario Vargas Llosa's *Aunt Julia and the Scriptwriter*." *Latin American Literary Review* 11 [22] (Spring–Summer 1983): 15–25.

Quijano, Aníbal. *Modernidad, identidad y utopía en América Latina*. Quito: Editorial El Conejo, 1990.

Quiroga, Horacio. *Cartas inéditas de Horacio Quiroga*. Vol. 1. Intr. Arturo Sergio Visca. Montevideo: Ministerio de Instrucción Pública y Previsión Social, 1959.

———. *Cartas inéditas de Horacio Quiroga*. Vol. 2. Intr. Mercedes Ramírez de Rossiello. Montevideo: Instituto Nacional de Investigaciones y Archivos Literarios, 1959.

———. *Cuentos*. Ed. and intr. Emir Rodríguez Monegal. Caracas: Biblioteca Ayacucho, 1981.

———. *Cuentos completos*. Ed. and intr. Alfonso Llambías de Azevedo. 2 vols. Montevideo: Ediciones de la Plaza, 1979.

———. *Sobre literatura*. In *Obras inéditas y desconocidas de Horacio Quiroga*, vol. 7, ed. Angel Rama. Montevideo: Ediciones Arca, 1969.

Rabasa, José. *Inventing America: Spanish Historiography and the Formation of Eurocentrism*. Norman: U of Oklahoma P, 1993.

Rama, Angel. *La ciudad letrada*. Hanover, N.H.: Ediciones del Norte, 1984.

———. *Las máscaras democráticas del modernismo*. Montevideo: Arca Editorial, 1985.

———. *Rubén Darío y el modernismo: circunstancia socioeconómica de un arte americano*. Caracas: Ediciones de la Biblioteca de la Universidad Central de Venezuela, 1970.

———. *Transculturación narrativa en América Latina*. Mexico City: Siglo XXI, 1982.

———, ed. *Más allá del boom: literatura y mercado*. Mexico City: Marcha, 1981.

Ramos, Julio. *Desencuentros de la modernidad en América Latina: literatura y política en el siglo XIX*. Mexico City: Fondo de Cultura Económica, 1989.

———. "Entre otros: *Una excursión a los indios Ranqueles* de Lucio Mansilla." *Filología* 21.1 (1986): 143–71.

———. "La ley es otra: literatura y constitución de la persona jurídica." *Revista de Crítica Literaria Latinoamericana* 20.40 (1994): 305–35.

Reiss, Timothy J. *The Discourse of Modernism*. Ithaca: Cornell UP, 1982.

Rela, Walter. *Horacio Quiroga: repertorio bibliográfico, 1897–1971*. Buenos Aires: Casa Pardo, 1972.

Richard, Nelly. "Postmodernism and Periphery." In *Postmodernism: A Reader*, ed. Thomas Docherty. Hertfordshire: Harvester Wheatsheaf, 1993, 463–70.

Rippy, J. Fred. *British Investments in Latin America, 1822–1949*. Minneapolis: U of Minnesota P, 1959.

Rivas, Mercedes. *Literatura y esclavitud en la novela cubana del siglo XIX*. Seville: Escuela de Estudios Hispano-Americanos de Sevilla, 1990.

Rivera, Juan Manuel. "*La peregrinación de Bayoán*: fragmentos de una lectura disidente." *Cuadernos Americanos* 35 (1992): 158–79.

Rodríguez Alcalá, Hugo, and Alberto Blasi, eds. *Essays on Lucio Victorio Mansilla*. Latin American Studies Program Commemorative Series, no. 5. Riverside, Calif.: Latin American Studies Program of the University of California, Riverside, 1981.

Rodríguez Monegal, Emir. *El desterrado: vida y obra de Horacio Quiroga*. Buenos Aires: Editorial Losada, 1968.

———. *Las raíces de Horacio Quiroga*. Montevideo: Editorial Alfa, 1961.

Romero, José Luis, and Luis Alberto Romero, eds. *Pensamiento político de la emancipación.* 2 vols. Caracas: Ayacucho, 1985.

Rosa, Richard. "Literatura y construcción de naciones en el Caribe: una lectura de los textos de Eugenio María de Hostos." Ph.D. diss., Harvard University, 1996.

Rotker, Susana. *La invención de la crónica.* Buenos Aires: Ediciones Letra Buena, 1992.

Rousso, Henry. *Le Syndrome de Vichy, 1944–198 . . .* Paris: Seuil, 1987.

Rowe, William. "Liberalism and Authority: The Case of Mario Vargas Llosa." In *On Edge: The Crisis of Contemporary Latin American Culture,* ed. George Yúdice, J. Franco, and Juan Flores. Minneapolis: U of Minnesota P, 1992, 45–64.

Rowe, William, and Vivian Schelling. *Memory and Modernity: Popular Culture in Latin America.* London: Verso, 1993.

Ruas, Charles. "Talk with Mario Vargas Llosa." *New York Times Book Review,* August 1, 1982, 15, 17–18.

Saco, José Antonio. *Historia de la esclavitud desde los tiempos más remotos hasta nuestros días.* Paris: Tipografía Lahure, 1875–77.

———. *Memoria sobre caminos.* New York: G. F. Bunce, 1830.

———. *Memoria sobre la vagancia en la Isla de Cuba.* Santiago de Cuba: Instituto Cubano del Libro, 1974.

———. "Mi primera pregunta: ¿La abolición del comercio de esclavos africanos arruinará o atrasará la agricultura cubana?" Madrid: M. Calero, 1837.

———. "Paralelo entre la isla de Cuba y algunas colonias inglesas." Madrid: Tomás Jordán, 1837.

Sahlins, Marshall. *Historical Metaphors and Mythical Realities.* Ann Arbor: Michigan UP, 1981.

Said, Edward. *Culture and Imperialism.* New York: Knopf, 1993.

———. "Secular Interpretation, the Geographical Element, and the Methodology of Imperialism." In *After Colonialism: Imperial Histories and Postcolonial Displacements,* ed. Gyan Prakash. Princeton: Princeton UP, 1995, 21–39.

Santí, Enrico Mario. "Latinamericanism and Restitution." *Latin American Literary Review* 20 (1992): 88–96.

Sarlo, Beatriz. "En el origen de la cultura argentina: Europa y el desierto. Búsqueda del fundamento." *10. Seminario Latinoamericano de Literatura Comparada (Porto Alegre, September 8–10, 1986).* Porto Alegre, Brazil: Universidade Federal do Rio Grande do Sul, 1987, 15–21.

———. *La imaginación técnica: sueños modernos de la cultura argentina.* Buenos Aires: Nueva Visión, 1992.

———. *El imperio de los sentimientos.* Buenos Aires: Diálogos, 1986.

———. *Una modernidad periférica: Buenos Aires, 1920 y 1930.* Buenos Aires: Nueva Visión, 1988.

Sarmiento, Domingo F. *Obras completas.* 51 vols. Ed. A. Belín Sarmiento. Buenos Aires: Imprenta y Litografía Mariano Moreno, 1899.

Schleifer, Ronald. *Rhetoric and Death: The Language of Modernism and Postmodern Discourse Theory.* Urbana: U of Illinois P, 1990.

Schulman, Ivan. Prologue to Juan Francisco Manzano, *Autobiografía de un esclavo.* Madrid: Guadarrama, 1975.

Schulman, Ivan and Evelyn Picón Garfield. *"Las entrañas del vacío": ensayos sobre la modernidad hispanoamericana.* Mexico City: Ediciones Cuadernos Americanos, 1984.

Schwarz, Roberto. *Misplaced Ideas: Essays on Brazilian Culture.* Ed. and trans. John Gledson. London: Verso, 1992.

Sebreli, José J. *El asedio a la modernidad: crítica del relativismo cultural.* Buenos Aires: Sudamericana, 1991.

Serres, Michel. "The Apparition of Hermes: *Dom Juan.*" In *Hermes: Literature, Science, Philosophy,* ed. J. Harari and D. Bell. Baltimore: Johns Hopkins UP, 1982, 3–14.

Shoemaker, Roy Howard. "El tema de la muerte en los cuentos de Horacio Quiroga." *Cuadernos Americanos* 220 (1978): 248–64.

Shumway, Nicolas. *The Invention of Argentina*. Berkeley: U of California P, 1991.

Smith, Barbara Herrnstein. *Poetic Closure: A Study of How Poems End*. Chicago: U of Chicago P, 1968.

Smith, Paul. *Discerning the Subject*. Minneapolis: U of Minnesota P, 1987.

Sommer, Doris. *Foundational Fictions: The National Romances of Latin America*. Berkeley: U of California P, 1991.

———. "Rigoberta's Secrets." *Latin American Perspectives* 18.3 (1991): 32–50.

———. "Who Can Tell?: Filling in Blanks for Villaverde." *American Literary History* 6.2 (1994): 213–33.

Sosnowski, Saúl. "Mario Vargas Llosa: entre radioteatros y escribidores." In *Latin American Fiction Today*, ed. Rose S. Minc. Taconic Parkway and Montclair State College: Ediciones Hispamérica, 1980, 75–82.

Soto, Hernando de. *El otro sendero: la revolución informal*. Lima: Instituto Libertad y Democracia, 1987.

Soubeyroux, J. "El narrador y sus dobles: *La tía Julia y el escribidor*." *Hommage à J. L. Flecmakosca par ses collègues*, 2 vols. Montpellier: Université Paul Valéry, 383–402.

Speratti-Piñero, Emma S. "Horacio Quiroga, precursor de la relación cine-literatura en la América Hispánica." *NRFH* 36.2 (1988): 1239–49.

Spillers, Hortense. "Changing the Letter: The Yokes, The Jokes of Discourse, or, Mrs. Stowe, Mr. Reed." In *Slavery and the Literary Imagination*, ed. Deborah E. McDowell and Arnold Rampersad. Baltimore: Johns Hopkins UP, 1989, 25–61.

Spivak, Gayatri. *In Other Worlds: Essays in Cultural Politics* London: Methuen, 1987.

Stamelman, Richard. *Lost beyond Telling: Representations of Death and Absence in Modern French Poetry*. Ithaca: Cornell UP, 1990.

Stern, Mirta. "*Una excursión a los indios Ranqueles*: espacio textual y ficción topográfica." *Filología* 20.2 (1985): 115–38.

Subirats, Eduardo. *El continente vacío: la conquista del Nuevo Mundo y la conciencia moderna*. Barcelona: Anaya & Mario Muchnik, 1994.

———. *La ilustración insuficiente*. Madrid: Taurus, 1981.

Swanson, Philip. *The New Novel in Latin America*. Manchester: Manchester UP, 1995.

Talens, Jenaro. *Romanticism and the Writing of Modernity: Espronceda and the Collapse of Literature as Institutionalized Discourse*. Valencia: Fundación Instituto Shakespeare, 1989.

Terdiman, Richard. *Discourse/Counter-Discourse: The Theory and Practice of Symbolic Resistance in Nineteenth-Century France*. Ithaca: Cornell UP, 1985.

Todorov, Tzvetan. "The Notion of Literature." *New Literary History* 1.1 (1973): 5–16.

Tollinchi, Esteban. *Romanticismo y modernidad: ideas fundamentales de la cultura del siglo XIX*. 2 vols. Río Piedras: U of Puerto Rico, 1989.

Torres, Camilo. "Memorial de agravios." In *Pensamiento político de la emancipación: 1790–1825*, 2 vols., ed. José L. Romero and Luis A. Romero. Caracas: Ayacucho, 1985, 1: 25–42.

Traube, Elizabeth. *Cosmology and Social Life: Ritual Exchange among the Mambai of East Timor*. Chicago: U of Chicago P, 1986.

Urquidi Illanes, Julia. *Lo que Varguitas no dijo*. La Paz: Khana Cruz, 1983.

Varela, Félix. *Escritos políticos*. Havana: Editorial de Ciencias Sociales, 1977.

Vargas Llosa, Mario *Aunt Julia and the Scriptwriter*. Trans. Helen R. Lane New York: Farrar, Straus, and Giroux, 1982.

———. *Contra viento y marea*. 2 vols. Barcelona: Seix Barral, 1986.

———. *García Márquez: historia de un deicidio*. Barcelona: Seix Barral, 1971.

———. *Kathie y el hipopótamo*. Barcelona: Seix Barral, 1983.

———. "My Son, the Rastafarian." *New York Times Magazine*, February 16, 1986, 20, 22–23.

———. *La orgía perpetua: Flaubert y "Madame Bovary."* Barcelona: Seix Barral, 1975.

———. "A Passion for Perú." *New York Times Magazine*, November 20, 1983, 75, 78–79.

———. Prologue to Hernando de Soto, *El otro sendero*. Lima: Instituto Libertad y Democracia, 1987, xvii–xxix.

————. *La tía Julia y el escribidor*. Barcelona: Seix Barral, 1987.

Vargas Llosa, Mario, and Angel Rama. *García Márquez y la problemática de la novela*. Buenos Aires: Corregidor, 1973.

Vattimo, Gianni. "Dialettica, differenza, pensiero debole." In *Il pensiero debole*, ed. Gianni Vattimo and P. Rovatti. Milan: Feltrinelli, 1983, 12–28.

Véliz, Claudio. *The Centralist Tradition of Latin America*. Princeton: Princeton UP, 1980.

————. *The New World of the Gothic Fox: Culture and Economy in English and Spanish America*. Berkeley: U of California P, 1994.

Vera León, Antonio. "Juan Francisco Manzano: el estilo bárbaro de la nación." *Hispamérica* 60 (1991): 3–22.

Villaverde, Cirilo. *Cecilia Valdés o la Loma del Angel*, 2 vols., ed. Olga Blondet Tudisco and Antonio Tudisco. New York: Anaya, 1971.

Weber, Max. *Economy and Society: An Outline of Interpretive Sociology*, 2 vols., ed. G. Roth and C. Wittich. Berkeley: U of California P, 1978.

————. *Max Weber on Charisma and Institution Building: Selected Papers*. Ed. S. Eisenstadt. Chicago: U of Chicago P, 1968.

Wicke, Jennifer. "Postmodern Identities and the Politics of the (Legal) Subject." *boundary 2* 19 (1992): 10–33.

Williams, Lorna Valerie. *The Representation of Slavery in Cuban Fiction*. Columbia: U of Missouri P, 1994.

Williams, Raymond L. *The Postmodern Novel in Latin America: Politics, Culture, and the Crisis of Truth*. New York: St. Martin's P, 1995.

Willis, Susan. "Crushed Geraniums: Juan Francisco Manzano and the Language of Slavery." In *The Slave's Narrative*, ed. Charles T. Davis and Henry Louis Gates Jr. New York: Oxford UP, 1985, 199–224.

Yndurain, Domingo. "Vargas Llosa y el escribidor." *Cuadernos Hispanoamericanos* 370 (1981): 150–57.

Yúdice, George. "¿Puede hablarse de postmodernidad en América Latina?" *Revista de Crítica Literaria Latinoamericana* 15.29 (1989): 105–28.

Zavala, Iris M. *Colonialism and Culture: Hispanic Modernisms and the Social Imaginary*. Bloomington: Indiana UP, 1992.

Zea, Leopoldo. *Discurso desde la marginación y la barbarie*. Barcelona: Anthropos, 1988.

Index